Nation Building in Baltic States

History, Memory and Identity

NATION BUILDING IN BALTIC STATES

HISTORY, MEMORY AND IDENTITY

Editor

K. B. Usha

ADROIT

Adroit Publishers

NEW DELHI • KATHMANDU

ISBN : 978-81-87393-42-9

2018

Published by
ADROIT PUBLISHERS 4675/21, Ganpati Bhawan, Ansari Road,
Daryaganj, New Delhi-110 002 Phone : 011-23266030
adroitpublishers@gmail.com
C/O Vajra books, Thamel, Jyatha,
Kathmandu, Nepal l KTM: +977-9808357451

Cover Design:

Typeset in Garamond Premier Pro by Arun Sharma, Akriti Graphic Solution,
Delhi-110081 E-mail: arun263923@gmail.com,
Ph: 9999414390

Dedicated

To

The People of Baltic States Who Sacrificed Their Lives for Guarding Hundred Years of Independence

CONTENTS

Preface and Acknowledgements

This book is the outcome of the understanding I have gained through research and course teaching on the Baltic states of Lithuania, Latvia and Estonia since 2009, and also the academic contributions of students and research scholars who are engaged in studies on Baltic states for the past several years under my supervision at the Centre for Russian and Central Asian Studies (CRCAS), School of International Studies, Jawaharlal Nehru University. The interest to initiate the study of Baltic states is primarily because, on the one hand, they are little known countries which are said to have had cultural interactions with India since antiquity. It is an underexplored area of research in Indian academic space. On the other hand, they represent several fateful chapters in history, i.e., domination by neighbouring powers, the appearance, disappearance and re-appearance as independent nations in the world map in twentieth century.

The historical events in Baltic states reveal somewhat a cyclical nature in the sense that they constantly fear the repeat of the past. The historical cycle, therefore, in the Baltic context means that during the past nearly 100 years' time Baltic states lost their home more than once and they fear such loss may occur in future as and when the events in the neighbourhood may unfold dangerous for them. They had little opportunities in shaping their own destinies and institutions because of their geopolitically significant location surrounded by powerful neighbours. Thus, they are in a situation of permanent vulnerability and insecurity not because of their own fault but it is their location in a geographically significant area that decides their destiny. This situation makes them a unique case of nationalizing small states in the international system in the 21st century.

The focus of this book is on the complex issues involved in the current nation building process in the Baltic states. The central argument of the book is that the post-Soviet nation-building and democratic transformation in Lithuania, Latvia and Estonia are founded on history, memory and identity as core elements. The thirteen chapters in the book broadly examines the way the Baltic "political community," "nationhood" and national and regional identities are imagined and constructed on the basis of history, memory and identity. It also seeks to explain how memory and history shaped securitization discourses and their implications for foreign policy. A range of theoretical insights from documented sources have been used by the authors to illuminate discussions pertaining to the above aspects.

A book takes its final shape after a great amount of reading, investigation in the relevant body of literature contributed by renowned scholars in the field of study, discussion, valuable comments and suggestions for improvement from colleagues, friends and other well-wishers and also of careful editing and proof reading. In this process, let me first express my sincere thanks to all those scholars whose works have been used for the purpose of discussion in this book. I am highly thankful to Centre for Russian and Central Asian studies for support for developing Baltic studies in the Centre. My sincere thanks are to Prof. A. K. Ramakrishnan, Prof. R. R. Sharma, Late Prof. Tulsiram and Late Prof. Arun Mohanty for extending to me and my students their inspirational support, encouragement, time for discussion and valuable comments for improvement.

I am extremely thankful to Prof. Vytis Ciubrinskas, Dr. Sarunas Paunksnis, Prof. Valdas Jaskunas, Prof. Algis Krupavicius, Prof. Giedrius Janauskas, Dr. Milda Paulikaite, and Prof. Egdunas Racius, faculty colleagues from Vilnius University, Vytautas Magnus University, and Kaunas University of Technology, Lithuania whose interactions and excellent lectures delivered in CRCAS extremely benefitted students of Baltic studies and also enabled the authors to articulate their ideas in this book. My special thanks to Laimonas Talat-Kelpsa, former Lithuanian Ambassador to India for his support and encouragement to develop academic collaboration, student and faculty exchange between JNU and Lithuanian universities which helped in strengthening Baltic Studies programme in CRCAS, JNU.

I highly appreciate the sincere efforts and hard work of all the authors for their valuable contributions to this book. I am grateful to Dr. R. Sugathan for his careful copyediting and proofreading of the manuscript. My sincere gratitude is to Mr. Akhil Sharma of Adroit Publishers, New Delhi for his interest in publishing this book. Thanks are due to Mohit Abrol for editorial support and Arun Sharma for typesetting the manuscript. It gives me great pleasure to recollect the care, compassion and constructive criticism I received from my daughters, Anu and Leenu while I was busy with this book's work.

K B Usha

Jawaharlal Nehru University, New Delhi

July 2018

List of Contributors

1. **Abdullakkutty K. P.** is a PhD scholar in Centre for Russian and Central Asian Studies (CRCAS), School of International Studies (SIS), Jawaharlal Nehru University (JNU), New Delhi. He submitted his PhD thesis on *Media Representations of Islam in Russia and India: A Comparative Study of Othering, Enemy Imaging and Gender Stereotyping, 2001-2005*. He has completed M. Phil in 2014 from CRCAS, SIS, JNU. Title of his dissertation is the *Role of Russian Media in International Political Communication: A Study of 'Arab Spring*. He did his M. A. in Mass Communication and Journalism from University of Calicut, Kerala, India. His main research interests are mass media, digital culture, political communication, globalization, cyber security, Islam, media representation, gender and minority issues.
2. **Saranya Antony A.** is a PhD scholar pursuing research on *Higher Education Reforms and Transformation of Public Universities in Lithuania and India in the Neoliberal Era* in the Centre for Russian and Central Asian Studies, School of International Studies, Jawaharlal Nehru University, New Delhi, India. She studied in Department of Educational Sciences, Faculty of Arts and Social Sciences, Kaunas Technological University, Lithuania for one semester under Erasmus+ Learning Mobility Fellowship in 2018. She completed her M. Phil in 2016 from CRCAS, SIS, JNU. The topic of her Dissertation is *Representation of Russia in the Baltic Media over Ukraine Crisis of 2014*. She did her M.A. in Politics (International Studies) from SIS, JNU. Her main research interests are international politics, neoliberalism, globalization, Higher Education, gender and democracy.
3. **Sarunas Paunksnis** is Associate Professor in the Faculty of Social Sciences, Arts and Humanities at Kaunas Technological University (KTU), Kaunas, Lithuania. He is the Head of Study Programmes Committee (Philosophy & Arts) and Digital Culture, Communication and Media Research Group at KTU. His main research interests are media philosophy, film studies,

post-colonial theories and Indian studies. He has published a number of articles and research papers in reputed international journals, periodicals and edited volumes. His recent edited book is titled *Dislocating Globality: Deterritorialization, Difference and Resistance* (Brill, 2016).

4. **Karamala Areesh Kumar** is an Assistant Professor of International Relations and World Politics at the Post Graduate Department of Political Science, Saint Joseph's College (Autonomous), Bangalore, India. He worked as a guest faculty in Department of Political Science at Sri Venkateshwara College (2014-15), University of Delhi, New Delhi, India. He completed his PhD from the Centre for Russian and Central Asian Studies, School of International Studies, Jawaharlal Nehru University, New Delhi, India. Topic of his PhD thesis is *Energy Politics between Baltic States, Russia and European Union; 1991- 2014.* He did his M.Phil from CRCAS, SIS, JNU. The title of his Dissertation is *Development of Multi-party System in Lithuania; 1991-2011.* He did his Masters in Politics (International Relations) from SIS, JNU. He has participated in various workshops, seminars national and international conferences and presented more than twenty research papers. His main areas of interest are international politics, nationalism, democracy, political parties, party system, gender, globalization and neoliberalism.

5. **V. Lenin Kumar** is an Assistant Professor at School of Government, MIT Word Peace University, Pune, Maharashtra, India. He completed his PhD from the Centre for Russian and Central Asian Studies, School of International Studies, Jawaharlal Nehru University, New Delhi. Topic of his PhD thesis is *Political Economy of Neoliberal Reforms in Estonia, 1991-2014.* He did his M.Phil. from CRCAS, SIS, JNU. Topic of his Dissertation is *Political Economy of Neoliberal Reforms in Estonia, 1991-2001.* He did his Masters in Politics (International Relations) from SIS, JNU and graduation from Presidency College Chennai, Madras University, Tamil Nadu. His main areas of interest include, political economy, Marxism-Leninism, globalization, neoliberalism, democracy, political leadership and social movements.

6. **Zakali Ayemi** is a PhD scholar in the Centre for Russian and Central Asian Studies, School of International Studies, Jawaharlal Nehru University, New Delhi, India. She submitted her PhD thesis titled *Gender, Higher Education and Labour Market in the Neoliberal Era: A Case Study of Russian Federation, 1991-2016* in 2018. She completed her MPhil in 2015 from the Centre for Russian and Central Asian Studies,

School of International Studies, Jawaharlal Nehru University. Topic of her Dissertation is *Women and Political Leadership in Soviet Union, 1917-1991*. She did her Masters degree from Centre for the Study of Regional Development, Jawaharlal Nehru University, New Delhi. Her main areas of research interest includes education, gender issues, globalization, labour market, women's rights and political leadership.

7. **Chinmaya Mahanand** is a Ph. D Scholar in Centre for Russian and Central Asian Studies, School of International Studies, Jawaharlal Nehru University, New Delhi. Topic of his thesis titled *Social and Political Ideas of Lenin and Ambedkar: A Comparative Study* is nearing completion. He completed his M. Phil in 2012 from CRCAS, SIS, JNU. His main areas of research interest are international politics, foreign policy, gender, social movements, social justice and political thought.

8. **Anju Devi** is a PhD Scholar in Centre for Russian and Central Asian Studies, School of International Studies, Jawaharlal Nehru University, New Delhi. She is currently pursuing her PhD research on *Memory Politics, Holocaust Revisionism and Jewish Identity in Contemporary Baltic States*. She has completed her M. Phil in 2012 and the topic of her Dissertation is *The Legacy of Holocaust in Contemporary Lithuania: the Rise of Anti-Semitism and Jewish Identity*. She did her M. A. in Political Science from Babasaheb Bhimrao Ambedkar University (BBAU) Lucknow, Uttar Pradesh, India. Her main areas of interests are international politics, minority issues, politics of identity and memory, Holocaust and cultural politics.

9. **Anoop Kumar** is a PhD Scholar in Centre for Russian and Central Asian Studies, School of International Studies, Jawaharlal Nehru University, New Delhi. He submitted his PhD thesis entitled *Cultural Diplomacy in International Relations: The Case of Russia-India Relations* in 2018. He completed his M. Phil in 2011 and the topic of his Dissertation is *Role of Baltic States in the War on Terror and Occupation of Afghanistan, 2001-2012*. His main areas of interest include culture, international relations, non-traditional security, social movements, globalization, inequality, culture, identity and foreign policy.

10. **Akanksha** is a PhD scholar in the Centre for European Studies (CES), School of International Studies, Jawaharlal Nehru University, New Delhi. She completed her M. Phil from CES, SIS, JNU in 2013. Topic of her M. Phil. Dissertation is *Integration of Sikh community in Britain since 1970s*. She did her M. A. in Politics (International Relations) from SIS, JNU. She

completed her graduation from Lady Shri Ram College, Delhi University, New Delhi. The main areas of her research interests are European politics, minority rights, human rights, migration, world politics and international organizations.

Illustrations

Figures

Map

Tables

Abbreviations

CoE	:	Council of Europe
CPSU	:	Communist Party of Soviet Union
CSCE	:	Conference on Security and Co-operation in Europe
ECHR	:	European Court of Human Rights
ECRML	:	European Charter for Regional Minority Languages
EP	:	European Parliament
EU	:	European Union
FCNM	:	Framework Convention for the Protection of Nation Minorities
HCNM	:	High Commissioner on National Minorities
HERA	:	Humanities in the European Research Area
HU	:	Homeland Union
LCU	:	Lithuanian Centre Union
LPP	:	Lithuanian Peasants Party
LPW	:	Lithuanian Party of Women
MAW	:	Memory at War
NATO	:	North Atlantic Treaty Organization
ND-WP	:	New Democracy-Women's Party
NHRO	:	National Human Rights Office
OSCE	:	Organization for Security and Cooperation in Europe
UNDP	:	United Nations Development Programme

http://www.kolovrat.org/map-of-the-baltic-states/baltblu-printable-map-of-map-of-the-baltic-states/

Chapter One

Introduction: Nation Building in Baltic States – History, Memory and Identity

K. B. Usha and Abdullakkutty K. P.

The Baltic states of Lithuania, Latvia and Estonia restored national independence in 1991 from the former Soviet Union through a nonviolent civil resistance movement known as the "Singing Revolution". In the post-Soviet period they are enthroned with the task of nation building, that is, to form a political community, build democratic institutions and nation states. It involves the transformation of the political system from the previous communist totalitarian one to liberal democracy and the planned economy to a free market economy, intending to give people a better future than in the past. The official narratives of Baltic political elites demonstrate that ethnic nationalism, identity, history and memory politics and practices play important roles in shaping their state and nation building processes. Their regime transition is oriented towards de-Sovietization and "return to Europe" by transforming the Baltic states as liberal democracies based on Western/European ideals/values such as freedom, justice, equality, minority rights, inclusion, diversity, well-being and so on.

However, in search of conceptualizing an independent national identity, political community and identification of nation with state through old symbols and collective memories, history has been reinterpreted, by and large, through conflating Soviet and Russian identities. A new public discourse about Soviet and Nazi periods, symbolic of the binary of Russian otherness and European sameness, has been constructed. In this hegemonic discourse, the rhetoric of Baltic states' victimhood, fragility, fear of Russia's expansionist ambitions and the need to ensure security relations with the West became core elements of identity. The national discourse characterized by historical continuity, homogeneity of Baltic majority ethnicity, "othering" of Russian identity as threat, and western/European as "self" which ensures security shows significant implications for democratization process in terms of citizenship, minority rights, political legitimacy, social cohesion and foreign policy. Apparently, the elite narratives further reveal the complexity of nation building process and the multiple dilemmas it created as there is no definite closure of the renewed debate over the past traumas and contested experiences of occupation, resistance and collaboration. How does "come to terms with history" remain a complicated question when they have the history of both being victim and sometimes, victimizers. This book outlines the complexities and challenges concerning nation building process permeated by ethno-nationalist agenda, dichotomy of ethnic versus civic nationalism and politics of memory, history and identity in a post-Soviet/socialist, postcolonial and pluralistic setting in Baltic societies.

Theoretical Considerations

For any newly independent nation state that chooses the path of democracy, its first task is to define its nation and state building processes. In democracy that originated from the Greek word *demokratia* it is important to define its *demos* (people) and *kratia* (rule/govern). The task, in other words, is to create a legitimate political community, identity and authority. Here some pertinent questions which scholars raised in the past need revisit: "what does it mean to rule," (government by the people) "who are the people" (inhabitants who live in the polity qualified to participate in democratic process, i.e., citizens) and "who constitutes people" (common/collective identity – a feeling of sameness) (Jolly 2007: 66-69). *Ethnos* (nation) belong to dominant ethnic groups becomes an important determinant of common identity. When people in a polity include members of different nations, ethnicity, shared memories, history, common ancestry, etc. emerge as elements of national identity (self/other) construction (Ibid: 69).

Apparently, history, memory and identity become constituent elements and source of politics in shaping the nation building and the nation states have to come to terms with their historical past and collective memory. Alberto Alesina and Bryony Reich define nation building as "a process which leads to the formation of countries in which the citizens feel a sufficient amount of commonality of interests, goals and preferences so that they do not wish to separate from each other" (Alesina and Reich 2015: 3). Nations are imaginative constructs and nation building is the very deliberate process that makes 'imagined communities' into real countries under certain geographic, linguistic or cultural affiliations and boundaries. State building is the creation of state machinery (ibid), i.e., the political system and structures of government such as constitution, president, prime minister, parliament, cabinet, judiciary and so on. Rodanthi Tzanelli (2008) sees nation building as a communitarian, emotional and dialogic reciprocity. It is "as an ongoing process that ends with the dismantling of the nation and not before that" (Ibid: 7). In terms of national integrity and legitimacy the formation of national identity is very much important in this process. Since nationalism, history, memory and culture are constitutive elements of political power and autonomy these factors play a significant role in defining national identity. When there are multiple memories and stories of the past these factors may become a source of contestation and irreconcilable differences.

Johann Gottfried Herder[1] who observed nations as the basic unit of humanity viewed language, history and culture[2] as inseparable elements in defining a nation and determining national identity (Herder cited in Piirimae 2012: 87-90). He viewed that without these three inseparable elements the conscious life of humanity would be meaningless. National individuality expressed through language and national consciousness played a decisive part in determining the future of mankind. Within the complex nature of these relationships, the people of each state had to complete a national mission, a mission devoted to the higher development of humanity among all the nations of the world (Herder, summarized in Liebel-Weckowicz 1986: 2). Herder found five principal components as causal determinants of national identity: "(1) the land, as the people's common heritage; (2) the law, as a covenant free entered into; (3) the existence of a shared language and folklore memory; (4) the emphasis on family ties, fostered and perpetuated by and (5) the love and reverence for their forefathers" (cited in Barnard 2003: 20). Ernest Andre Gellner (1987) also points out the significance of language in identity formation. For him, identity is related to nationalism, and culture and politics are interrelated in the modern world. He argues that political freedom should follow cultural and social cohesion (Gellner 1987).

Anthony D. Smith focuses on the social processes and cultural resources of the formation and persistence of nations. He argues that in order to understand nations and nationalism comprehensively, it is necessary to treat them as cultural phenomena rather than understanding them merely as ideology or politics. The ideology of nationalism is closely related to national identity, which is multidimensional concept that covers aspects of a specific language, sentiments and symbolism (Smith 1991). He identifies seven modern characteristics in an ideal type of nation:

1. A well-defined territory, with a fixed center and clearly demarcated and monitored borders;
2. A unified legal system and common legal institutions within a given territory, creating a legal and political community;
3. Participation in the social life and politics of the nation by all the members or "citizens";
4. A mass public culture disseminated by means of a public, standardized, mass education system;
5. Collective autonomy institutionalized in a sovereign territorial state for a given nation;

6. Membership of the nation in an "inter-national" system of the community of nations;
7. Legitimation, if not creation, of the nation by and through the ideology of nationalism (Smith 2008: 13-14).

Depending upon the specificities of the cases, these factors influence definition of nationhood. Smith defines "national identity" as "the continuous reproduction and reinterpretation of the pattern of values, symbols, memories, myths, and traditions that compose the distinctive heritage of nations, and the identification of individuals with that pattern and heritage" (Smith 2008: 19). The national identity reflects in social, cultural and political practices pursued by nations in preserving and maintaining independence and political power. It also sets the goals and agenda for the future development of nation and people.

The definition of nation as "imagined communities" offered by Benedict Anderson is the widely accepted model in political science for explaining identity and nationalism. Political communities are created through political discourse and practices. These discourses and practices involve deciding insider/outsider or identity/difference. Political practices are manifested in state policies. Political discourses are shaped by intelligentsia (Anderson 1983). The identification of self/other differences is manifested in the discourses of identity by political elites and state policies like citizenship law, language and education policies, etc.

Paulos Mar Gregorios invites our attention to how identity is being exercised in relation to the "other". He explains the complexity of self-other relation as an essential constituent in national identity. He states:

> There is first, relation of origin; second, relation of each to its own past – a past which is also full of relations; third, relation to the future as hope and commitment; and fourth, present relations and interactions which are in constant flux. Identity is not defined by self-understanding; yet self-understanding, also constantly in flux, is an integral part of one's identity (Gregorios 1989: 8-9).

In this formulation inter-relations of past, present and future matter. To elaborate his argument further he points out the aspect of tension between various groups in the social fabric of a given nation, which has roots in the past and has implications in the present. The nation's relation with outside world, perceived commonality of interests, perceived conflict of interests, alliances and hostilities, prejudices and predispositions against or in favour of other nations, apprehensions, threats, competition for higher esteem among nations are significant aspects of national identity. The tension between the identity of people and the identity of ruling class are significant in understanding national identity. These two identities are rarely same in a nation. Most often there is conflict between the interests of the ruling group and those of the people. The former try to convince the latter that whatever they are doing is in the interests of the latter. In actual reality the interests of the ruling class dominate, and they forge the national identity in terms of their own interests (Gregorios 1989: 11). If identity is taken as a product of social relations, memory and historical experience play an important role in defining it. Memory is important in understanding nationalism and also politics of exclusion and inclusion.

Memory studies scholars throw light on politics of memory centred on the legacy of 20th century history of socialism relevant to European politics. Since Maurice Halbwachs (1925) theorized the collective nature of memory and social frames of memory many attempts to study memory have been pursued by scholars of philosophy, sociology, psychology, communications, literature, and culture studies. Smirnov (2015: 59) defines politics of memory as "a range of measures to promote certain interpretations of the events of the past to achieve certain political goals. The agent of the politics of memory is either the state or political parties/influential social groups ... In a broad sense, the politics of memory facilitates the 'invention' of traditions in line with certain political goals of the power groups". Maria Paula et al. (2009: 77) say, "Memory operates as a selective process and may become a political weapon for the victims of war and genocide when forgetting has established its hegemony". Pierrie Nora (1984) explored "the places of memory" and many ways of looking at the past. Irina Matonye (2013) takes "narratives and representation" as two building blocks of memory for interpreting and understanding the past. Aleida Assmann (2012) views memory as also involved in forgetting in the context of democratic transition.

Zheng Wang (2018: 4) conceptualizes the political aspects of memory in an International Relations (IR) point of view combining insights from liberal, constructivist and instrumentalist traditions. Wang sees historical memory "as a variable to explain political action and social movements" and as a source of "collective identity" in his conceptualization of the link of historical memory with national identity formation, perceptions and policy making. Given the link between "historical memory and rise of nationalism", the author argues that collective memory is an integral part of nation building (Zheng 2018: 31), as historical memory has multiple functions, links and effects. Historical memory influences political "actor's perceptions, interpretations and decision-making process" in myriad ways. It acts as "a key element in the construction of national identity formation" and "the lens and motivational tool" (Ibid: 29) for framing and reframing memories by mobilizing the memory of a particular time and space of the past for present use and future policy formation. A nation's "identity determines national interests, which in turn determines policy and state action" (Ibid: 31). "Chosen trauma" and "chosen glory" could be elements of identity. The link between collective memory and history is manifested in the education system, social discourses and state policies (Ibid).

Michael Bernhard and Jan Kubik consider three important premises of politics of memory in post-communist states:

> First people always strive to come to terms with the past of their communities in order to generate a sense of order in their personal and collective lives. Second, new leaders often find it advantageous to call for the punishment of the political and coercive authorities of fallen regimes. Whether and how they do depends heavily on their interpretation and assessment of the collective past. They, remembering the past, particularly collective, is a political process; thus, the politics of memory and commemoration needs to be studied as an integral part of the establishment of new collective identities and new principles of political legitimacy (Bernhard and Kubik 2014: 2-3).

Two concepts: mnemonic actors and memory regimes are important in this framework. The politics of memory focus on "strategies that political actors employ to make others remember in certain, specific ways and the effects of such mnemonic manipulations" (Kubik and Bernhard 2014: 7). Reconstruction of memory is related to contemporary purposes of specific political actors including state authorities, political parties, mass media, education system, and so on. It is not necessary that everything that happened in the past may be used in the present political context.

Considering the "collective memory as a form of social consciousness socially shared beliefs and attitudes towards the past", Marek Ziolkowski identifies four basic functions of memory and claims:

> It can constitute (1) an instrument for restoring the knowledge of the past; (2) a tool of a deepened reflection on the history of a particular nation, on the role of determination and fortuity, and of fate and choice in the nation's experience, and on the notions of "normality" and "obviousness" the way they are taught to every generation; (3) a basis for an emotional evaluation of the past and present, a stimulus that evokes the feeling of either satisfaction with the befallen changes or else a nostalgic, no-claim mourning for the past irrevocably lost, and finally, (4) a basis for taking action or putting forwards claims aimed at a restitution, at least partial, of the past state of affairs" (Ziolkowski 2000: 297-303).

It is the historical memory which is usable for present political purposes. Obviously, memory can be used as a political resource and, given memory diversity, in a polity it could become a source of contestation while constructing national identity.

In politics of identity the process of identification initiated by state institutions for the purpose of solving social problems is important. Politically speaking, identities in a modern state are not static but constructed and distributed in a given time and space through discourses. As Calhoun states, "In the modern era identity is always constructed and situated in a field and amid a flow of contending cultural discourses" (Calhoun 1994: 13). Modern nation states use different methods to build "nation". Homogenization is one thing that is important in nation building in Europe. As Charles Tilly (1975: 43-44) notes, "almost all European governments eventually took steps which homogenized their populations: the adoption of state religions, expulsion of minorities like the Moors and the Jews, institution of a national language, eventually and the organization of mass public instruction." Culture becomes a powerful element in defining identity in the modern times. This becomes problematic when the majority ethnic or social groups try to homogenize and force the minority to follow their language and culture. Critics say that nationalist claims of people tend to ignore internal diversity and conflict. As Richard White states, nationalism "irrational, and self-serving ... promotes ignorance and self-deception on a massive scale" (White 2005: 169). In this sense nationalism and homogenizing tendencies can, to a certain extent, be destructive in terms of social harmony and cohesion. The marker of "self" can cause continuation of "otherness" and marginalization of minorities for long. Thus, in the process of transformation of democracies, ethnicity based nationalism play a significant role in defining the nation.

In order to understand minority nationalism, Rogers Brubaker (1996) offers a conceptual model, "triad nexus", comprised of three analytical components: "national minorities, the newly nationalizing states in which they live, and the external "homelands" to which they belong". This framework has widely been used in many studies on Russian speakers adding to new elements such as international institutions and arguments linking to 'an ascendant and expansive "Euro-Atlantic space"' (Smith et al. 2002; Kelley 2004; Galbreath 2005). In the post-Soviet Baltic states, in their attempt of transforming to democracy revived nationalism in nation building in which culture and identity becomes integral components of political process. According to Eric Hobsbawm (1990: 62) "states would use the increasingly powerful machinery for communicating with their inhabitants, above all the primary schools, to spread the image and heritage of the 'nation' and to inculcate attachment to it." He also notes that "the official or culture-language of rulers and elites usually came to be the actual language of modern states via public education and other administrative mechanisms." Thus, language and education become means of communicating particular idea of nation.

Divergent interpretations of history of experience of Second World War play an important role today in all European countries while discussing the basic ideas and values that should guide contemporary politics and society (Sierp 2014: 1). The political significance of history is emphasized by the then president of the German Bundestag in 2007 as he said: "History does not pass, it cannot be overcome. It is a prerequisite for the present, and dealing with history shapes the future of any society.

Therefore, the preservation of memory is a political, that is, a shared responsibility" (N. Lammert, quoted in Sierp 2014: 1). Thus, history is important in shaping not only the present, but future also. Therefore, preserving historical memory is a shared responsibility of political elites and citizens. Memory also has the power to act as a source for political change (Verovsek 2017). Obviously, historical memory is constructed with a priority objective of creating or strengthening collective identity and cohesiveness. Such identity construction is mostly "from above" by political elites to impose on society for advancing their own political purposes. When the official narratives of the past and commemoration practices insist certain space of past should be remembered in a specific way, the official collective and cultural memories act as political resource and source of contestations. Obviously, in post-Soviet Baltic states collective memory, history and identity could be seen as the dominant ingredients in nation building, state politics, public discourse and policy making.

Nation Building in Baltic States: Politicization of History, Memory and Identity

Lithuania, Latvia and Estonia restored independence through mobilization of ethnic nationalism, historical past and collective memory during the freedom movement. The legacy of centuries-old intense nationalistic identity of the Baltic people contributed to a strong sense of nationalism in the Baltic quest for autonomy and independence. Evoked by popular nationalist movements that struggled to free the 'Baltic self' from oppressive 'others' the Baltic nations emerged as a geopolitical and cultural entity between Western and Eastern Europe. And the Baltic nationalism, according to Hartman, evolved around a few distinct entities which are 'key ingredients' of history, geography, language, religion, economics, and legal and political systems (Hartman 1992). Thus, Baltic nationalism could find its legendry images and heroic icons from the historical narratives on golden years of Baltic regimes that were destroyed by both Western and Eastern powers.

The Baltic states have a tragic and complex history of political repression, bloodshed, appearance, disappearance and re-appearance as independent states. The Baltic states were dominated in the past by neighbouring powers and subjected to foreign rule for centuries. The Germans, Danes, Poles, Swedes and Russians occupied Baltic states at different points of time in history. They experienced various wars in different historical periods from Teutonic Order's Crusades to Second World War (Kasekamp 2010). The Second World War established that the Baltic security and sovereignty depend on the great power's willingness to guarantee these to them. The location of Baltic states between two giant neighbours, Soviet Union and Germany, remained as the main cause of their vulnerability and victimhood in the region, especially during Second World War period. In view of the troubled history of foreign domination during different historical times, the geopolitics and power dynamics on the eve of the Second World War once again confirmed their permanent vulnerability (Roucek 1949).

Apparently, today one can see that the historical events in Baltic states in the past 100 years show somewhat a cyclical nature in the sense that they constantly fear the repeat of past. The historical cycle, therefore, in the Baltic context means that during the past over 100 years' time Baltic states lost their nationhood more than once and they fear such loss may repeat in future as and when the events in the neighbourhood unfold unfavourable and dangerous for them. They had little opportunities in the past in shaping their destinies and institutions on their own because of their geopolitically vulnerable location surrounded by powerful neighbours. They are caught in a situation of permanent vulnerability and insecurity not because of their own fault and but because of their location in a geographically significant area that decides their destiny.

The modern era sovereignty of Baltic states began in the interwar period (1918-1940). They were made provinces of the Russian Empire in the 18th century. Although Lithuania had independent state structures since 13th century unlike Estonia and Latvia, they were also finally brought under the rule of Russian Empire. Thereafter, they had undergone severe Russification reforms in the 19th century. However, they miraculously achieved independent statehood for the first time in modern era in 1918 by fighting successfully against the mighty Russian and German forces after the First World War. In the nation building process they could consolidate their nationhood without much domestic problems as the majority ethnic groups, i.e., Lithuanians, Latvians and Estonians, were demographically dominant. Since the ethnic composition was favourable, the question of minorities had been politically less problematic throughout the interwar period (Smith 1994).

They introduced a constitution and succeeded in building democratic institutions, establishing parliamentary system, cultivating political pluralism, restructuring economies and reshaping national cultures comparable to that of their Scandinavian neighbours (Smith 1994). They developed their agriculture based economies, introduced land reforms and expanded industries. The Soviet and Western powers granted them recognition. The Soviet Union signed treaties with Estonia, Latvia and Lithuania on 2 February, 1 August and 12 July respectively in 1920, granting them *de jure* recognition. The Allied powers granted *de jure* recognition to Estonia and Latvia in January 1921 and Lithuania in December 1922 (White 1994: 35). They were granted memberships in international agencies such as League of Nations in 1921.

However, the liberal democratic phase initiated after centuries of feudal servitude did not survive its consolidation and popular legitimacy in the midst of interwar crisis. The economic crisis as a result of the great depression of 1929-1930 hit hard the three Baltic states causing political instability. All the three Baltic states gave way to dictatorship and succumbed to authoritarian mode of presidential regimes of a nationalist stamp, Lithuania in 1926, Latvia and Estonia in 1934. The nationalist authoritarian regimes under Presidents Antanas Smetona in Lithuania, Karlis Ulmanis in Latvia and Konstantin Pats in Estonia were distinguished as benign rather than malign dictatorships.

During the interwar period, Estonia, Latvia and Lithuania were worried about their security. The question of how to defend their independence and sovereignty in the shadow of two neighbouring great powers Russia and Germany shaped their perspectives and policies (Hope 1994). They remained fragile because of the perceived indifference of the great powers towards their independent status and lack of resources to protect themselves through coordinated foreign and security policies. However, cooperation between the three countries was also in a poor state due to mutual suspicion (Kirby 1994). During this period, Baltic states' relation with the Soviet Union was relatively normal despite their mistrust and dislike to Soviet Russia. But given the legacy of presence of German minorities Baltic states had very friendly relation with Nazi Germany. Soviet interests in Baltic territories were opened with Soviet access to Baltic Sea ports. Baltic governments also understood the strategic significance of Baltic coastline for both Soviet Union and Germany and identified the dangers to them in case of war between both great powers. Hitler thought of Lithuania, Latvia and Estonia as "glacis of the European anti-bolshevist powers against Russia" (Hiden and Salmon 1994: 102).

Given the geopolitical situation and material realities emerged at that time Estonia and Latvia signed agreement with Germany in 1934 for closer cooperation with Germany. But Lithuania was preoccupied with confrontation with Poland over Vilna question and German occupied Lithuanian territory of Memel (Klaipeda). They were in a situation of potential conflict with Germany. Baltic states were not in the priorities of Hitler but they were very significant for Soviet Union as a border zone with potential vulnerabilities. Panicked by the talks between Britain, France and Soviet Union for a plan of tripartite guarantee for Baltic states, Estonia and Latvia turned to Germany to counteract it over the fear of Soviet interference in their internal affairs and signed non-aggression treaties with Germany on 7 June 1938. The pro-German actions of Estonia and Latvia provided grounds for more Soviet suspicion on them and their capability to observe neutrality. Since the British and French talks were slow on the issue of security guarantee for Baltic states and not agreeing with the Soviet demands fully, Soviet Union made deal with Germany and signed Nazi-Soviet non-aggression pact on 23 August 1939 (Kirby 1994). Hitler ensured Soviet neutrality which he thought would end the threat of potential western aggression. The secret protocol of the Pact granted Soviet Union Finland, the Baltic states, eastern Poland and the Romanian province of Bessarabia within its sphere of influence. The secret protocol in the Pact further suggested, "In the event of a territorial and political transformation in the territories belonging to the Baltic states, the northern frontier of Lithuania shall represent the frontier of the spheres of interest both of Germany and the USSR ..." (Overy 2017: 125).

The relation between Soviet Union and Baltic states entered a critical phase after the Hitler-Stalin Pact of 1939, especially when the rumours regarding German attack on Soviet Union spread. The *Baltic Entente* of Lithuania, Latvia, and Estonia were alleged to be preparing provocative actions against the Soviet state. They were, thus, forced to sign Pacts of Defence and Mutual Assistance with Soviet Union, accept Soviet troops on their soil, and became in effect Soviet protectorates. The Pact was signed by Estonia on 25 September, Latvia on 5 October and Lithuania on 10 October 1939. Thereafter, Soviet troops were brought to the Baltic frontiers. Elections were held under Soviet supervision. People elected new "People's Assemblies" in each country and installed pro-Soviet governments which requested their incorporation into the Soviet Union. On the pretext of invitation Soviet troops entered Lithuania on 15 June and Estonia and Latvia on 17 June 1940. Second World War broke out when Germany attacked Soviet Union code named as "Operation Barbarossa on 22 June 1940 to finish its "Jewish-Bolshevik" enemy. The Baltic states were incorporated into the USSR in August 1940 (Misiunas and Taagepera 1983; Senn 1990).

Lithuania, Latvia and Estonia experienced many difficult situations during 1939-1991 as a result of Nazi German and Soviet invasions and occupation. The Baltic people had experienced horrendous crimes against humanity both under Soviet and Nazi German invasions from 1940 to 1944 during the War. Almost 90-95 percent of the Jewish population was exterminated by Nazi German forces. Under Soviet invasion and occupation they experienced mass deportation of Balts to Siberian Gulags, arbitrary arrests, imprisonment and repression. In the post-War era Baltic states were forcibly annexed into Soviet Union by Stalinist regime and Soviet occupation continued for more than fifty years until 1991 when they restored independence. In the post-independent period they have somehow managed to establish democratic regime compared to other states in the post-Soviet space, and became members of NATO and European Union in 2004. Thus, in the 21st century they look somewhat in a more secure situation but their frightening past is still haunting them. The history of Second World War experience remains the most contentious and complicated one with regard to their nation building in the post-Soviet era.

Apparently, the current nation building and democratic transformation in Baltic states is based on contemporary Baltic nationalisms, culture and legal continuity as the basis of national identity formation, especially in Latvia and Estonia (Hartman 1992; Lane 1994; Kasekamp 2010; Plakans 2012; Auers 2015), predominance of culture and language, historical injustice and "two genocide" narratives (Rummel 1990; Onken 2007, 2010), de-Sovietization and memory politics of "becoming European" (Malksoo 2010), and historical revisionism and obfuscation of Holocaust (Levin 2001; Donskis 2009; Katz 2009, 2017). Consequent upon the above factors Baltic states face multiple dilemmas related to history, identity and memory politics.

Baltic nationalism promoted a kind of inter-nationalism between three states, Lithuania, Latvia and Estonia, instead of infusing all diversities into a single Baltic nation state. Despite having different linguistic and socio-cultural traditions all the three countries put emphasis on their Baltic national identity to be survived during the years of struggle for independence and the nation building process thereafter. Though the people across three countries formed a united struggle with Baltic nationalist motives and set a model of nonviolent protests through human chain, the 'Baltic Way'. There were no demands for a unified Baltic nation state. In that sense, the Baltic nationalism accommodated the local and traditional diversities within the region and formed three distinctive nation states that kept and asserted their Baltic identity. And the nationalist movements that finally orchestrated across three states in the form of 'Singing Revolution' also set a distinctive model in the process of nation building.

In the contemporary nation building process the re-established Baltic states as Benedict Anderson (1991) suggests have to imagine a "political community" having shared national consciousness and construct, a national identity founded on very different historical and social experiences. They are bound to reconstruct new boundaries of "self" and "other" for which history and memory are important instruments to decide strategies of inclusion and exclusion. The political elites especially in Latvia and Estonia dominantly used history of their short span of democracy in the inter-war era to argue for legal continuity, to reject Soviet legacy and assert the victimhood narratives on memory of the bitter experience under Soviet occupation to define their political system and construct national identity. The natural antagonism towards 'colonial masters' has been the part of Baltic national identity formation and emergence of independent states in the region that experienced the yoke of German and Russian powers time and again. And the Baltic region's 'organic nationalism' could even survive internal challenges from Soviet supported anti-secessionists 'contrived nationalism' since the former one was derived from an internally-initiated, organic sense of national identity that could flourish and enjoy popular support (Hartman 1992).

The nation building process in Baltic States has been no way different from the European and other experiences of homogenizing certain diversities under a single 'national' umbrella. Actually, the Baltic nation building methods were similar to the typical European nation building measures such as homogenizing diverse populations, adopting a state religion, excluding minorities, constituting a national language and restructuring means and method of public instruction. To maintain its national cohesiveness Baltic states kept the non-Baltic people, language and culture at bay and often followed exclusive practices towards different identities. The historical experiences and social memories always got reflected in the nation building process of Baltic states in the form its relations with Western and Eastern European countries and people. The so-called Molotov-Ribbentrop Pact of 23 August 1939 signed during the Second World War is considered as the historic injustice to the Baltic people and therefore the decades of sufferings and dependence have constructed an image of 'victimized Baltic nation' vis-à-vis the hegemonic power struggle of 20th century.

Lithuania, Latvia and Estonia view themselves as part of "civic Europe/West" to which they want to return and reclaim their real past and right to national historiography. They consider Soviet Union as a colonizer which coercively annexed "illegally occupied" and deprived them of their independence. In the post-colonial setting of Baltic nation building and democratic transformation in the post-Soviet era under the framework of Russian otherness and European sameness, the politics of "othering" is focused on narratives of victimization and innocence of majority ethnicity, historical injustice, cultural domination, "illegal occupation", and contested interpretation of the experience of Second World War. Russian speaking minority is framed as "illegal migrants" and "colonists" who cannot be imagined as natural members of post-Soviet political community at par with Baltic majority ethnicity. Russia, thus, is implicated as external enemy/existential threat and Europe is accepted as protector and guarantor of security and development.

When looking at the Baltic nation building narrative depicting Nazi and Soviet crimes as "equal genocides" through the prism of Holocaust, it reflects an irreconcilable and contested victimhood challenging the fragility and innocence of Baltic majority ethnicity who were also collaborators and perpetrators in Holocaust. Narratives on Holocaust reflect a controversial treatment as Jews are considered more oriented toward Soviet Union and associated with communist Bolsheviks. History, memory and identity are, thus, infused with politics and therefore, important requirement in the current democratization process, political discourses and practices. Hence, arguably, the Baltic nation building project is impregnated with complexity and multiple dilemmas related to history, memory and identity manifested in issues of citizenship, statelessness, minority rights, social integration, democratization, security and foreign policy. Their victimhood discourse also includes their experience under Nazi German invasion and extermination of Jews, but after nearly three decades of independence, the Baltic states are still struggling to "coming to terms with the past" in the quest for gaining acknowledgement of dominant narrative of victimhood suffered due to atrocities committed by the Soviet Union. Their political imagination of nationhood using collective memory, selective history, homogenization attempts and reinterpretation of history accordingly are causing multiple dilemmas.

Structure of the Book

This book is a collection of thirteen scholarly papers that explore the multifarious dimensions of nation building process in Baltic states and the challenges they face in the new geopolitical world order. It tries to address certain pertinent questions: how Baltic states' past influences the present politics and policies and future directions; why memory and history are important in defining and understanding nationalism, nation building and identity in contemporary Lithuania, Latvia and Estonia; how the historical memory politics is manifested in Baltic states; how the legacies of past injustices in political and historical memory influence the contemporary projects of transitional justice and redressal in producing new forms of revisionism; how Holocaust and the issue of local collaboration with Nazis are viewed in Baltic states; what are the implications of memory and commemoration politics for democracy and political pluralism in Baltic states; how politics of history, memory and identity impacts Baltic international relations, especially with Russia and Europe; and what kind of complexities and moral and integration dilemmas memory politics generate in Baltic societies.

The central argument of the book is that the contemporary nation building and democratic transformation in the Baltic states is primarily founded on the national symbols, themes, and nationalist political elites' narratives and understanding of victimhood, politics of collective memory, common history and identity of majority ethnicity. Anything related to Soviet Union is considered as bad in contemporary Baltic states. Soviet nostalgia is not encouraged. Such conceptualization has both domestic and international repercussions. K. B. Usha and Abdullakkutty K. P. in *Introduction: Nation Building in Baltic States – History, Memory and Identity* (Chapter 1) introduce the post-Soviet context of Baltic politics, theoretical framework, core arguments, main contents and structure of the book.

Baltic states regained independence through their freedom movement known as the "Singing Revolution". Emphasizing the influence of historical origin of the nation, culture, religion, language and political identification of citizens in the national imagination and identity formation of the Baltic states, Saranya Antony A. in *The Singing Revolution, Independence and Democratic Transition of Baltic States: Nationalism, Culture and Identity* (Chapter 2) discusses the role of ethnic nationalism, culture and identity in the nonviolent Baltic national freedom movement and the democratic transformation. Saranya argues that Singing Revolution worked like music therapy to boost the self-sacrificing spirit of the masses in independence movement and democratic transformation thereafter. The origin of "the Singing Revolution" was from the titular majority's fear of elimination of their culture and language and also the demographic change consequent upon the policies imposed by the Soviet regime. In the current democratic transformation in Lithuania, Latvia and Estonia nationalism, identity and culture play important roles in defining political community, identity and establishing political institutions of the state.

Sarunas Paunksnis in *Nationalism and Nation Building in Contemporary Lithuania* (Chapter 3) takes us to an important debate on the political character of Baltic states that whether they should be considered as post-colonial countries like India. Considering the independent states after the collapse of the USSR as the postcolonial countries may jeopardize the 'self' understanding of Baltic states as European. To construct the nation and mobilize the nationalist movement the intelligentsia resurrected the historical greatness of Baltic countries and popularized it through folk-songs, stories, fairytales and myths that ultimately led to the Singing Revolution. However, there are short comings in conceptualizing a nation and in the process of nation building through homogenization in a multicultural state like Lithuania. And the author clearly warns that the brand pacifist version of nationalism popularized during Singing Revolution is slowly giving way to radical nationalism in Lithuania and in Baltic states in general.

The media especially radio popularized nationalist narratives that could unite people of three countries, Latvia, Lithuania and Estonia to fight for a common cause. Constructing an 'imagined Baltic community' in a buffer zone between Eastern and Western Europe the media mobilized the 'Baltic Way' of nationalism to achieve independence for Baltic states. The nationalist discourses were disseminated and popularized with the rise of strong intelligentsia across Baltic states, and different genres of printed literature appeared in vernacular languages. Baltic media worked instrumental in retention of the 'revolutionary cooperation' between Bolsheviks and Baltic nationalists before the so-called Soviet-Nazi secret pact had changed the scenario. Abdullakkutty K. P. in *Media-ted Nationalism: The 'Baltic Way' of National Imagination* (Chapter 4) explores the way popular literature and media constructed and circulated the notion of Balt and Baltic nationalism that evolved through long struggle for national identity and cultural sovereignty.

Since the Baltic states experienced political transition from authoritarianism to parliamentary democracy, these countries try to incorporate the norms and values of western democratic models. Political parties played important role as potential actors in the establishment and consolidation of new democratic regimes across Baltic states. Karamala Areesh Kumar argues that political parties especially in Lithuania emerged as a result of national awakening and political movements for national independence that resulted in the formation of democratic parliamentary system. He in *Democratic Transition and Emergence of Multi-Party System in Lithuania* (Chapter 5) explores the very political culture of Baltic nation building process analysing the development of political parties and multi-party system in Lithuania in the broader context of post-communist democratization and democratic consolidation.

Baltic states restored independence at a time the process of globalization is intensified and neoliberal economic reforms are recognized as universal policy model worldwide. Baltic states quickly embraced neoliberal economic model and initiated reform policies as a crucial element in the post-Soviet nation building process that keeps a distance from Russia and integrates with Europe. Estonia became the most successful case in the neoliberal transformation of economy according to the conditions of international financial institutions such as IMF, World Bank and WTO. The neoliberal transformation resulted in the withdrawal of the state's social role from all sectors. Consequently, the neoliberal policies adopted by Baltic States forced the state to play the role of protecting the market that resulted in drafting comprehensive laws for privatization and withdrawing all subsides from agriculture, industries and the service sector. Focusing on the political economy aspect of the nation building process in Baltic states, V. Lenin Kumar in *Political Economy of Neoliberal Reforms in Baltic States: The Case of Estonia* (Chapter 6) discusses the issues of economic reforms in post-Soviet Estonia. He argues that Baltic economy more than any other sectors did face the de-Sovietisation process such as institutional restructuring and market-oriented reforms.

Among the major reform policies adopted by post-Soviet Baltic states the language reform turned to be one of the most critical reforms. The new language policy in the education sphere explicitly affected the rights of huge monolingual Russian speaking minorities. And the current language politics retrieve the memory of Polish, German and Russian dominance and the intense Russification of the society, culture, and education during Soviet times. Zakali Ayemi in *The Impact of Language Politics on Education in Baltic States: The Case of Russian Speaking Minority* (Chapter 7) analyzes the politicization of language and its impact on education of the Russian minorities across the region. Language policy is used as a tool to revenge the Soviet treatment of the Baltic states especially in Latvia and Estonia. To survive this challenge Russians are forced either to naturalize themselves and learn titular language to reside in Baltic states or remain deprived of educational and employment opportunities.

The critical views of Baltic intelligentsia, especially minority rights and political morality in contemporary times contributed to the nation building process. Lithuanian liberal philosopher, political theorist and former member of European Parliament Leonidas Donskis played a key role in the nation building process through strong social critique of the Lithuanian society, politics and mainstream social science discourse. Constructing unparalleled debates on nationalism and nationalist notions Donskis has stunned the academia and policy makers both at home and abroad. Chinmaya Mahanand in *Socio-Political Ideas of Leonidas Donskis: Nationalism, Anti-Semitism and Predicaments of Modernity in Lithuania* (Chapter 8) introduces the thoughts of Leonidas Donskis who philosophically engaged with the nationalist notions and critiqued the socio-political discourses in the contemporary Baltic states. Being a Lithuanian native of Jewish origin, Donskis strongly opposes the anti-Semitism influenced by the radical 'blood and soil' ultra-nationalism, and defends the historical, egalitarian, inclusive, multicultural legacy of Lithuania. He understood the mainstream intellectual discourse as responsible for the transition of Lithuania in the past and also its transformation in the future. As a human rights defender he considered oppression and discrimination on the basis of caste, race, gender and religion as a global problem. He was a staunch critique of caste discrimination and oppression of Dalits in India. He called the caste based discrimination of Dalits in India and elsewhere "one of the biggest paradoxes of 21st century".

The Holocaust history reveals the complexity of the Baltic nation building by simultaneously following two irreconcilable political goals of sympathizing with both victims and perpetrators. When looking at the nation building process of Baltic states through the prism of Holocaust, the history of Jewish experience during Second World War reveals an untold aspect of ethno-national understanding of nation and national identity asserted by Baltic national majority. Hence, the paradox of the attempts to hide their own crimes for which they can use Soviet crimes as an excuse for Holocaust obfuscation calls into question the Baltic democratic system. K. B. Usha in *Historical Memory of Holocaust, "Double Genocide" Politics and Revival of Anti-Semitism in Contemporary Baltic States* (Chapter 9) discusses the dilemma of historical memory related to the ethno-nationalist agenda of nation building and memory politics and the revival of anti-Semitism in the Baltic states of Estonia, Latvia and Lithuania while addressing contested narratives of victimhood caused by Soviet occupation and Holocaust as two "equal genocides".

Exploring the discourses of ethnicity, exclusion and minority rights, Anju Devi traces the history and development of anti-Semitism and its impact on the Jewish community in Baltic states with special reference to Lithuania in *Ethnicity, Exclusion and Minority Rights in Baltic States: The Case of Jewish Community in*

Lithuania (Chapter 10). Despite their contribution in the nation building process Jews are victims of 'memory politics' and face challenges regarding status of citizenship, native language, security, identity, equality, freedom of speech etc. As the Jewish fight for their human rights continues, the 'historical injustice' to this minority group prevails in the context of post-Soviet democratic nation building process of Baltic states which is based on western liberal norms and values. As ethno-nationalism and identity politics are getting stronger the Jews are struck between the debates of "return to Europe" or "return to west" whereas the Baltic states have the history of massive extermination of almost 95 percent of Jews. The social attitude of animosity, Holocaust revisionism and discriminatory policies towards Jews still continue in re-independent Lithuania, Latvia and Estonia.

Political participation of women in Lithuania is an important issue in the process of nation building. Despite having constitutional support for equal status for men and women and having numerical strength representing 53.2 percent of total population Lithuanian women do not have equal share in power structure. While there was considerable women representation in Lithuanian politics and parliament after the Russian revolution, women's political rights were denied under the Soviet regime. But things are changing after restoration of independence. Karamala Areesh Kumar in *Political Participation of Women in Lithuania* (Chapter 11) throws light on gender politics in Lithuania. Though Lithuania adopted education and health policies for women's empowerment and witnessed their political strengthening, as Dalia Grybauskaite was elected as first women president in 2009, Kumar finds that lack of trust on the state institutions, trade unions and political parties still affects political representation of women negatively.

Since Baltic states define Russia as an external threat and Russian speakers as internal threat, their security policy is formulated to deter potential Russian aggression, use of Baltic Russian speaking minority as a soft power asset, and leave the responsibility of protection of Baltic states to NATO. Eastward expansion of NATO and the increased military build-up of NATO in the Baltic Sea over Russian border after Ukraine Crisis reveal this perception. Therefore, Baltic states are always in strenuous relation with Russia, although they depend on Russia for energy resources. The security policy and identity politics, thus, could generate a situation of security dilemma as a result of Baltic states' constructing Russian identity as both internal and external threats in the region. Anoop Kumar in *Baltic States' Policy towards Russia: Problems of Politics of Identity and Securitization* (Chapter 12) discusses the nexus between the politics of identity and securitization of Russia and its implications for the foreign policy and bilateral relations between Baltic states and Russia, which are strenuous from the very beginning in the post-Soviet period.

The issue of minority rights is one of the major challenges of nation building process in contemporary Baltic states. Their exclusionary policies, especially of Estonia and Latvia, unleashed international criticism and invited the role of supranational bodies like European Union in such discourses in these sovereign member states. Baltic states, under EU obligations, have to deal with the issues of ethnic, linguistic and religious minorities living in three countries. Minority issue was an important issue even in the wake of EU accession negotiations. Akanksha in *Baltic States and Europe: The Role of European Union in the Baltic Minority Rights Discourse* (Chapter 13) makes an attempt to understand the issue of minority rights in Lithuania, Latvia and Estonia in a larger context of historical evolution of the concept of minority protection in Europe and the impact of the same on the standard setting of membership criteria of EU for the Baltic countries. Given the membership of Baltic states in the EU and their obligation to abide by EU norms and principles on minority question she raises the concern on minority rights policy followed in Baltic states with a negative record regarding the question of citizenship of their minority citizens, especially in Latvia and Estonia calling their evolving democracy into question.

Ultimately, this book is part of an attempt to scholarly engage with the diverse issues regarding the nation building process of Baltic states in the post-Soviet/post-communist context. While the book discusses a range of issues related to nation building, it is not without limitations. It is really a difficult task to analyze the reality of developments in Baltic states for those who do not know language and have less access to primary data, media narratives and speeches from the field. Therefore, given the complex ethnic, linguistic, socio-political, economic, geopolitical and strategic issues of Baltic region, the analysis in this book is partial as many areas are left to scrutiny by further research and comprehensive understanding. Being a strategically important region between Western and Eastern Europe, the nation building process of Baltic states would attract the scholarly attention of both academic and policy-oriented researchers.

Notes

1. Johann Gottfried Herder (1744-1803) is known as father of cultural nationalism (Schmid 1956). He was a student of Immanuel Kant, one of the great philosophers in modern western philosophy, at Konigsberg (Kaliningrad) University. Herder spent his formative years in Riga (1764-69). He was a teacher at the cathedral school in Riga. He also worked as an assistant preacher at the various churches in Riga. In 1864 Herder's statue was eructed in Riga. Kurt Stavenhagen, a prominent Baltic German phenomenologist believes that "the Herderian in Herder emerged in Riga." He argued Herder contributed the concept of national

identity as grounded in language to all the Central and Eastern European nations (Piirimae 2012). The Baltic debate, national thinking and actions resemble Herderian ideas of cultural nationalism and national identity. Hence, Herder's views provide useful insights in understanding the role of identity and culture in history and politics of Baltic states.

2. Herder was subjected to criticism as an advocate of racism, although his writings reflected the dangers of ethnic fanaticism.

References

Anderson, Benedict (1983, 1991), *Imagined Communities: Reflections on the Origin and Spread of Nationalism*, London: Verso.

Alesina, Alberto and Bryony Reich (February 2013), "Nation building," National Bureau of Economic Research (NBER), Cambridge, Working Paper, 18839, retrieved from http://www.nber.org/papers/w18839.pdf

Araújo, Maria Paula Nascimento and Myrian Sepúlveda dos Santos (2009), "History, Memory and Forgetting: Political Implications", Translator: Sheena Caldwell, *RCCS Annual Review*, September, 1(1): 77-94.

Assmann, Aleida (2012), "To Remember or to Forget: Which Way out of a Shared Memory", in Aleida Assmann and Linda Shortt eds. (2012), *Memory and Political Change*, New York: Palgrave Macmillan, pp. 53-71.

Auers, Danis (2015), *Comparative Politics and Government of the Baltic States: Estonia, Latvia and Lithuania in the 21st Century*, New York: Palgrave Macmillan.

Barnard, Frederick M. (2003), *Herder on Nationality, Humanity and History*, Quebec: McGill-Queen's University Press.

Bernhard, Michael and Jan Kubik, eds. (2014), *Twenty Years after Communism: The Politics of Memory and Commemoration,* Oxford: Oxford University Press

Brubaker, Rogers (1996), *Nationalism Reframed: Nationhood and the National Question in the New Europe*, United Kingdom: Cambridge University Press.

Bruggemann, Karsten and Andres Kasekamp (July 2008), "The Politics of History and the "War of Monuments" in Estonia", *Nationalities Papers*, 36 (3): 425-448.

Calhoun, C. (1994) *Social Theory and the Politics of Identity*, Oxford: MA: Blackwell.

Donskis, Leonidas (2009), *Troubled Identity and the Modern World*, New York: Palgrave Macmillan.

Galbreath, David J. (2005), *Nation building and Minority Politics in Post-Socialist States: Interests, Influence and Identities in Estonia and Latvia*, Stuttgart: Ibidem Verlag.

Gellner, Ernest Andre (1987), *Culture, Identity and Politics*, Cambridge: Cambridge University Press.

Gregorios, Paulos Mar (1989), *Enlightenment: East and West, Pointers in the Quest for India's Secular Identity*, Shimla: Indian Institute for Advanced Study.

Hartman, Gary (1992), "The Origins and Growth of Baltic Nationalism as a Force for Independence", LITUANUS, *Lithuanian Quarterly Journal of Arts And Sciences*, 38 (3).

Hackmann, Jorg and Marko Lehti (2008), "Introduction: Contested and Shared Places of Memory, History and Politics in North Eastern Europe," *Journal of Baltic Studies*, 39 (4): 377-379.

Halbwachs, Maurice. (1925), *The Collective Memory*, trans. Francis J. Ditter and Vida Yezdi Ditter, New York: Harper and Collins.

Hiden, John and Patrick Salmon (1994), *The Baltic Nations and Europe: Estonia, Latvia and Lithuania in the Twentieth Century*, London: Longman.

Hobsbawm, Eric (1990), *Nations and Nationalism since 1780: Programme, Myth and Reality*, Cambridge: Cambridge University Press.

Hope, Nicholas (1994), "Interwar Statehood: Symbol and Reality", in Graham Smith, ed. (1994), *The Baltic States: The National Self-Determination of Estonia, Latvia and Lithuania*, London: Macmillan Press Limited, pp. 41-68.

Jolly, Mette (2007), *The European Union and the People*, Oxford: Oxford University Press.

Kasekamp, Andres (2010), *The History of the Baltic States*, New York: Palgrave Macmillan.

Katz, Dovid (2009), "On Three Definitions: Genocide; Holocaust Denial; Holocaust Obfuscation", in Leonid Donskis, ed., *The Litmus Test Case of Modernity: Examining Modern Sensibilities and the Public Domain in Baltic States at the Turn of the Century*, Bern: Peter Lang AG, pp. 259-278.

Katz, Dovid (December 2017), "The Extraordinary Recent History of Holocaust Studies in Lithuania", *Dapim: Studies on the Holocaust*, 31 (3): 285-295.

Kelley, Judith (summer 2004), "International Actors on the Domestic Scene: Membership Conditionality and Socialization by International Institutions", *International Organization*, 58: 425-457.

Kirby, David (1994), "Incorporation: Molotov-Ribbentrop Pact", in Graham Smith, ed. (1994), *The Baltic States: The National Self-Determination of Estonia, Latvia and Lithuania*, London: Macmillan Press Limited, pp. 69-85.

Klumbytė, N. (2010), "Memory, Identity, and Citizenship in Lithuania", *Journal of Baltic Studies*, 41 (3): 295-313.

Kubik, Jan and Michael Bernhard (2014), "Theory of the Politics of Memory", in Michael Bernhard and Jan Kubik, eds. (2014), *Twenty Years after Communism: The Politics of Memory and Commemoration*, Oxford: Oxford University Press, pp. 7-32.

Lane, Thomas (1994), "Nationalism and National Identity in the Baltic States", *Journal of Area Studies*, 2: 56-70.

Liebel-Weckowicz, Helen (April 1986), "Nations and Peoples: Baltic-Russian History and the Development of Herder's Theory of Culture", *Canadian Journal of History*, 21: 11-24.

Levin, Dov (2001), "Disinformation and Antisemitism: Holocaust Denial in the Baltic States, 1945–1999", in John K. Roth, Elisabeth Maxwell, Margot Levy and Wendy Whitworth, eds. (2001), *Remembering for the Future: The Holocaust in the Age of Genocide*, London: Palgrave Macmillan, pp. 847-857.

Malksoo, Maria (2010), *The Politics of Becoming European A study of Polish and Baltic post-Cold War security imaginaries*, Oxon: Routledge.

Matonye, Irina (2013), "The Elites Games in the Field of Memory: Insights from Lithuania", in Georges Mink and Laure Neumayer eds., (2013), *History, Memory and Politics in Central and Eastern Europe: Memory Games*, New York: Palgrave Macmillan, pp. 195-120.

Misiunas, Romuald J. and Rein Taagepera (1983), *Baltic States: Years of Dependence, 1940-1980*, Berkeley: University of California Press.

Nora, Pierrie (1989), "Between Memory and History: Les Lieux de Mémoire", *Representations*, Special Issue: Memory and Counter-Memory, Spring, 26: 7-24. Retrieved from https://is.muni.cz/el/1423/jaro2013/SOC564/um/40802691/Nora_Between_Memory_and_History.pdf

Onken, Eva-Clarita (2007), "The Baltic States and Moscow's 9 May Commemoration: Analysing Memory Politics in Europe." *Europe-Asia Studies*, 59 (1): 23-46.

Onken, Eva-Clarita (2010), "Memory and Democratic Pluralism in the Baltic States - Rethinking the Relationship," *Journal of Baltic Studies*, 41 (3): 277-294.

Overy, Richard (2017), *The Origins of the Second World War*, London: Routledge.

Plakans, Andrejs (2012), *A Concise History of the Baltic States*, Cambridge: Cambridge University Press.

Piirimae, Eva (2012), "*Humanität versus* Nationalismas the Moral Foundation of the Russian Empire: Jegor Von Sivers' Herderian Cosmopolitanism", *Ajalooline Ajakiri*, 2012, 1/2 (139/140), 79–113, retrieved from https://ojs.utlib.ee/index.php/EAA/article/view/589/574

Rummel, R. J. (1990), *Lethal Politics: Soviet Genocide and Mass Murder Since 1917,* New Brunswick and London: Transaction Publishers.

Roucek, Joseph S. (January 1949), The Geopolitics of Baltic States", *The American Journal of Economics and Sociology*, 8 (2): 171-175.

Senn, Alfred Erich (January 1990), "Perestroika in Lithuanian Historiography: The Molotov-Ribbentrop Pact", *The Russian Review*, 49 (1): 43-56.

Senn, Alfred Erich (1999), "Introduction", in Edvardas Tuskenis, ed. (1999), *Lithuania in European Politics: The Years of the First Republic, 1918-1940*, New York: St. Martin's Press, pp. 1-11.

Sierp, Aline (2014), *History, Memory, and Trans-European Identity: Unifying Divisions*, London: Routledge.

Smirnov, V. (2015), "The Role of Political Elites in the Development of the Politics of Memory in the Baltic States" *Baltic region*. 2015. № 2 (24). P. 58—72. Retrieved from https://journals.kantiana.ru/upload/iblock/752/Smirnov_58-72.pdf

Smith, Anthony D. (1991), *National Identity*, London: Penguin Books.

Smith, Anthony D. (2008), *The Cultural Foundations of Nations: Hierarchy, Movement, and Republic*, Oxford: Blackwell Publishing.

Smith, David J., Artis Pabriks, Aldis Purs and Thomas Lane (2002), *The Baltic States: Estonia, Latvia and Lithuania*, London: Routledge.

Smith, Graham (1994), "Introduction: The Baltic Nations and The National Self-Determination", in Graham Smith, ed. (1994), *The Baltic States: The National Self-Determination of Estonia, Latvia and Lithuania*, New York: St. Martin Press, pp. 1-12.

Tzanelli, Rodanthi (2008), *Nation building and Identity in Europe: The Dialogics of Reciprocity*, London: Palgrave Macmillan.

Verovsek, Peter J. (2017), "Memory, narrative, and rupture: The power of the past as a resource for political change", *Memory Studies*, August, retrieved from http://journals.sagepub.com/doi/full/10.1177/1750698017720256

White, James D. (1994), "Nationalism and Socialism in Historical Perspective", in Graham Smith ed. (1994), *The Baltic States: The National Self-Determination of Estonia, Latvia and Lithuania*, New York: St. Martin Press, 13-40.

White, Richard (2005), "Herder: On the Ethics of Nationalism", *Humanitas*, 18 (1&2): 166-181.

Zheng Wang (2018), *Memory Politics, Identity and Conflict: Historical Memory as a Variable*, New York: Palgrave Macmillan.

Ziółkowski, Marek (2000), "Four Functions of Memory", *Polish Sociological Review*, 131: 291-308.

Chapter Two

The Singing Revolution, Independence and Democratic Transformation of Baltic States: Nationalism, Identity and Culture

Saranya Antony A.

Introduction

This chapter focuses on the role of ethnicity based nationalism, identity and culture in mobilizing the masses for collective action during the non-violent "Singing Revolution" that led to the restoration of independence and the aftermath democratic transformation in the Baltic states of Lithuania, Latvia and Estonia. The origin of the Singing Revolution was from the titular majority's fear of elimination of their language, culture and demographic change consequent upon the policies imposed by the Soviet regime. In the current democratic transformation in Baltic states nationalism, historical memory, identity and culture play important roles in defining political community and establishing political institutions of state. The state and nation building processes aimed at quickly removing the legacies inherited from Soviet era and integrate with Europe. The Baltic political elites sought to reclaim their preferred past to get rid of Soviet legacies. New narratives of national identity formation considered the elements of common history, collective memory, ethnicity, culture, religion and language as symbols of political identification of citizens with their respective states.

The Baltic states' independence movement developed into one of the successful nonviolent mass movements in the recent international history. It derived its entire strength from culture, i.e., the folk songs, music concerts and the self-sacrificing spirit of the masses. Songs helped to keep the movement non-violent throughout the whole period of freedom struggle. Thus, songs turned as symbols of national identity and political action. In the Baltic case, Johan Gottfried Herder's philosophy played an important role in articulating national culture and nationalism. He identified songs being symbols of heritage could be used as instruments of social change. Herder's interest in Baltic folk poetry in the 18th century influenced the emergence of Baltic national cultures and singing traditions and song festivals which later helped mobilize Singing Revolution (Smidchens 2014).

Nationalist sentiments among people were awakened in the late 1980s, in view of their historical experiences and ethnic pride. Nationalism in Baltic states is a multi-faceted process. To understand nationalism and identity conception of Baltic states, one has to come across with various assimilation policies formulated by Germany, Russia and the former Soviet Union. The contemporary culture of Baltic states is a mixture of German and Russian cultural assimilation process. Besides, in the thirteenth century, prior to the Russian occupation, there were German merchants in Baltic states. It was the Baltic-Germans who dominate the social realm of Estonia and Latvia during this period. Most of the German merchants were followers of Lutheranism. The majority of Estonians and Latvians had faith in Lutheran religion. Estonia's literacy rate over Lutheran religious tradition was high and since the association of the Lutheran church with Baltic German was close and strong. The integration of Lutheranism was allowed as an attribute to the Estonian nationalism and identity (Person 2014).

Since independence, the Baltic states started redrawing political system and reconstructing the national identity. In the meantime, due to linguistic clashes, citizenship abandonment has emerged within the Baltic states. The initial schemes of Baltic states were mainly concentrated to depart from the continuation of the Soviet legacy. The Baltic states began identifying the Soviet Union and its successor Russia as an 'Othering' national identity different from European 'Us' (Kesa 2011). The European Union was defined as the friend and supporter of development and security. Therefore, they decided to integrate into the Euro-Atlantic security structure and joined NATO and the European Union in 2004. Mainly, the EU enlargement policies that have been initiated to include same geographical, socio-cultural and national identities helped promote of the Baltic interest.

Nationhood, Nationalism, Identity and Culture: Theoretical Perspectives

Nationalism and national identity are contested concepts and multifaceted processes evolved over time. The formulation of nationalism has been rooted in the sense of belonging among the inhabitants of a nation or a group. Nation's incoherent treatment of dissent of citizen leads to vacillation on origins of national identity. In fact, a number of factors determine the notion of nationalism and identity formulation such as language, symbols, history of a nation, kinship and culture (Guibernau 2004). The strong feeling of nationalist sentiments caused to turn up with strong patriotism or chauvinism. Major discourses regarding nationalism and national identity are related to cultural and social studies.

Stuart Hall (1992) is one of the cultural theorists, who advocates the question of cultural identity. His major argument is that there are two types of identity: identity as a being or a sense of unity and commonality; identity as becoming or a process of identification that shows the discontinuity in the identity formation. According to him, national identities are not things we are born with but are formed and transformed within and in relation to representation (Hall 1992). Paul Gilroy has raised the discussion of the relationship between race, ethnicity and nationalism, finds these as a sign to shape the national identity. According to Gilroy, national identity is a melting pot which has the assimilating character by depending on the notion of citizenship and patriotism (Gilroy quoted in Inac and Unal 2013).

Benedict Anderson (1983) in his best known work *Imagined Communities: Reflection on the Origin and Spread of Nationalism* interprets the anomaly of nationalism. He states that national identity is imagined and constructed. According to him, nation is an imagined community; but, he is strictly delimiting the boundaries of the nation – who is in and who is out – but in doing so he also signals a limitation of what the nation as imagined community can contain. National identity operates through a process of exclusion, not only of those who are outside of it but also of those aspects of its members that cannot readily be encompassed by the description in terms of national identity (Salhi 2003).

Anthony D. Smith (1991), one of the prominent theorists of ethno-symbolism, provides the nature, cause and consequences of national identity as collective phenomena. In his conceptualisation, national identity is a multi-dimensional concept, extended to include a specific language, sentiments and symbolism. Smith (1992) explains features of national identity as composing a historic territory or homeland, common myths and historical memories, a common mass public culture, common legal rights and duties for all members, and a common economy with territorial mobility for its members. Smith examines the origins of nations and national identity and finds them in ethnic identity as a pre-modern form of collective cultural identity (Smith 1992).

Samuel P. Huntington (1996) claims that the culture and cultural identities which at the broadest level are civilisation identities are shaping the patterns of cohesion, disintegration and conflict in the post-cold war world. He argues that the 'civilisational us' and the extra 'civilisational them' is a constant feature a factor in human history. Huntington correctly pointed out that historical relations between states or other entities of the same civilisation have differed from relations between states or entities of different civilisations. Separate codes governed behaviour towards those who are 'like us' and the 'barbarians' who are not. The contradictions among

'Us' and 'Them' reinforce to appropriate various national identities (Segers 2004).

Roger Brubaker is an American sociologist, whose works are mainly focussed on the subjects related to immigration, citizenship, nationalism, ethnicity and social theory. His major work was *Nationalism Reframed: Nationhood and the Nation Question in the New Europe* (1996). According to Brubaker nationalism is interlocking and interactive, bound together in a single relational nexus called triadic nexus. The triadic nexus explains three distinct aspects such as nationalising nationalism, the external national homeland and the national minorities (Rogers 1996).

Hence it led to understand minority nationalism in post-communist central and Eastern Europe. Many researchers utilise these frameworks for the research on Russian speakers in Baltic states. Certain authors have added a fourth node in the study of post-independent Soviet states, that is international institutions. Smith (2002: 3) notes that quadratic approach is more appropriate for the Baltic states as it links an ascendant and expansive Euro-Atlantic Space' to the existing framework. In the Baltic context, this approach has been employed successfully in determining the interplay between the international organisation (the EU, OSCE, and Council of Europe), external homeland (Russia) nationalising states (Estonia, Latvia and Lithuania) and National Minorities (Russian speakers) (Cheskin 2015).

The post-communist Central Eastern Europe is comprised of loosely integrated, poly ethnic, poly religious and poly linguistic states that nevertheless almost exclusively engaged in the process of nation building based on the model of an ethnic nation state. Therefore, in the Soviet successor states a politics of citizenship was shaped by claims of politicized ethnicity, or by ethnic nationalism, which was more exclusive and more irreconcilable with democracy than civic nationalism (Budryte 2005). History and memory of victimhood due to Soviet and Nazi Germany's crimes shapes the present politics in contemporary Baltic states as has seen from the days of mobilization of national independent movement, Singing Revolution.

Singing Revolution: Ethno-Nationalism, Culture and Non-Violent Civil Resistance

Singing Revolution is a series of resistance movement occurred from 1987 to 1991 in Estonia, Latvia and Lithuania. People began calendar demonstrations to signify their protests. The fundamental problem which led to this struggle was because the freedom of speech and assembly was forbidden in the Soviet period. Baltic people used singing as a method of protest to resist Soviet policies. They publicized different styles of music, rock, folk, and choral. The situation and singing together of these songs become significant rather than the type and meaning of the songs. The songs had the power to drive away the fear of people and avoided the war (Loraine 2017).

Figure 1: Singing Protest demonstration for Baltic freedom
Source: https://namba.net/movies/1923756-the-singing-revolution

Baltic independence movement got the name "Singing Revolution" from Estonian journalist Heinz Valk's, editorial titled "Laulev Revolutsioon" (Singing Revolution) after a mass singing event in June 1988. He wrote: "A nation who makes its revolution by singing and smiling should be a sublime example to all". "It is impossible to even imagine in Estonia's city streets the riots, barricades, burning automobiles and similar features of mass revolt by large nations. This is not our way!" (Quoted in Smidchens 2014: 3). "This is our flag, not Soviet, this is our nation," peoples were lauding this way in a 1988 gathering; and people holding flags in hand, sang songs. That had enduring the nationalism and national identity among the Baltic people. Songs, flags, nonviolent resistance and national identity are something different from all the political struggles that happened in the nineteenth century (Tedla 2011). Thus, Singing Revolution led to the restoration of independence lost during Second World War, nation building and the formation of national identity.

Before independence, three Baltic states went through various assimilation policies of Russia and the Soviet Union such as a unified language policy called Russification. A compulsory assimilation of Baltic states into Russian culture, or in other words to create a non-Russian into a Russian[1] was an important goal of Russification policy. The key aim of Russification was to establish the Russian dominance over the Polish language, German and Tatar (Pavlenko 2011). In addition, the language policies help emerge national movements. The period from 1860 to 1914 witnessed a blossom of non-Russian national cultures and the development of modern political movements among non-Russian nationalities to demand their civil and political rights. After the First World War Lithuania, Latvia and Estonia achieved independent statehood for the first time in the modern time.

However, their independence during the interwar period (1918-1940) was short-lived due to geopolitical developments on the eve of Second World War. The Molotov-Ribbentrop Pact of 23 August 1939 that brought Baltic states under the spheres of influence of Soviet Union. They lost their independence after the War as Estonia, Latvia and Lithuania have been insisted to integrate with the Soviet Union. The three Baltic republics join the Soviet Union as fourteenth, fifteenth and sixteenth members in 1940 (Kasekamp 2010). They have undergone Sovietization process. Nationalisation of property, abolition of religious propaganda and belief, and collectivization of agriculture were the national policies of the Soviet period (Paine 2010: 1). They remained under Soviet occupation until 1991. Throughout the Soviet rule they showed discontent but the Soviet leadership suppressed dissent.

When Mikahil Gorbachev introduced glasnost and perestroika reforms they got the political opportunity to mobilise national independence. They mobilized politically on the pretext of protest against environmental problems generated by Soviet industrialization projects throughout Lithuania, Latvia and Estonia. People organized for an agitation of environmentalists against the Moscow plan to build the expansion of phosphate mine and began a resistance movement of indigenous people in Latvia and similar anti-Soviet protest against environmental damage in Lithuania and Estonia also. The demographic shift of indigenous population was because of massive migration of workers and it made the indigenous population a minority in their own country. All these caused resentment among the people and became the part of resistance against Soviet Union. People were mobilised through organizations such as Helsinki 86, and popular movements were led by popular fronts. Most of the agitations become the broad spectrum of the national movement of Baltic states (Mole 2012) known as Singing Revolution.

Singing Revolution is a mode of protest initiated by Baltic people to condemn the Soviet policies. Baltic people sang songs to express disagreements and wished to acquire liberation. It was a method followed by cultural assets to strengthen nationalism, identity and ultimate independence. Anatol Lieven wrote:

> ... no-one, Balt or non-Balt, who witnessed the great pro-independence demonstrations of 1988-1991 will forget them or the tremendous emotional impact they had: the songs, the tears, the sense of relief as people were able to say in public things for years they had been scared even to whisper in private (Lieven 1993: 219).

The movement was supported by intelligentsia and also had institutional support from people in leadership positions in the respective Republics.

Singing Revolution is the protest movement of intellectuals and students against *Russification* of culture. A song festival is conducted every five years as a part of the tradition known as Laulupidu or Tallinn song festival. Since 1869, the Estonians

Figure 2: Commemoration of Song Festival (Laulupidu) of Singing Revolution in Estonia
Source: https://merilinsretro.files.wordpress.com/2016/01/img_42831.jpg
Song festival was one of the important events during freedom movement in which people raised national flags and sang banned songs as a method of non-violent resistance.

have been following this tradition. Johann Voldemar Jannsen was the leader who organised the song festival nationwide. He wrote patriotic songs and one of these later became the Estonian national anthem (Jaan 2017). Baltic people had shown their resistance through the songs and other cultural performance during Singing Revolution. The relevance of bloodless movements had increased. Instead of the aggressive movements, they initiated the peaceful movement. Resistance had taken different forms of movements all over the Baltic states. They revisited their history of bitter experience and organized calendar demonstrations on dates such as 23 August related to their loss of independence (Ibid).

Hitler's Nazi Germany and Stalin's Soviet Union signed on 23 August 1939 a non-aggression treaty which is also called Molotov-Ribbentrop Pact. In addition to stipulations of non-aggression, the *treaty* included a secret protocol that divided territories of Poland, Lithuania, Latvia, Estonia, Finland, and Romania into German and Soviet "spheres of influence", anticipating "territorial and political rearrangements" of these countries. Thereafter, Germany invaded Poland. The pact was confirmed by the supplementary protocol of the German-Soviet Frontier Treaty, which was amended after the more or less simultaneous invasion of Poland and sharing it. It remained in force for nearly two years, until the German government of Adolf Hitler ended the pact by launching an attack on the Soviet positions in Eastern Poland during "Operation Barbarossa" on 22 June 1941. When the Germans turned against the Soviets, this ended up in the Second World War as we know now. The Baltic states were incorporated into the Soviet Union. Baltic states had to follow communism, prohibit the national songs and national flags of the Estonians, Latvians and Lithuanians (Kulbok-Lattik 2014).

Later on, the Soviet Union reissued Russification policy in the Baltic states, and it was severe in the period of Brezhnev. It created a division among the native peoples and immigrant Russian-speaking workers in Baltic states. After Mikhail Gorbachev has brought two policy changes called Glasnost (openness) and perestroika (restructuring), the Baltic peoples could see a new face of Soviet Union. This policy was the strong factor which helped the Baltic people is more aware and awake. Finally, it culminated into the harmony of the Baltic people (Zelce 2011).

The popular fronts were formed in Estonia and Latvia. Intellectuals met in the Institute of an Academy of Science. In the case of Lithuania, the intelligentsia established a group called perestroika movement, which later on known as *Sajudis* movement. and *Sajudis* were endowed with human resources such as organisers, lawyers, economist and journalists. The popular front and *Sajudis* have motivated for self-determination of Baltic states. Since 1988 both popular front and *Sajudis* have started to organise programs across the Baltic states. They had established a Baltic Assembly in 1989 (Raun 1994). They decided to meet periodically and follow the strategy of nonviolent resistance. Initially, the *Sajudis* were organised and functioned in support of Moscow, and the main slogan was the "Glasnost, democracy and sovereignty". The nature of *Sajudis* was cultural and ecological rather than political. On the one hand, *Sajudis* have focused on the distortions of socialism and on the other hand, they were followed and support other social movements within the Soviet Union (Bulota 2008).

Prominent Lithuanian writer and member of the initiative groups of *Sajudis* Vytautas Petkevicius expressed the official position of *Sajudis* in one of the early meetings this way: "Restructuring (perestroika) - is a revolution, it is the returning to the Leninist norms of life. We are internationalist and will always remain such. But often the internationalism got distorted here. It is impossible without national self-respect, without loving the own language, culture and country (*komjaunimo Tiesa*

28/6/88)" (quoted in ibid). The *Sajudis* founding congress was held on October 22. They had sung the national anthem on the event. In fact, Gorbachev said that *Sajudis* was a force able to increase the prestige of Lithuania more. The full support of Gorbachev's reform was reflected in every nook and corner of the Soviet Union. This has been part of a popular movement deliberately led by allies of Gorbachev. Therefore, Gorbachev began to accept them (Bulota 2008).

Later, the popular fronts and *Sajudis* Baltic states began calendar demonstrations demanding political independence. There were several social movements occurred at that time. The pioneering movement of Baltic states was the environmental movement. The environmental security was deteriorated due to the Soviet policies in the Baltic states. The Soviet Union's Ministry of Fertilisers and Industries decided to initiate large-scale mining project in the region of Virumaa in Estonia. In 1987 the students at Tartu University organised a conference where they accused against the Soviet Union of damaging their natural resources and social effects. This conference was later known as Aula meeting. It was the first resistance environment movement by the students. However, these protests have been influenced by the huge population of the Baltic states. It became the root of the independent movement of Baltic states. In Latvia environmental demonstrations began with opposition to the construction of hydroelectric power station on Daugava River. Baltic states were against the Chernobyl power plant. Latvians took part of accident clean-up works of Chernobyl power plant from the 1989 to 1991. The Chernobyl power plant disaster occurred in April 1986 led to the Baltic countries to concentrate on the ecological issues (Zaharchenko 1990).

One of the important sources of non-violence of Singing Revolution was Mahatma Gandhi's principles of non-violence in formulating their own civilian defence strategy. A participant of freedom struggle explains Lithuania government's policy during the later phase of independence movement against Soviet provocation, "At that time we used repeat; We won't fight! We follow Gandhi! We are peaceful people!" (Tamosaityte 2017: 131). Richard Attenborough's film *Gandhi* was telecasted in the national television in Lithuania for the purpose of educating people about non-violence (Usha 2012).

The cultural interaction of Baltic states during ancient times attracted their attention to India. During Singing Revolution, they studied non-violent Indian freedom struggle led by Gandhi which defeated the mighty British Empire after 200 years of colonial rule (Usha 2017a, 2017b).

On 23 August 1989, Baltic states organised a unique and peaceful movement of long human chain, which later came to be known as "the Baltic Way",[2] a significant event in the history of Baltic states' pacific methods. It was formed by a line of about two million peoples holding hands stretching for 600 km from Vilnius to Tallinn.

Figure 3: Baltic Way

Source: http://coldwarsites.net/country/estonia/museum-of-the-popular-front-tallinn/

The Baltic popular fronts organized a 600-km-long human chain, the Baltic Way, from Tallinn to Vilnius on the 50th anniversary of the Molotov-Ribbentrop Pact. Around two million people participated in the event organized on 23 August 1989. This event is also known as Baltic Way of Peace.

It was a popular movement to defy the Soviet Union and a non-violent method of expressing discomfort of the existing political setup (Govardhan 2015). In fact, "The Baltic Way" was one of the latest national freedom movements in the world that used Gandhian non-violence for achieving political independence. Scholar of nonviolence exclaimed, what Estonians, Latvians, and Lithuanians did, "stands as a major milestone in the history of the modern world" (Quoted in Smidchens 2014: 3). The Baltic Council, an association that was formed along with the independence movement helped keeping of Baltic states' unity during the freedom movement till the declaration of independence in 1990-1991. After the restoration of independence the three Baltic states have chosen the path of democratic transformation on western liberal norms.

Democratic Transition and National Identity Formation

After the restoration of independence in 1991, construction of national identity and citizenship has become vital components in the democratic transformation of Baltic states that is based on western/European norms. Return to historic homeland, language, culture, collective memory, history and de-Sovietization remain the key elements of formation of national identity and defining citizenship in Baltic states. Homeland is a mirage concept. Every people have a homeland; peoples who are not part of any particular state also have a homeland. A homeland is not a legal term, but essentially a psychological, emotional, historical and cultural concept (Ginor 1998). Even the nomadic peoples have a homeland related to their memory, myth, and legend and fantasy that spells beauty, warmth and idealised perfection. In fact, in the Baltic states, the demarcation, cultivation and transmission of symbols and myths of homeland have emerged as an important means to define competing representations of nationalism. A nation is more than an imagined community of people, for a homeland has also to be imagined (Billig 1995).

The discussions for making of a homeland is mediated between power and identity (Kaiser 2000). In Baltic states, homeland making could be traced back to the Russian regime. The policies of Russian tsars have contributed to the migration of peoples from Russia to Baltic states. The feeling of homeland hindered to endeavour the formation of Baltic states' nationalism and identity. However, in a 1965 festival in Estonia, audience of about 120,000 demanded a repeat performance of the song 'My Homeland and My Love', an unofficial anthem of the Estonian people (O`Connor 2003). The emotional attachment to homeland creates internal frictions among the Baltic citizens. In Estonia, Russian community survives separately because many ethnic Russians allegedly have stronger links to their historic homeland than to their country of permanent residence (Cheskin 2015).

"Return to the Homeland" and "Disloyal Russian Immigrants" are the terms used to address ethnic Russians in Baltic states. This was an important confrontation over the ethnic issues regarding the political statements of the Estonian, Latvian and Lithuanian official's during the first half of independence. The conflict regarding the "Lihula monument can be seen as an attempt to reinforce Estonian identity and pride" (Ehala 2009). "One of their leaflets stated that the Estonian elite aims to tear away Estonian-Russian roots, to break their emotional ties to their historic homeland ...Russians are being made into well-fed slaves of the nationalist elite" (Ibid). There is no homeland for the present inhabitants of national minoretions of Baltic states. The nation's persistent fall for the paranoia of nationalism produces inequality among people. As national majority's language became the core elements defining identity, citizenship and social integration, minority began feeling discrimination and exclusion.

Baltic states' languages are not same for all three states. Estonia follows the language of Finno-Ugric origin; it is completely distinct from the Indo-European language followed by the Latvia and Lithuania. Apart from the difference, they unite for the preservation of native language at the period of Soviet Union. Baltic languages became an important element of the Baltic nationalism. Baltic nationalism has originated from the internally initiated organic sense of national identity (Hartman 1992).

Before Russian invasion, the German language was superior in the public life of Baltic states. Thereafter, Tsar's policy of Russification enthroned over public life in Baltic states. A multinational and multilingual Soviet Union came into power. They had a linguistic policy that the Russian language became the first language; the native languages of each state became the secondary language. The language policy of the Soviet Union has been categorised by scholars as "language-status planning rather than language-corpus planning" (Sallabank 2010).

The linguistic phases of Baltic states can be analysed as a place for the language of conquerors. Post-Soviet Baltic states adopted laws on language. The Baltic states' constitutions announced languages such as Estonian, Latvian and Lithuanian will be their respective state language. The protection and preservation of state language ensure the language law of each Baltic state. In Estonia, any language other than Estonian and Estonian sign language is foreign language (Riigikogu, Language Act 2011). The language law has been justified by arguing that they are a necessary and legitimate assertion of state power to counteract the legacy of Russification. Latvia marked the national language law as a feature for nationalism (Encyclopedia Lituanica 1970-1978).

There are discussions regarding minority communities who are linguistically dissimilar to the state language in post-soviet Baltic states. Many Russian speakers or ethnic Russians are settled in Baltic states during the strict era. In fact, they are currently considered as mainly representing them as a citizen of the Soviet Union rather than the Russian. It is obvious that Russian speakers in Baltic states have the fundamental difference with Russians in Russia. In 1998 David Laitin proposed that "Russian speakers would assimilate into Baltic societies" both linguistically and culturally (quoted in Cheskin 2015: 76).

Various kinds of opinions turn up such as that the Russian language arises as a threat to state languages. Anatolijis Gorbunovs, Chairman of the Latvia Supreme Council, explained why the Russian language was considered as a threat to the Latvian language:

> No other country in the world, as a result of occupation by two criminal regimes, the communist and the Nazi, has lost many of its native inhabitants. But this has happened

in Latvia. Therefore now the Latvian state has taken huge efforts devoted to saving the country's language, the basic mark of the Latvian nation (Gorbunovs quoted in Mole 2012: 83-84).

Language is the most important factor of identification forging national identity. If a person is proficient in one language, it means he can understand a community. Therefore, the use of native language is representing a community and also a large entity. The emotional attachment of a person to certain symbols, scripts or native language has produced nationalism or the ethnic identity (Tamosiunas 1980). In a wider perspective languages are with centripetal and centrifugal tendencies to reinforce unity among the people or the contradictory, especially to make it distinguish from other nations.

Common history and collective memory have a close connection in Baltic states in defining nationalism, political mobilization during independence movement and the democratization process. Collective memory transfers from generation to generations regarding the events a person experienced. Memory is a product of social communication and interaction. Collective memory has a strong link between the collective identities of social groups. History and collective memory are constituent parts of the politics of memory. Estonia, Latvia and Lithuania have common shared experience regarding the Russian and Soviet rule. Pagan time's folklore and folk arts have influenced the Estonian, Latvian and Lithuanian music, literature and art (O`Connor 2003). Since the geographical location of these three states shares a common annexation history, their shared history has an inter-connection with collective memory.

Collective memory and history have a significant role to integrate different ethnic groups. "One of the most significant factors in the failure of Latvian integration policy remains "collective memory and the inability to achieve a convergence of historical perceptions' between different ethnic groups" (Zelce 2009: 72-93; Cheskin 2015). The 2007 *bronze soldier* incident was an example of the failed state integration policy. The separated historical interpretation and "collective memories centred on the competing narratives of Soviet history", led protests of discrigions what Maria *Mälksoo* talks as the "memory war" (Cheskin 2015).[3] Memory war is clarifying two specific divisions on the consumption of common history and memory. The Russian speakers or Russian minorities in Baltic states have denied the claim of Soviet Union's occupation of Baltic states, rather they describe the Soviet Union's accomplishments: the foundation of industry, job security and other welfare provisions (Mikeladze 2010: 80).

The celebration of past events is a way to reconstruct country's dominant narratives produced by Baltic political elites. The memory conflict between the Russian speakers and the Estonians, Latvians and Lithuanians is part of the Baltic political community. In general, major conflict occurred on the issue of the Soviet occupation or the Liberation of Baltic states. One-third of Estonians has strong admittance to the Soviet Union's victory in Second World War. Most of the veterans in the red army were the Estonians. Automatically, the new generation has attachment over ancestors' victory placed as a symbol of memory. Estonia has a history of the destruction of monuments and the restoration of monuments. In 1920, a monument of *Peter the Great* in the centre of Tallinn was removed by signing of the Tartu Peace Treaty (Ehala 2009). In 1940 onwards, many of the monuments were demolished when Estonia went separate from the Soviet Union. When Nazi Germany occupied Estonia they restored some of the pro-German monuments. At the end of the Second World War, the Soviet Union came and destroyed them again. The *Bronze solider* memorial of Second World War was depicted as the Soviet liberator of Estonians. The Russophone[4] community of Estonia feels pride and high status over the narratives of Estonian liberation movement of the period (Ibid).

Algirdas Brazauskas, the former president of Lithuania, proclaimed that:

> In spite of our differences, the unity between Lithuania, Latvia and Estonia as well as the cooperation between our countries should survive and constitute one of our priorities. At the same time, this cooperation should not, in any case, be closed space in which Lithuania locks itself. We belong simultaneously to many regions: to the space around the Baltic Sea, to Central Europe and to the Baltic states. The development of our relations with Central Europeans consolidates the historical place of Lithuania in Central Europe (quoted in Kesa 2011: 88).

Culture is a system of shared knowledge, beliefs, procedures, attitudes and artefacts that exist among the group of humans. Culture has strongly influenced the behaviour of an individual. Culture mainly describes patterns, explicit and implicit, of and for behaviour acquired and transmitted by symbols, constituting the distinctive achievements of the human group (Oatey 2012). Traditionally, the system follows a pattern of practices that may be in a particular community or in states. Shared culture is a component of the formulation of nationalism. Protection and preservation of cultural identity within the domestic level as well as outside are the main policies of the Baltic states (Gill 2013).

The Soviet culture was assimilated into Estonia but in an incomplete assimilation process. In 1993, "59% of Estonian Russophones considered them as representatives of Soviet culture in Estonia. The identification of Russian ethnic identity has increased from 85% in 1992 to 92% in 1993" (Ehala 2009: 148-149). Estonians and Russophones have prominent differences, and national history contributes to the creation of their identity: for Russophone, "this feature was rather suppressed: only four out of ten mentioned in history as a significant part of their identity" (Ibid).

Latvians are the only Baltic people who continue to emphasise the common past and future of the Baltic states and also want to preserve the Baltic unity (Eglitis and Ardava 2012). Latvia is situated in between north and south direction. Estonia has located them as a Nordic identity. Lithuania keeps its Central European identity. Making loyal inhabitant in Baltic states became a complicated and less dilute process. A common feature of the Baltic states is based on cultural and ethnic rather than civic and territorial criteria. Both Latvia and Estonia believed in Lutheran religion and Lithuania follows the Catholic religion. The Baltic peoples have commonly shared experiences under Russia and the Soviet Union (Norgaard and Johannsen 1999).

Democratic Pluralism, Citizenship and Minority Rights

In a democracy pluralism is accepted norm and rights of minorities are guaranteed trough constitutional means. In Baltic states citizenship is a factor that strengthens nationalism, identity and nation state building. Citizenship has rooted in the issues of nationality, identity and language. Traditionally an individual's citizenship is determined by the citizenship or the nationality of parents or citizenship based on blood or descent. Citizenship is a status bestowed on those who are full members of a community. All who possess the status are equal with respect to the rights and duties with which the status is endowed (Grant 1999). The meaning of citizenship grew from a shared network of individuals within the same city, municipality or ethnic region, to a much larger, more abstract imagined community (Anderson 1983). The shared networks communicate through the common language of the particular city or municipality. There are two types of citizenship: granting and naturalisation. Granting citizenship means citizenship based on the territory of birth or citizenship '*Jus Soli*' (Arnold 2004).

In general there are three types of citizenship such as citizenship by birth, citizenship by registration, citizenship by naturalisation. Individuals receive membership through birth in the territory has called *Jus Soli*, this membership has determine by the geography. The literal meaning of the *Jus soli* is "Law on Soil". Second type is *Jus Sanguinis* means membership by decent referred as bloodlines (law of blood). The other type is citizenship by naturalisation based on certain factors such as age, residence, lack of criminal record, and means of support. Traditionally, it is considered as discretionary act of public authority, later on it has transmitted to the automatic acquisition of citizenship. Kee Gorenedijik has introduced a new concept on the context of Baltic states. It is the concept which explains the *dentizen* is an individual who is somewhere between being an alien (non citizen) and a full-fledged citizen (cited in Dobson 2003).

It is important to know the Soviet citizenship law before understanding the post-Soviet Baltic states' citizenship laws. According to Soviet Socialist Republic common federal citizenship provision, each and every citizen of a union republic shall be citizen of the USSR. USSR citizenship shall be equal for all Soviet citizens irrespective of the grounds for its acquisition (article 1). The foreign citizen and the stateless peoples can acquire USSR citizenship through their request, irrespective of race, nationality, sex, education, language and place of residence (article 15) (Tunkin 1980). Now a large Russian-speaking minority is part of Baltic states.

Post-Soviet Baltic states' citizenship laws are entirely different from the Soviet citizenship law. The foundation of citizenship law paved the way to new nation building. An Estonian citizen is a person who holds Estonian citizenship at the time of entry into force of the Citizenship Act of 1995 (Citizenship Act of Estonia 1995). The proficiency of the Estonian language is a requirement of attaining Estonian citizenship. The Estonian citizenship is acquired through birth or by naturalisation process. A person who wishes to acquire Estonian citizenship by naturalisation must know the general principles of Estonian constitutional order which are provided in chapters I and III of the Constitution of the Republic of Estonia (Citizenship Act of Estonia 2011).

The "citizenship of Latvia is a person's permanent legal connection with the state of Latvia. The substance of Latvia citizenship is the total complex of the mutually interrelated rights and obligations of both a citizen and the state" (Law on Citizenship, Republic of Latvia 1994). Article 10 deals with "the right to obtain the citizenship of Latvia" through the naturalisation process (Ibid). There are restrictions upon naturalization of Latvian citizenship; one of the important restrictions to grant citizenship after 4 May 1990, is to have propagated fascist, chauvinist, national-socialist, communist or other totalitarian ideas or have stirred up ethnic or radical hatred or discord, and provided such a thing has been established by a court decree (Ibid). The Latvian citizens are persons who were Latvian citizens on 17 June 1940, and their descendants who were registered in accordance with the procedures set out in law, except persons who have become citizens of another state after 4 May 1990. The Latvian language fluency is a criterion to determine the naturalisation process of Latvia (Citizenship Law, Republic of Latvia 1995).

Article I of the Lithuanian Law on Citizenship states:

> A person shall be citizen of the Republic of Lithuania prior to 15 June 1940, their children, grandchildren and great-grandchildren, provided that the persons are not citizens of another state, persons who were habitually resident in the present-day territory of the Republic of Lithuania in the period from 9 January 1919 to 15 June 1940 as well as their children, grandchildren and great-grandchildren, provided that on the day of coming into force of the Law on Citizenship enacted on 3 November 1989 they were and at the present time are habitually resident in the territory of the Republic of Lithuania and are not citizens of any other state (Law on Citizenship, Republic of Lithuania 2002).

To seek Lithuanian citizenship, the person has to pass the Lithuanian language examination (Law on Citizenship, Republic of Lithuania 2002).

The exclusionary citizenship policy in Latvia and Estonia and homogenization of culture and language of state in terms of titular ethnic majority's aspirations created problems challenging democracy. Such measures left a strong sense of economic and social insecurity among Russian speakers as national minority. There emerged trust deficit among the minority potentially damaging to the effective functioning of welfare state and economy. Trust, convenience and sense of community are factors which uphold the effective functioning of the shared economy (Consumer Intelligence Series, "The Sharing Economy" 2014). David Miller argues that national identity is fundamental to sustain viable welfare states (Miller 1995; Johnston et al. 2010). Nationhood makes redistribution within the community by generating a sense of fellow feeling and sympathetic attachment to the interest of co-nationals and by generating a trust in the willingness of others to reciprocate benefits when the need arises (Miller 1997).

The vulnerable economic sector was a threat to the newly independent states, particularly in the Baltic states. Due to the two World Wars, the human capital and the economy has fallen into diminishing level. After 1991, the patriotic sentiments contributed to collect a good rate of tax. Hence, the economic factor influences the Russian speakers to integrate with the Baltic states. However, the unequal distribution of wealth among the Russian speaking minority is prevalent in the economic sectors of Baltic states (Gotz 2014).

The sense of economic security has increased among Baltic states and it widely reflects the life of the ethnic Russians. Many economic policies of Baltic states have led the Russophones to associate with them. The Baltic states have shown low cultural attraction to the Russian speakers but comparatively "high economic attraction and contradictory levels of political attraction". Internal consolidation through this policy and the socio-political conditions are leading them to compromise with the internal identity disparities. Non-Latvian and non-Estonian segregation has been based on the level of education and language skills for a job. There is a wage gap between the ethnic Estonian and the non-Estonian as in other Baltic states. Magdalens Solska noted "the economic performance of the Estonian government which has led to increased trust in political institutions and therefore increased value in Estonian citizenship compared with either Lithuania or Latvia" (cited in Cheskin 2015: 79-93).

Baltic Democratization Process: Issues and Challenges

The Baltic states' nationalism and identity narratives have begun to be discussed since the post-Soviet era within international politics. Baltic nationalism and identity are based on the past historical and social experiences. Since 1992, Baltic states had proceeded with the process of de-Sovietisation, which included the removal of symbols, political institutions and persons representing Soviet power in the past from the social and political landscape.

The shift of content of national identity was seen in the policies of Baltic states over the period of time. Earlier, nationalism and identity was studied within the context of a right to independent statehood and sovereignty. Now the European and non-European powers have been an influential element of shaping Baltic nationalism. The Baltic national identity conception was strong within Estonia, Latvia and Lithuania. A European Commission Survey observed:

> The presence of large Russian minorities, the geographical closeness to Russia and the 20th century social and political experience explain why the Baltic states' nation building process after the declaration of independence in 1991 has been set in terms of survival of the nation and preservation of national identity. Nationalism in Baltic states is connected to the survival of the independent state (European Commission Survey 1998).

The peoples of Baltic states have shown "a sharp dichotomy between themselves and the hegemony across multiple attributes of national identity in an attempt to maximise the cultural distance between us and them" (Person 2014: 3). The Baltic states reassert their identity through the culture. As Estonian, Latvian and Lithuanian national identities came to be defined in opposition to Soviet other. The conflation of Soviet/Russian meant that the stabilization of nationalism and national identity of Baltic states, and especially Estonia and Latvia entailed the exclusion as far as possible of the *Russian-speaking* minority and Russian language and culture (Mole 2012).

The Baltic states desired conception of nationalism is different from the existing political reality. The geographical proximity between West and East, internal instabilities, external dependence are some of the factors that delimit the transformation of Baltic states' national identity. In many ways, the Baltic states' national identity is connected to the survival of the independent states. At present, the large number of Russian minority is part of Baltic states due to the Soviet integration in the past. In fact, these countries in their attempt to build democracy follow homogenization process in a multi-ethnic/multi-cultural society.

Since 1991-94, despite cultural differences Baltic states are treated as a single geopolitical unit due to shared common history. However, there exists a difference among them challenging Baltic unity. Since independence rivalries began among them like the fish war between Latvia and Estonia and pork war between Lithuania and Latvia in 1991. Over the course of time, Estonia, Latvia and Lithuania are fighting for a prominent and priority position in the European Union. General public opinion is that Baltic states maintain an unsatisfactory relation among themselves. A kind of non-cooperation emerged between them on the matters related to economic and political competition. Former Lithuanian Foreign Minister Algirdas Saudargas "called the unity of the Baltic states a mere fiction that only exists in western politicians' minds. There is also difference regarding their regional identity Landsbergis[5] and Saudargas mentioned Lithuania as a central European or central Baltic European country" (Miniotaite 2003: 218). Former Estonian President Toomas Ilves[6] in 1998 said that "I saw that for years Estonia has suffered from the unsuccessfully planned policies of the other Baltic states. Estonia is a post-communist Nordic country not a Baltic country" (Ilves 1999: 1). Then the politicians of Latvia construe Latvia as a northern European Baltic Sea country.

A British historian David Kirby pointed out the specificity of the concept of Baltic states. He states:

> Often the term Baltic is essentially outsider's construct and this may have hindered the development of a strong sense of common regional identity. After Russia's revolution, Lithuania was grouped with Estonia and Latvia as the Baltic states, in spite of obvious cultural and historical- political differences. Since the late 1980s, when the western world learnt once more to know these peoples, they have increasingly been lumped together as Balts or even Baltic, a term with which none of these states is particularly happy to be associated. Integration in the west and disintegration in the east may if anything has jeopardised the chance of creating a firm and viable Baltic identity (Kirby 1998:2 quoted in Miniotaite 2003: 213).

National identity is built by a contradiction between inside and outside or us and them. Independent Baltic states have been locating "narratives of belonging to the west, with the east as their threatening other" (Miniotaite 2003: 214). Europe becomes the Promised Land for those countries to change identity in accordance with the process of transition and democratisation. The conception of civilizational conflicts has been seen in the Baltic states' wall divisions between western civilization and the non-western Russia (Ilves 1999: 1).

During 1992-1994, Baltic states used a common metaphor to represent their nationalism and identity as a bridge between the East and the West or as neutrality in relation with others such as the European Union and Russia. Aftermath, when Baltic states were enthroned into NATO and EU, then the old metaphor was replayed as the bridgehead state of western civilisation. On the accession to EU and NATO the political elites of Baltic states emphasised the foreign and security policies as the instrument of accession to the European Union. "Return to Europe" became central theme of the policy formulation of Baltic states (Vilpisauskas 2003).

The dominant narratives of history are socially constructed, and rooted in the needs, interest, beliefs and aspiration of the present, as well as the events of the past. The Soviet institutions, ideology and the dominant narratives are kept into the history; there are tensions regarding post-Soviet narratives of Baltic states about the minority community of Russians at the domestic and international levels. The politics centred on history, identity and memory, thus, continues as these are central themes on which the current nation/state building are occurring in Baltic states.

Conclusion

Baltic states regained independence from the former Soviet Union through Singing Revolution. Nationalism, identity and memory politics reflected in the post-independent nation building process. Nationalism and identity formation of Baltic republics is a gradual process, and changes occurred over a period of time. The Baltic states try to delegitimize the Soviet past and also to depart from Russia. Baltic states favour a European identity and prefer to follow European culture and tradition. In fact, the three states had a competition to seek a place in the European Union immediately after restoring independence.

Russian language and culture create binary fission among Baltic states. Baltic states had the binary composition within the system on the field of political structure and the socio-economic facilities of citizens. A national identity construction does not imply denial of the reality of historical events and their material consequences. Estonia, Latvia and Lithuania are generally known as Baltic states, but now each state tries to acquire self-determination and self-promotion rather than remaining a unified identity in the Baltic Sea region. Thus, Moreover, the identify construction has both domestic international level implications in terms of integration of Russian speaking monarchy & cultivation normal selection with Russian. Issues related to history, memory, identity and ethnic nationalism constantly remain as big challenges to their security, development and foreign policy.

Notes

1. Russification was an assimilation policy initiated under the reign of Tsar, Alexander II who enforced it in the Baltic states. This policy was an effort to impose Russian language and orthodoxy (Miller 2008).
2. Baltic way is a 600 kms long human chain from Tallinn to Riga to Vilnius organized on 23 August 1989 with the participation of around 2 million people. It refers to a peaceful demonstration arranged by peoples of the Baltic states for the restoration of independence from Soviet Union (Huang 1999).
3. Memory war is a HERA collaborative research project led by University of Cambridge, Memory at War: Culture Dynamics in Poland, Russia and

Ukraine (MAW). Memory war is a war over memories that explain the cause of war and consequence of the war. Memory at War regarded as emerging division between West and East European memory. It aims at mapped and analysed dynamics of cultural memory and the identity and political developments in the region. The working hypothesis of MAW is that the public memory of twentieth-century traumas mediates the variety of ways in which nations develop in post-socialist space (Cheskin 2015).

4. Russphones is a term to refer those peoples who are proficient in Russian language (Ehala 2009).
5. Professor Vytautas Landsbergis is a Lithuanian conservative politician and Member of the European Parliament. He was the first head of state of Lithuania after its declaration of independence from the Soviet Union.
6. Toomas Hendrik Ilves is an Estonian politician who was the fourth President of Estonia from 2006 to 2016. *Ilves* worked as a diplomat and journalist. He was the leader of the Social Democratic Party in the 1990s.

References

Anderson, Benedict (1983), *Imagined Communities: Reflection on the Origin and Spread of Nationalism*, London: Verso.

Arnold K. R. (2004), *Homelessness, Citizenship, and Identity: The Uncanniness of Late Modernity,* Albany: State University of New York Press.

Billig, Michael (1995), *Banal Nationalism*, New Delhi: Sage Publication

Brubaker, Rogers (1996), *Nationalism Reframed: Nationhood and the National Question in the New Europe*, United Kingdom: Cambridge University Press.

Budryte, Dovile (2005), *Taming Nationalism? Political Community Building in the Post-Soviet Baltic states*, Landon and New York: Ashgate publishing.

Bulota, Rytis (2008), *National Movements in Central East Europe*, Kaunas: Vytauto Didziojo Universitetas:

Cheskin, Ammon (2015), "Identity and Integration of Russian Speakers in the Baltic states: A Framework for Analysis", *Ethnopolitics*, 14 (1): 79-93.

Citizenship Act of Estonia (1995), retrieved from http://www.google.co.in Search?q_ Citizenship+ of+Estonia

Citizenship Law, (1995), Republic of Latvia Saeima, retrieved from https://likumi.lv/ta/en/id/57512-citizenship-law

Dobson, Andrew (2003), *Citizenship and the Environment*, New York: Oxford University Press.

Dreifelds, Juris (1995) Latvia, Iwaskiw R Walter(ed) *Area handbook series Estonia, Latvia, Lithuania country studies*, Washington DC :Federal Research Division Library of Congress.

Eglitis, Daina and Laura Ardava (2012), "The Politics of Memory: Remembering the Baltic way 20 Years After 1989", *Europe-Asian Studies*, 64 (6): 1033-1059.

Ehala, Martin (2009), "The Bronze Soldier: Identity Threat and Maintenance in Estonia", *Journal of Baltic Studies*, 40 (1): 139-158.

European Commission, The Forward Studies Unit, (1998), "Survey of National Identity And Deep-Seated Attitudes towards European Integration in the Ten Applicant Countries of Central and Eastern Europe", Working Paper: 1-31, retrieved from http://www.pedz.unimannheim.de/daten/edzmr/pbs/00/survey_of_national_identity.pdf

Gill, T. Grandon (2013), "Culture, Complexity, and Informing: How Shared Beliefs Can Enhance Our Search for Fitness", *Informing Science: the International Journal of an Emerging Transdicipline*, 16: 71-98.

Gilroy, Paul (1987), *There Ain't No Black In The Union Jack*, London: Routledge.

Ginor, Zvia (1998), *Essays on Jewish Thought, American Judaism, and Jewish-Christian Relations*, New York: Temple Israel Of Great Neck.

Gotz, Norbert (2014), "Introduction: Collective Identities in Baltic and East Central Europe", in N. Gotz, ed., (2014), *The Sea of Identities: A Century of Baltic and East European Experiences with Nationality, Class, and Gender*, Stockholm: Södertörn University, Elanders, pp. 11-28.

Govardhan (2015), "Influence of Gandhian Principles of Nonviolence in the Singing Revolution (Sàjûdis Movement) of Lithuania", *International Journal of Applied Social Sciences* (2) : 146-156.

Grant D. (1999), "Citizenship and Justice", in Alexander Kouzmin, and Andrew Hayne eds., (1999), *Essays in Economic Globalization, Transnational Policies and Vulnerabilities*, Amsterdam: IOS Press and International Institute of Administrative Sciences; pp 101-112.

Gromilova, Anna (2007), "Changing Identities of the Baltic states: Three Memories in Stone", *CES Working Paper*, 4 (2A): 94-110.

Guibernau, Montserrat (2004), "Anthony D. Smith on Nations and National Identity: A Critical Assessment", *Nations and Nationalism*, 10(1/2): 125-141.

Hall, Stuart (1992), "The Question of Cultural Identity" From Modernity and Its Future, Cambridge: Polity Press; pp 274-316.

Hartman, Gary (1992), "The Origins and Growth of Baltic Nationalism as A Force for Independence", *LITUANUS, Lithuanian Quarterly Journal of Arts and Sciences*, 38 (3).

Hoggard, Mandy L. (2016), *Touched by Time: Geopolitical Themes of Estonian National Identity through Song Festival,* Thesis submitted for Master of Science, to Department of Political Science, Utah State University.

Huntington, Samuel P. (1996), *The Clash of Civilisations and the Remaking of World Order*, New York: Touchstone.

Huntington, Samuel P. (1993), "The Clash of Civilisations?" *Foreign Affairs*, 72 (3): 22-49.

Ilves, Toomas Hendrik (1999), "*Estonia as a Nordic Country*", *American Rhetoric Online Speech Bank*. Retrieved from http://www.americanrhetoric.com/speeches/toomasilvesestonianordiccountry.htm

Jaan, Mina (2017), "History, Facts and Figures of the Estonian Song Celebration", retrieved from http://2017.laulupidu.ee/wp-content/uploads/2017/06/History.pdf.

Kasekamp, Andres (2010), *A History of the Baltic states*, New York; Palgrave Macmillan.

Kesa, Katerina (2011), "Latvian and Lithuanian Policy in the Eastern Neighbourhood: Between Solidarity and Self Promotion", *Perspectives*, 19 (2): 81-100.

Kirby, D. (1998) "Locating the Baltic: Keynote address delivered at the 16th Conference on Baltic Studies", *Baltic Studies Newsletter*, 22(3): 2–3.

Krebber, Victoria (2012), *Identity Questions in the Baltic states An Analysis of Estonia, Latvia and Lithuania Regarding Their Attitudes towards European Identity*, Bachelor Thesis, European Studies, University of Twente.

Kulbok-Lattik, Egge (2014), "The Sovietization of Estonian Community Houses (Rahvamaja): Soviet Guidelines", *Acta Historica Tallinnensia*, 20 (1): 157-190. Retrieved from Language Act 2011,Republic of Estonia Riigikogu, retrieved from https://www.riigiteataja.ee/en/eli/506112013016/.

Law on Citizenship, Republic of Latvia (1994), retrieved from http://webcache.googleusercontent.com/search?q=cache:http://www.humanrights.lv/doc/latlik/citiz1.htm&gws_rd=cr&dcr=0&ei=kF9QWt6yLcSGvQSS66fQDg.

Law on Citizenship, Republic of Lithuania (2002), Vilnius, pp. 1-21. Retrieved from http://www.refworld.org/pdfid/4e65e95c2.pdf.

Law on State Language (1995), Republic of Lithuania Seimas, retrieved from https://www.uta.edu/cpsees/lithlang.htm

Lieven, Anatol (1993), *The Baltic Revolution Estonia, Latvia, Lithuania and the Path to Independence*, New Haven and London: Yale University Press

Suziedelis,Simas(1970), Lithuanian Resistance (1970-1978), Encyclopedia Lituanica I-VI, Boston : Juozas Kapocius.

Loraine Sophie and Pettee Scharlin (2017), "A Nation in Concert: The Role of the National Song Festivals in the Estonian Independence Movement, 1987-1991", University of Vermont, Scholar Works @ UVM, Undergraduate Theses. Retrieved from https://scholarworks.uvm.edu/cgi/viewcontent.cgi?article=1208&context=hcoltheses

Mikeladze, Davit (2010), "Russian-speaking Population in the Baltic states: Russian-speaking Population in the Baltic states: A Fifth Column or An Integral Part of the Local Society?", LAP LAMBERT Academic Publishing

Miniotaite, Grazina (2003), "Convergent Geography and Divergent Identities: A Decade of Transformation in the Baltic states", *Cambridge Review of International Affairs*,16 (2): 210-222.

Mol, Lennart (2014), *Towards an Inclusive National Identity? The Development of National Identity in Estonia, 1991-Present*, Master Thesis, Rotterdam: Erasmus University.

Mole, Richard C.M. (2012), *The Baltic states from the Soviet Union to the European Union: Identity, Discourse and Power in the Post-Communist Tradition of Estonia, Latvia and Lithuania,* Abingdon: Routledge.

Norgaard, Ole, and Lars Johannsen (1999), *The Baltic states After Independence*, London: Edward Elgar Publishing Limited.

O'Connor, Kevin (2003), *The History of the Baltic states*, Westport, CT: Greenwood Press.

Oatey, Spencer (2012), "What Is Culture? A Compilation of Quotations", *Global pad Core Concept*, 1-20.

Parliament of the Republic of Latvia (1999), *Official Language Law*, Riga. Retrieved from https://likum.lv/ta/en/id/14740-official-language-law.

Pavlenko, Aneta (2011), "Linguistic Russification in the Russian Empire: Peasants into Russians?" *Russian Linguistics: International Journal for the Study of Russian and other Slavic Languages*, 35 (3): 331-350.

Pavlovaite, Inga (2003), "Being European by Joining Europe: Accession and Identity Politics in Lithuania", *Cambridge Review of International Affairs*, 26(2): 240-255.

Person, Robert (2014), "Resisting Hegemony: Transformations of National Identity under Foreign Occupation," Working Paper 396: 1-31, Notre Dame: Kellongg Institute For International Studies, retrieved from https://kellogg.nd.edu/sites/default/files/old_files/documents/396_0.pdf.

Raun, Toivo (1994), *Baltic Independence, 1917-1920 And 1988-1994 : Comparative Perspectives*, Washington, D .C: The National Council For Soviet And East European Research.

Ross, Alistair (2012), "Communities and Others: Young People's Constructions of Identities and Citizenship in the Baltic countries", JSSE, 11(3): 1618-5293

Salhi, Kamal (2003), "Introduction" in Kamal Salhi (eds), *Francophone Post-Colonial Culture: Critical Essays*, New York: Lexington Books, pp xi-1.

Sallabank, Julia (2010), "Language documentation and language policy", in Peter K. Austin (ed.), (2010), *Language Documentation and Description*, vol. 7, London: SOAS, pp. 144-171.

Segers, Rien T. (2004), "The *Underestimated Strength* of *Cultural Identity*: *Between.*

Localising and *Globalising Tendencies* in the *European. Union*", in Jari, Kupiainen, Erkki Sevanen, and John A. Stototesbury eds. (2004), *Cultural Identity in Transition Contemporary Conditions, Practices and Politics of a Global Phenomenon*, New Delhi: Atlantic Publishers and Distributors, pp. 85-88.

Smidchens, Guntis (2013), "Remembering the Baltic Singing Revolution on the National Mall, 1998", Washington DC: Smithsonian Folklife Festival.

Šmidchens, Guntis (2014), *The Power of Song: Nonviolent National Cultures in the Baltic Singing Revolution*, University of Washington Press and Museum Tusculanum Press.

Smith, D. Anthony (1992), "National Identity and the Idea of European Unity", *International Affairs*, 68 (1): 55-76.

Smith, David J. (2002), *The Baltic states: Estonia, Latvia and Lithuania*, New York: Routledge.

Smith, Graham, Vivien Law, Andrew Wilson, Annette Bohr, and Edward Allworth (1998), *National-Building in the Post-Soviet Borderlands: the Politics of National Identities*, Cambridge: Cambridge University Press.

Spencer-Oatey, Helen. (2012), "What is Culture? A Compilation of Quotations", Global PAD Open House

Spencer-Oatey, Helen and P. Franklin (2012), "What is Culture? A Compilation of Quotations", *Global PAD Core Concepts*, Available at Global PAD Open House, retrieved from http://go.warwick.ac.uk/globalpadintercultural.

Tambur, Silver (2017), "Estonia's Youth Song and Dance Celebration Created a Thrill in Tallinn", *Estonian World, retrieved from http://estonianworld.com/culture/estonias-youth-song-dance-celebration-creates-thrill-tallinn/*

Tamosiunas, Algis (1980), "The Linguistic Russification of Titular Baltic nationalities", *Lithuanian Quarterly Journal of Arts and Science*, 26 (1).

Tamosaityte, Daiva. (2017), "Gandhism: Similarities between Lithuanian and Indian Independence Movements", in Laimonas Talat-Kelpsa ed., (2017), *India and Lithuania: A Personal Bond*, New Delhi: Lithuanian Embassy, 131-141.

Tedla, Aden (2011), "Estonian Campaign for Independence (The Singing Revolution), 1987-1991", Global Nonviolent Action Database, retrieved from https://nvdatabase.swarthmore.edu/content/estonians-campaign-independence-singing-revolution-1987-1991.

Tunkin, G.I. (1980), "The Law on Citizenship of the USSR", *Soviet Law and Government,* 18 (4): 22-36.

Union of Soviet Socialist Republics (1978), *Law on Citizenship*, Moscow: Chairman of the Presidium of the Supreme Soviet of the USSR.

Usha, K. B. (2012), "The Evolving Relations between India and Baltic states", *Lithuanian Foreign Policy Review,* (January-June), 27: 83-109.

-------------- (2017a), "India-Lithuania Cultural Interactions: A Contemporary Perspective", *IUP Journal of International Relations*, 11 (1): 27-51.

-------------- (2017b), "Memory Politics and Identity Dilemmas in Contemporary Baltic states", unpublished paper presented at Silver Jubilee Celebrations of India-Baltic Relations Workshop on *India and the Baltics: Prospects and Challenges*, organized by Centre for European Studies, School of International Studies, Jawaharlal Nehru University, New Delhi, on 21 November 2017.

Vilpisauskas, Ramunas (2003), "The final stage of the EU-accession game: The Baltic states – the likely victims of their own success?" A draft paper for the EUSA conference (27-29 March 2003), the panel on *EU*, pp. 1-20. Retrieved from http://aei.pitt.edu/view/conference/CC001002.html

Zaharchenko Tatiana (1990), "The Environmental Movement and Ecological Law in the Soviet Union: The Process of Transformation", *Ecology Law Quarterly*, 17(3); 455-475.

Zelce, Vita (2009), "History-responsibility-memory: Latvia's case", in J. Rozenvalds and I. Ijabs eds., (2009) *Latvia. Human development report, 2008/2009: Accountability and responsibility*, Riga: University of Latvia, pp 44-57.

Chapter Three

Nationalism and Nation Building in Contemporary Lithuania

Sarunas Paunksnis

Lithuania, just like India is a postcolonial country. As postcolonial countries, they share a crucial element in the struggles for freedom, or anti-colonial struggles – that is, nationalist movements, which were instrumental in attaining the independence. Lithuanian experiences, of course, are very different from the Indian ones, but India for almost two centuries was a colony of the British Empire, and Lithuania initially experienced Russian empire's colonialism from the late 18th century until the end of the First World War, and later in the 20th century – as being incorporated into the Soviet Union. I am using these terms, though it is still debatable in academic circles if we could call Soviet Union a colonial empire similar to British, or French, and a post-Soviet period a postcolonial one (Kelertas 2006). It is also debatable whether we can call countries that became independent after the collapse of the USSR the postcolonial countries. Lithuania does not like to see itself as a postcolonial country, as this would jeopardize the understanding of the self as a European country. This has a lot to do with self-worth – as if being a postcolonial nation diminishes that worth. Lithuania always emphasizes that it has always been part of Europe, and experience of being a part of the Russian empire and later of the Soviet Union was rather brief, a mistake, that we were victims for some time separated from where we really belong, from out 'home' so to speak – Europe, in a political sense of the word, in terms of identity, culture, shared heritage.

De-colonization as a political process is understood in a very narrow procedural sense, not taking into account the effect of Russian and Soviet colonization on society and culture. Some scholars call for de-colonization of the mind, and I would say that this type of de-colonization, which Lithuania rejects, would be a very long process, as the effect of being the colonized would be felt for many years to come. I will not go into the details about the effects regarding culture, mentality, self-perception, but the sum of it all does indicate quite well that Lithuania is a postcolonial state, only refusing to accept it, as on some imaginary level this would place Lithuania where it wants to be placed the least – in the same league as India, other Asian, Middle Eastern, African and Latin American countries. Moreover, this would undoubtedly hurt the national feelings of belonging to Europe, and the feeling of being equal to Western European and North American countries.

Unlike India, Lithuania had a brief moment of independence in the inter-war period. However, Lithuania's problem was always being a small country having hostile neighbours. Democracy in India has deeper roots; Lithuania became independent quite recently in 1990.

Among other things, in terms of colonial and postcolonial experience, that Lithuania shares with many other former colonies is nationalism in terms of it being instrumental in achieving independence – both in 1918, and in 1990. There are many similarities in anti-colonial nationalisms in Lithuania and in different parts of the world, including India. Nationalism in Lithuania at the end of the 19th century emerged among the intelligentsia, many of them were educated in Russia, St. Petersburg in particular – these were mainly medical doctors and the Catholic clergymen, like Jonas Basanavicius and Vincas Kudirka, who, in addition to their own respective professions, were writers, poets, secretly publishing anti-colonial newspapers and newsletters, being distributed across the country. Therefore, what I would call the first wave of anti-colonial nationalism did not really involve the masses. Lithuania till the middle and largely till the second half of the 20th century was agrarian country, cities were small, majority of the population lived in the countryside, and a large portion of the rural population were uneducated, often illiterate. Thus, the project of independence and nationalist ideas circled among the intelligentsia.

As any nationalism anywhere in the world, Lithuanian nationalism produced a nation. It imagined a nation, to quote Benedict Anderson (2006). Nationalist intelligentsia of early 20th century wrote a lot about glorious Lithuanian past, were pointing out Lithuania's might, or the might of the Grand Duchy of Lithuania that existed from the13th till mid-16th century, and the strength of Polish and Lithuanian state (Poland and Lithuania were one state from 1569 to 1785). So, initially the late 19th century nationalist project focused on resurrecting the Polish-Lithuanian state, later – on resurrecting Lithuanian state of the pre-16th century – Lithuania at that time included territories that today are Belarus, a part of Russia and Ukraine, and its borders in 15th century stretched till the Black sea – something Lithuanians are proud of even today, and never fail to mention – that at one time Lithuania was the largest country in Europe in terms of size, that we were the last to adopt Christianity, that German crusades in the Medieval period against Lithuania were never successful and European armies were defeated every time they came to

Lithuania. Sometimes Lithuanians even mention, with some pride, that from time to time Lithuanians used to sail across the Baltic Sea to Sweden, and the Swedes were militarily inferior. What Lithuanians do not mention though is that they used to sail to Sweden as raiders on looting expeditions, and they used to steal and rape.

In constructing the nation the nationalist intelligentsia of the time was resurrecting the historical greatness, were compiling Lithuanian folk songs, stories, fairy tales, myths, sometimes even inventing myths. Paradoxically, while being devout Catholic at that time, Lithuanians were emphasizing Lithuanian uniqueness in terms of pre-Christian religion, indigenous beliefs. Of course, Lithuanian language was a major element in constructing the nation. Written Lithuanian language was banned in Lithuania in the 19th century, but books were circulating in the underground, and they were being printed in Prussia, *Konigsberg*, present day Kaliningrad. In the early 20th century, language as well became a part of Lithuania's image of being unique in the world. What helped in this was the fact that Lithuanian language does not share any similarities with other languages in the region, is not part of the Slavic languages, and is one of the oldest still used languages in the world. At the same time, modern Lithuanian literature began to form, as well as modern poetry.

Another significant problem nationalism was facing in Lithuania was the definition of the nation. This is a general problem of nationalism, where one group, either linguistic, religious, ethnic, is perceived as forming a core of the nation while other groups are subordinate, marginal. The narrow concept of the nation, who can be included, and who should be excluded was a problem. Anti-colonial nationalism was emphasizing Lithuania's past glory, but Lithuania was always a very multicultural state. Most of the people in Lithuania before it became part of the Russian empire were not ethnic Lithuanians, as it was a very large country in terms of size. The same goes with the period of Grand Duchy of Lithuania. Lithuanian language was also considered the language of the peasantry, while Latin was the language of the clergy, and Polish, the language of the cultured. On top of that, a large section of society in Lithuania was Jewish, especially in the cities. Before Second World War, 45 percent of the population in capital Vilnius was Jewish, in Lithuania 7 percent, and today there are only about 2000 Jews in Lithuania in total. Ethnic Lithuanians in such multicultural country, if it ever were re-established, would have constituted a minority. Nationalism in general has a problem with minorities. Of course, the concept of a nation in such scenario cannot be based on minority – something ethnic Lithuanians were facing if such model of Lithuania was adopted. Therefore, after much debate during the early 20th century, and during the First World War, the agreement was to declare independent Lithuania on ethnic and linguistic grounds, and it is geographically and territorially the Lithuania that exists today.

Minority Problem

Problem with the minorities in Lithuania, namely Polish, Russian and to a very small extent Jewish exists still today. Poles in Lithuania, and Russians, and Jews in a popular understanding are not considered Lithuanians, even though they have all the legal rights and have lived in Lithuania since time immemorial. Lithuania also has a small Muslim community – Tartars who migrated to Lithuania at around 15th century, but Islam in Lithuania is regarded as something new and alien.

The history has been reshaped in the early 20th century in such a way, that the Lithuanian golden age was began to be perceived as the time before Lithuania entered into the union with Poland. There was no animosity between the Poles and Lithuanians at that time. In fact, Lithuania's golden age in terms of intellectual, political, artistic achievements, were precisely the centuries when Lithuania and Poland were one country. However, in rewriting history Poland was constructed as an enemy – it was constructed as a country that occupied Lithuania, and in many ways, a country responsible for all the misery Lithuania had to go through. Also, the relationship with Poland was hostile between the first and second world wars, as Poland had occupied a portion of Lithuania with Lithuania's capital Vilnius, and only during the Second World War Lithuania got it back. This fuelled anti-Polish sentiments that are alive even today. Therefore, until today this type of history, a distorted past is taught at schools, and is very much part of the collective memory, if we can call it this way. If you ask an average Lithuanian what he or she thinks about the Poles, you may not receive a very positive evaluation.

A decisive factor in Lithuania's independence, and I would call our independence in 1918 a luck by chance, an accidental independence, was First World War, and the collapse of the Russian empire. During that tumultuous period, Lithuania declared independence. Wars with the Soviet Union and Poland ensued, and lasted until 1920. Poland occupied a portion of Lithuania, and the Soviet Union in the end retreated. The interwar period was the time of nation building – a process, which was interrupted by the Second World War and the Soviet occupation, which lasted until 1990. In the interwar period, Lithuania enjoyed some years of democracy, but mostly it was an authoritarian state under the presidency of Antanas Smetona (from 1926 to 1940). There were some persecutions of the leftists at that time, but largely it was a peaceful time, with no atrocities committed against the citizens, or other things one may expect from the authoritarian rule.

Second World War marked a sad and horrific chapter in Lithuania's history. As a small country, it found itself between the interests of two powers – Nazi Germany and the Soviet Union. Although at the beginning of the war Lithuania maintained its neutrality and tried to have friendly relationship with both countries, it did not succeed. In 1940 it was annexed by the Soviet Union, in 1941, when Nazi Germany was pushing the Red Army back, it was occupied by the Nazis till 1944, when the Soviet Union invaded once again, towards the end of the war pushing the Nazis westwards. In 1941 USSR started mass deportations of the population to Siberia (then, and after the war around 300000 people were exiled, many of them died either on the way to Siberia, or shortly after the arrival as the living conditions were inhuman). Apart from this, another tragedy happened. During the Nazi occupation, although it was brief, a majority of Lithuania's Jewish population was killed. This history is something few people in Lithuania want to talk about, as most of the killings were done by Lithuanian collaborators, and not by the Nazis. Anti-Semitism was strong in Lithuania, as in many other European countries at that time.

Even before the war, there was nothing wrong to make fun of Jews, although they were not discriminated. However, in contemporary Lithuania there is just silence about it. During the Nazi occupation, Lithuania formed an interim government, which was very friendly with Nazis, and largely shared their ideology. Very right-wing nationalists, who saw an opportunity in Nazi Germany's occupation – an opportunity to end Soviet occupation, which was perceived as a far worse option, and the government hoped that if Nazis were successful, this would help, in the end, to restore Lithuania's independence. Nevertheless, this did not happen; Lithuania was occupied by the Soviets again, and remained in the USSR until 1990.

After decades of being part of USSR, nationalism in Lithuania began gathering a momentum in late 1980s as the effect of perestroika. But, this time the situation was very different. The country was no longer squarely agrarian. Intelligentsia was large; cities and urban culture were there. Therefore, anti-Soviet nationalism was a mass movement, and mobilization of the masses was not a difficult talk to achieve, as a vast majority of Lithuanians never accepted Soviet Union as their country, only that these feelings were repressed, and more often than not people could not express their political positions openly. Therefore, nationalism, but only silent, repressed, was always there in Lithuania even under the Soviet rule.

What we may call the anti-Soviet, or anti-colonial Lithuanian nationalism managed to mobilize the masses, and the favourable political conditions such as the weakening of the Soviet Union, etc. managed to achieve Lithuania's independence in 1990. In 1987 a political organization named *Sajudis*, or Movement, Rising was established, later becoming a political party, which was instrumental in establishing Lithuania's independence.

The act of independence in 1990 is usually termed as the restoration of independence, but this term is not accurate. The Lithuanian state in the interwar period was very different one from the one in late 20th century. Though it can be understood as a restoration, I would say that it involved a good deal of newness, as the society was extremely different. But, nationalism during the peaceful so-called 'singing' revolution had similarities with the one in early 20th century. Same symbols were being used, an emphasis on glorious past, and very strongly an emphasis on the earlier nationalist movement and the interwar period of independence. Almost all writings of late 19th century and early 20th century writers were banned as ideologically unacceptable, but in late 1980s, they started to be republished. As I mentioned, the restoration of independence was termed a 'singing' revolution, and not only in Lithuania, but in Latvia and Estonia also. That was because people used to gather at large political meetings during which patriotic songs, either folk songs or those written in late 19th-early 20th century were sung. This 'revolution' if we may call it this way was peaceful. There was aggression from the side of the Soviet army, KGB, Special Forces, but Lithuanians never retaliated.

Let me divert a bit into my personal experience, as I remember the events in late 1980s and early 1990s quite well, even though I was only a child back then. The atmosphere was much politicized during those years, and we, as children, were not insulated from that. So, as a child living through and experiencing the tumultuous times I was never far away from politics. I was too young to understand it, but politics was everywhere. Teachers were talking about the events that were happening, parents were. We, as kids, were thrown into a political, anti-Soviet, anti-colonial, nationalist discourse at a very young age. At school, we used to draw cartoons of the politicians we did not like. Sometimes we, ten year olds, used to fight if it appeared that we had different political positions, or our parents supported different politicians. There was a lot of hope, a lot of euphoria, but at the same time a lot of fear. There were Red army soldiers patrolling in the streets, tanks at strategic locations. Near my house, in a quiet street several trucks full of soldiers used to stand throughout the days. I used to pass them on my way to school, and I remember my fear, as well as childish curiosity, because the soldiers were heavily armed, and I, as a boy of ten, naturally, was interested in guns and similar boyish things. However, as I said, there was a lot of fear and tension. I used to see my parents scared while watching TV or listening to the radio, and discussing the events.

Early 1991 were perhaps the worst period. At that time, we faced a military assault on strategic objects in the country, primarily in the capital Vilnius. It happened one night, and my parents talked in the evening before, that something bad was about to happen. They even talked what would happen if there were a full-scale assault, and Lithuania's re-incorporation into Soviet Union, which was collapsing at that time. They talked about possible deportations and reprisals, and genocide – something Lithuania faced during and immediately after the Second World War. Lithuania lost about a quarter of population – people being deported to Siberia, labour camps, most of them did not survive – the whole intellectual core was wiped out in this way. I have some members of my family deported in this way and never came back). The topic of deportations to Siberia under Stalin's rule was a taboo topic in schools. However, in late 1980s and early 1990s there was a lot of talk about this. Therefore, I knew what happened at that time, and I feared it would happen again. I remember even thinking what I should pack if they deport my family and me. Nevertheless, these fears never materialized.

I remember quite well the change in the school curricula. At around 1987 we used to read many texts about Soviet Union, about Lenin, there was a portrait of Lenin hanging in the classroom, right above the blackboard. However, around 1989, and especially in 1990 things began to change. At school, we started learning poems by earlier banned poets, we read books that were not available before, written in early 20th century. I was too young to comprehend exactly what was happening, but now, as I reflect on those times, I realize that I, as well as my generation, went through a historical shift, a massive social and cultural transformation. In the kindergarten, we had lessons in Russian language. In my first years at school, we learned about Soviet Union, read Soviet poetry and literature, and little by little, we were being produced as Soviet citizens. This was interrupted by the collapse of the USSR and Lithuania's independence movement. I would say that I am privileged in this sense. The earlier generations, who completed their education in the USSR and had their identities formed as the Soviet people are very different from my generation. The generation that was born in independent Lithuania after 1991 has an entirely different identity, for them Soviet Union and the independence movement is what they read in school textbooks, and what they hear from their parents, but never experienced – they experienced only independent Lithuania.

My generation, I would say, is an interrupted generation, a generation in-between, hybrid generation, whose production of Soviet identity was interrupted, and diverted into an extremely different direction. I feel privileged, because my hybrid identity gives me an altogether different perspective of the world, not to mention that I myself am a social scientist, and to a large extent work in the field of postcolonial theory. I was shaped by two different worlds – the Soviet and the so-called Western. I do not feel I fully belong to either of them, but both worlds are part of what I am. I understand very well what Edward Said felt when he was saying that he felt homeless, intellectually, felt not belonging, echoing Theodor Adorno in many ways, who wrote on what it means being homeless in one's home (Said 1994; Adorno 2005). Said says that such position, hybrid and complex identity gives a "bird's eye view" on society, politics, culture. One can observe from the distance without fully participating, fully belonging. My position, in this sense, goes against the general Lithuanian position about its identity, formation of which was heavily influenced by nationalism. The liberation movement emphasized very clearly that Lithuania wants to go where it belongs – to Europe, to be part of the West again.

Nationalism in general denies hybridity and understands identities in a very simplistic way as clearly demarcated. It is not so in reality. Such clear demarcation in terms of identity is very much part of an identity crisis Lithuania has been going through since 1990. We imagine we belong to Europe, in terms of political and cultural identity, although we are marginal. We are postcolonial, but we do not want to identify with that. We cannot accept being marginal, and this inability is a source of great anxiety, as well as feelings of inferiority. As many scholars working in postcolonial theory have emphasized, marginality is not necessarily negative, it can be empowering if accepted as part of identity. However, Lithuania cannot make use of this, and is in a perpetual state of mimicry. Lithuanian identity is very fragile, because we deny so many elements of our Self. We always need to identify with a larger structure, be it the European Union, or USSR; we constantly mimic; I would say we are a country of mimic men and women, echoing V.S. Naipaul and Homi Bhabha (Naipaul 2011; Bhabha 2004). I think many Lithuanians would find it hard to accept what I am saying – so strong are the feelings of Lithuanian exceptionality. I am not talking about pride or patriotism. Those are there, but there is also a hollow feeling of us being exceptional in some way, having some kind of mission either in the world, or at least in Eastern Europe. This is a destructive feeling producing what one may call a collective anxiety, a feeling of inferiority, a discontent of being small and invisible. There is a joke in Lithuania told by some critical scholars who deal with nationalism and Lithuanian post-Soviet identity: only basketball is a stable element of Lithuanian identity, as identity is so focused on exceptionality. Basketball is as popular in Lithuania as cricket is in India, and we have one of the best national teams in the world. They say that only during the world championship, European championship and the Olympics we can feel pride, we no longer feel inferior or marginal, as we have a strong identity that binds us all, even if for a brief moment.

Lithuanian nationalism was strong throughout the past 25 years of independence, and played a major role in politics, but not decisive. As it should happen, it took a back seat after the independence was achieved, but it is always present. However, some real disturbing tendencies we can observe in Lithuania today. The brand of nationalism that was crucial in establishing independent Lithuania, a pacifist version of nationalism, is slowly torn apart, giving way to radical nationalism. Similar processes can be observed all across the European Union. This relates primarily with the financial meltdown of 2008, and this heavily affected Lithuania. Many young people had to leave the nation looking for jobs in other European countries and never came back. I would say that due to our difficult past and the traumatic experiences that occurred not so long ago, Lithuanians could adapt to very harsh material conditions very well, and in Lithuania, we did not see much objection regarding economic austerity that was implemented in 2009, and devastated the country, especially the poor. Most people suffered in silence, and still are suffering, accepting the material conditions as unavoidable. During that time, radical nationalism and blaming the EU began to rise, but it always was marginal. Lithuania, since it joined the EU in 2005 was one of the most supportive countries of the union, but this started to change, although even today Lithuania is among the countries that have the most positive position towards the EU. A process similar to Brexit would never happen in Lithuania, and largely the Russian faction is crucial, especially since the war in Ukraine. Feelings that what happened to Ukraine may happen to Lithuania and other Baltic states and such possibility is strong.

The rise of radical nationalism and to some mild extent – an anti-EU position in Lithuania today – was triggered due to the refugee crisis of 2015, as well as the terror attacks in France, Belgium and Germany since 2015. Lithuania is taking an anti-immigration position, though not as harsh as, let us say Hungary, and there are signs of rising racism, and Islamophobia. Every day in Lithuanian press, one can read fear-mongering articles regarding the refugees, the immigrants – that they would destroy Europe and Lithuania as well; one can read conspiracy theories that the crisis was devised by Russia in order to destroy Europe, and so on. Most of the political parties demonstrate, although mildly, such attitudes, but the perceptions of the crisis in the EU among the people, perceptions that are highly influenced by media, are quite radical and disturbing.

Lithuania does have, and always had neo-Nazi groups, skinheads, pretending to be the guardians of Lithuanian culture and traditions, and they are well known especially for their anti-Semitic positions. These groups were always marginal and barely visible in the public space. However, today we can observe a rise of such rhetoric in the mainstream. Last year in the general election a populist party, The Green and Peasants' Union, won a landslide victory. This party earlier was very much anti-EU and anti-NATO, but over the past few years their rhetoric has become more mellow. They are, on the one hand, very vocal proponents of what they call Christian values, especially in terms of definition of a family, are anti-gay, anti-abortion, though ban on abortions is a long way to go. At the same time, they try to incorporate ancient, pre-Christian Baltic religious rhetoric as part of Lithuania's exceptionality – something that has never been done before by any political power. The current PM was until recently was a high-ranking law enforcement officer, so having a person who has just been wearing a uniform in one of the highest civilian posts in a country is met with quite a lot of criticism from a liberal press.

Processes occurring in Lithuania clearly correlate with what is happening elsewhere in the EU – radical nationalism is on the rise everywhere – Hungary, Sweden, Denmark, Germany, France, UK, etc. The future of the EU is also one of the main themes of political life, and also everyday life. Brexit caused a lot of panic in Lithuania, as the UK is number one destination of economic migrants from

Lithuania. With tensions with Russia, and uncertainty with the EU, Lithuania once again feels being a country on the borders of Europe, uncertain about its future.

References

Adorno, Theodor (2005), *Minima Moralia*, translated by E. F. N. Jephcott, London and New York: Verso.

Anderson, Benedict (2006), *Imagined Communities: Reflections on the Origin and Spread of Nationalism*, London: Verso.

Bhabha, Homi K. (2004), *The Location of Culture*, London: Routledge.

Kelertas, Violeta (ed. 2006), *Baltic Postcolonialism*, Amsterdam and New York: Rodopi.

Naipaul, V.S. (2011), *The Mimic Men*, London: Picador.

Said, Edward W. (1994), *Representations of the Intellectual*, New York: Vintage.

Chapter Four

Media-ted Nationalism: The "Baltic Way" of National Imagination

K. P. Abdullakkutty

Disseminating nationalist discourses during the years of struggle for independence, Baltic media played a pivotal role in the construction of an 'imagined Baltic community' in a buffer zone between Eastern and Western Europe. When the "Baltic Way" of nationalism emerged as powerful movement, media, especially radio, popularized nationalist narratives that could unite people of three countries, Latvia, Lithuania and Estonia, to fight for a common cause. The notion of Balt and Baltic nationalism that evolved through centuries of struggle for national identity and cultural sovereignty has been circulated through popular literature and media. Surviving too many challenges of foreign occupations in different time and space, the national character of Baltic countries has been kept alive in diverse forms of media even beyond the boundaries of nation states. Given such a unique experience of national awakening, this chapter attempts to explore the role of media in constructing and popularizing the Baltic national imagination throughout the years of struggle for independence.

Conceptualizing Media-ted Nationalism

Media especially the press has been considered as the medium of nationalist narratives or the space where "imagined communities" are formed. McLuhan (1964) and Eisenstein (1979) had underscored the role of print literature in the development of nationalism in the post-Gutenberg era. Tracing the theoretical account on mediated nationalism Madianou (2002) suggests that Deutsch (1953) may be the first one to theorize the role of communication in nationalism discourse. Though Gellner (1983) emphasized role of culture in the spread of nationalism he made only a passing argument about the role of the media that also echoed McLuhan's concept of medium. According to Gellner, "media do not transmit an idea that happens to have been fed into them...it is the media... itself [that] automatically engenders the core idea of nationalism quite irrespective of what in particular is being put into the specific messages transmitted" (Cited in Madianou 2002: 35).

In this regard, Anderson (1983, 2006) conceptualized the idea of media-ted nationalism arguing that vernacular media played a great role in the construction of the notion of "horizontal comradeship" or national imagination. Anderson emphasized the rise of "national consciousness" or creation of "imagined community" among people of diverse linguistic and cultural background as a result of the "revolutionary vernacularizing thrust of capitalism." The revolutionary impact of print capitalism, apart from its role in devaluing of Latin and inspiring Reformation, was the rise of national consciousness among the readers or media audience. Despite having any face to face meeting, print capitalism connected "fellow-readers" to form "the embryo of the nationally imagined community" (Anderson 1983: 44).

Subsequently print media worked like a connecting element that helps people for simultaneous mediated communication across the nation state and feel them as part of an "imagined community". Thus Anderson summarizes his arguments: "the convergence of capitalism and print technology on the fatal diversity of human language created the possibility of a new form of imagined community, which in its basic morphology set the stage for the modern nation" (Anderson 1983: 46). Considering the questions on relevance of mediated nationalism in the age of new technological advancement, Anderson reiterates that instead of strengthening globalism new media technologies form 'long distance nationalism' and rework and redefine nationalistic politics and attachments in a global context (Anderson 1983: 46).

Hobsbawm (1992) asserted media's role in linking the public and private worlds and breaking the so-called "division between the national public sphere and the private lives of citizens". Thus rather than acknowledging it as a medium of disseminating political ideologies, Hobswam identified media as "one of the significant forces that have shaped nationalism and identity in the 20th century" (Cited in Madianou 2002: 35). Billing (1995) made theoretical elaboration of media-ted nationalism introducing a new concept of 'banal nationalism' that, according to Madianou, focuses on the reproduction of nationalism in the established nations. In such a context the national press disseminates the regular and familiar forms of nationalism known as 'banal nationalism' that could ensure the reassertion of identity (Madianou 2002: 36).

However, these theories have faced severe criticism from post-colonial scholars for the Eurocentric approach and nation state framework that could not include transnational and supra-national experiences of nationalism. Constructing a binary of 'civic' and 'ethnic' nationalisms, Eurocentric theories mostly avoided the experiences of national imaginations even from the margins of Europe (Mihelj 2011).

An international comparative approach to the study of media-ted nationalism would give more insight to the theoretical as well as the empirical research in this field. Hence, this chapter tries to explore the development of nationalist narratives in Baltic states and enquires how the media played a vital role in the construction of a "Baltic Way" of national imagination.

Evolution of Baltic Nationalism

Three provinces of the Russian Empire, earlier known as *Livland*, *Estland* and *Courland* (*Kurland*) are now familiar as Baltic states comprising Lithuania, Estonia and Latvia. Located east of Baltic Sea these countries were ethnically inhabited by peoples of Finno-Ugric origins and linguistically composed by Finnish and Indo-European languages. Peoples and ethnic groups speaking Baltic languages are being called Balts (Boiko 2002: 7). Due to the geo-political location, being in the west of East and east of West, Baltic states remained in the geopolitical, cultural and linguistic margins of West and East. Even though Baltic countries have "repeatedly faded in and out of the European history" for centuries, these countries manifest diversity in cultural, linguistic, and ethnic composition (Balcytiene 2002).

Despite certain similarities in recent past Baltic countries never had an identical way in their historical experiences. Lithuania has been the largest among the three with an ancient culture, rich history and strong political power since the years of Grand Duchy of Lithuania. Lithuania experienced the nationalist power in 14th and 15th centuries under Jogaila and Vytautas Grand Duke (Lithuanian-Polish dynasty), could beat Teutonic Knights and expand the boundaries to Black Sea and even resisted Tatar advance into the region. Latvia and Estonia, on the other hand, had lost their statehood in 13th century and came under the spheres of Baltic German influence. These countries after the decline of Teutonic Order got certain benefits in education and their peasantry under Swedish rule caused emergence of nationalist waves, especially after abolition of serfdom in 1681(Balcytiene 2002; Hartman 1992: 72; Sharma 1998: 19)

The Tsarist colonial rule of Russia in later centuries caused the nationalist awakening in Baltic countries due to the abolition of serfdom and the advancement of capitalism. Nationalist movements like National Patriotic Association of Lithuania (NPAL) (182I) and "Young Latvia" (1869) emerged as a result of Tsarist reforms while strong intelligentsia from Vilnius and Tartu Universities popularized the nationalist cause. Baltic nationalism intensified in 20th century when a 'revolutionary co-operation' developed between Russian Bolsheviks and Baltic nationalists against Tsarist regime. Thus the early phase of the Baltic nationalism evolved around Baltic people's continuous struggle for independence from different European powers such as the Dutch, Germany and Russia (Sharma 1998: 25, 50; Hartman 1992: 76).

The contemporary historical identity of three Baltic countries is also defined according to their struggle for national independence from both Russia and Germany during the years of World Wars. The very experiences of Nazi and Soviet regimes evoked the Baltic nationalism in the form of preserving the culture and language that helped these countries ensure the power for self-determination during the final years of Soviet Union. Unlike the ideas of class conflicts in the Western Europe, the political mobilization and party systems across Baltic countries were based on issues like national identity and cultural autonomy (Balcytiene 2002).

Therefore, Baltic struggle for independence and autonomy were the outcome of a strong nationalistic sense rooted in the intense 'nationalistic identity' of the Baltic people. Since the Baltic nationalism was based on internally-initiated organic sense of national identity, Hartman (1992) argues, it could win popular support and survive the challenge of Soviet nationalism. The strategic location and the economic advancement of the region could reinforce the notion of Baltic superiority whereas Baltic languages and literatures became source of national pride. Religiously, the pagan identity of Balts also worked as a factor in the nationalist assertion of the Baltic people when they were confronted earlier by Christianization and later by Sovietization (Hartman 1992: 75). Among a number of facts that supported the Baltic nationalism the high literacy rate of Estonian and Latvian population is considered very important one (Sharma 1998: 35).

Media-ted Baltic Nationalism

With the rise of strong intelligentsia across Baltic states, different genres of printed literature appeared in vernacular languages to disseminate nationalist discourses. Even though the first newspapers in Baltic national languages were published later than many other European languages, there were more than two hundred Polish journals published in Lithuania since 1760 and continued until 1918. The vernacular press began to flourish when Estonians started *Luhhike Oppetus in* 1776 and Latvians published *Latviesu Arste* in 1768 followed by *Nusidavimai Dievo Karalystėje*by Lithuanians in 1823. When Tsarist rulers banned publishing of printed materials in Lithuanian language in 1864 to curb national awakening, such materials were printed outside the country. To overcome such bans, journals in English, German and French languages were also published to raise the Baltic nationalist question before international community (Balcytiene 2008: 47; Hartman 1992: 76).

The Lithuanian Literary Society founded in 1879 worked for reviving vernacular literature and circulating printed materials in Lithuanian language. In this regard, a literary magazine *'Aura'*, though banned in 1864 thus published outside Lithuania, contributed a lot articulating narratives of national rebirth, liberation and independent Lithuanian culture. A number of periodicals like *Varpas* joined in the nationalist imagination propagating ideas of national solidarity, democracy and tolerance (Hartman 1992: 73; Sharma 1998: 36).

Demanding equal rights for Latvian people with other nations, students of Tartu University started a national newspaper *Majas Viesis* and the almanacs *Seta, Daba, Pasaule*. Latvian intellectuals, authors, writers and poets contributed to this paper and constructed nationalist narratives of Baltic people. To strengthen the nationalism movement, young Latvian journalists also published a radical newspaper called *Peterburgs Avizez*. Similarly, Estonian intelligentsia mobilized the masses for nationalist cause with a couple of newspapers like *Perno Postimees* in 1857 published from Parnu and *Eesti Postimees* from Tartu in 1860s. Johann Waldemar Jannsen, the editor of *Perno Postimees* articulated the concept of Estonian nation and circulated the idea among the peasants to fight for equal rights for Estonians. *Eesti Postimees* started by Jannsen in 1864, also circulated among intellectuals and peasants, developed as the mouthpiece of Estonian national movement. This newspaper strongly opposed the Germanization and asserted patriotic notions demanding the vernacularization of Estonian educational system. Articles in *Eesti Postimees* by journalists like Carl Robert Jakobson, who later started a weekly newspaper *Sakala* in the southern Estonian town of Viljandi, attacked the Baltic German nobility and voiced for poor peasantry (Hoyer et al. 1993: 70).

Two leading radical newspapers, *Jauna Strava* and *Dienas Lapa* published in 1886 also fanned the nationalist wave. Since the editors of these papers, poet Janis Rainis and lawyer Peteris Stucka, were leaders of the radical national movement, the Tsarist army muzzled their voice arresting and sending them for exile. During the revolutionary phase of 1905, newspapers like *Uudised* published memorandum that demanded autonomy for different nationalities including sections under Russian empire. Estonian Social Democratic Party leader Peter Speek, the editor of *Uudised*, proposed a charter of demands for autonomous self-governments across Baltic region (Hoyer et al. 1993: 79).

Baltic media constructed a nationalist public sphere and articulated nationalist narratives that connected all spheres of society during the revolutionary phase. While *Eesti Postimees* worked as the organ of the Estonian Progressive People's Party, *Uudised* became the organ of Social Democratic Party and supported even the bourgeois ideology for the nationalist cause. During these years, newspapers *Uudised* along with *Teataja* and the two *Postimees* led the fight for freedom and voiced for a range of issues like rights of the working class, tenants, farmers and women. With a series of radical articles, Latvian newspaper *Cina*, the organ of Latvian Social Democratic Worker's Party, became popular while papers like *Darty* and *Dzimtenes Vastness* attracted public for their revolutionary images (Sharma 1998: 44; Hoyer et al. 1993: 82).

Lithuanian newspaper *Darbininku Balsas* published between 1901 and 1906 strongly supported national liberation movement. To mobilize the peasants, Lithuanian Peasant League published a newspaper titled *Lietuvos Ukininkas*. Once the ban on Lithuanian language press lifted in 1904, the media and political parties demanded true press freedom that could ensure national independence. Baltic newspapers like *Eesti Postimees* and *Virulanc* strongly criticized the 1905 Tsarist press law which reinforced the censorship and fought for total freedom. As a result of such struggles, more than 12 daily newspapers emerged by 1907 from Estonia where *Eesti Postimees* was the only daily earlier. Thus, we can see the strong role of media in articulating and disseminating nationalist narratives across the Baltic states during the Tsarist and revolutionary periods of last century (Hoyer et al. 1993: 107).

National Narrative of Soviet Phase

Baltic media could keep the momentum of the 'revolutionary cooperation' between the Bolsheviks and Baltic nationalists during the years after the 1905 revolution. Along with nationalist movements, Bolshevik party organizations spread across Baltic states whereas a Latvian organization even published a newspaper *Okopnaya Pravda* prior to the October Revolution in 1917. Contrary to the earlier demands of autonomy for Baltic states, the October Revolution strengthened the demand for social and national liberation and independence from Russia also. Though Bolsheviks supported sovereignty of nationalities in the early years, regime changed the policy once Baltic states declared their autonomy and independence. When Baltic states became the 'war zone' and were occupied by Germany but finally defeated (Russia also) in the First World War, the nationalist demands of Baltic people regained with the help of Western powers until they got independence for two decades during1919-1939 (Hoyer et al. 1993 ; Sharma 1998).

Enjoying two decades of independence, the Baltic media tried to revive its nationalistic narratives as nations having rich and diverse socio-religious traditions and cultural heritage. However, the Soviet and German annexations of Baltic states in 1939, following the Molotov-Ribbentrop treaty, brought back the challenges to the media to struggle for the survival of national identities. The Baltic intellectuals and media had to face the bitter experiences of censorship, muzzling and life threat from Soviet regime under Stalin. The situation changed in the post-Stalinist era with the spread of literary works and media outlets especially radio (Hoyer et al. 1993: 200).

Magazines like *Looming* and *Loomnigu Raamatukogu*, started in 1957, became popular in Estonia reviving the national and cultural discourses whereas the readership of media also increased. Diverse magazines such as *Eesti Loodus* in science, *Keel ja Kirjandus* in academics and *Siluett* in fashion emerged. In Latvia, circulation of the magazine *Padomju Jaunatne* grew more than six fold while circulation of newspapers increased many a time. *Lisema, Podomju Latvijas Sieviete, Skola un Gimene, Lauku Dzive* and *Maksla* were magazines published for ladies, family and art. Newspapers in Lithuania also turned popular while specialized magazines emerged such as *Tarybine Moteris* for women, *Moksleivis* for youth, *Nemunas* for literature, *Musu Gamta*, and *Musu Sodai*for nature, *Mokslas ir Gyvenimas* for academics· *Mokslas ir Technika* for science, *Kulturos* and *Barai* for culture, *Tarybinis Mokytojas* for teachers, and *sportds* for sports for sports fans (Sharma 1998: 102; Hoyer et al. 1993: 203).

Though the number of media outlets increased during the Khrushchev era, the control and censorship muzzled the nationalist discourses. Then, journalists like Oiev Anton of Tartu paper *Edasi* developed new method of narration, storytelling of farmers and countryside, to challenge Soviet ideological restrictions. Lithuanian entertainment program *Linksmasis Subatvakaris*, Estonian news program *Reporteritund* and *Pacvakaja*, and *Latvianthe* information and music show *Milrofons* were popular radio programs that awakened the Baltic cultural and national feelings in the pre-television era. Once television stations started in Latvia in 1954, Estonia in 1955 and Lithuania in 1957, it marked a new era in Baltic media laying the foundations of national television traditions, later popularized by people like Valdo Pant with popular episodes of 'Today 25 years ago' (Hoyer et al. 1993: 206; Sharma 1998: 105).

Despite certain setbacks in the nationalist media narratives in post-war years, Baltic media and literary fields fought back the hegemonic measures of Russification under Soviet regime. To challenge the Soviet control, Baltic media joined the East European International Radio and Television organizations of Poland and Finland. In the later decades, Samizdat (clandestine literature banned by the state) periodicals and religious magazines also revived the nationalist discourse in Baltic states. *Ausra*, the secular Samizdat magazine published since 1975 and religious magazines like *Dievas Ir Tevyne* and *Rupintojelis* became popular. A host of periodicals including *Varpas* (1977), *Alma Mater* (1979), *Postage, Perspektivos, Tassokelias* and *Laisves* šauklys emerged in diverse fields but articulated the nationalist way and popularized the Baltic notion (Sharma 1998: 125; Hoyer et al. 1993: 208).

The Gorbachev's *glasnost* and *perestroika* helped Baltic media to revive its role as the public sphere that could construct the ideas of national liberation and independence instead of Soviet nationalism. Party organs were replaced by independent press and foreign and local journalists worked for national cause rather than becoming party propagandists. And, in the final years of Soviet regime, party affiliations disappeared and an era of so-called "free and independent" Baltic media emerged that could ferment 'national morale' (Balcytiene 2008: 48).

Media Constructed "Baltic Way"

Baltic media and journalists became the frontrunners of independence movements as mainstream media worked along with underground publications like *Auseklis* and *Staburags* disseminating the voice of national leaders and organizations. Journalists like Dainis Īvāns who led the Latvian Popular Front even followed 'oral journalism' bringing everyday voices into the press and making everyday views heard. While official media dropped many stories of protests and demonstrations, alternative press like *Padomju Januatne, Cīņa*, and *Atmoda* took the baton of mass movements and united the Baltic voice. As the source of information and inspiration for movements, media-orchestrated the famous 'Singing Revolution' that united the Baltic people for a peaceful spring against the Soviet regime.

Figure 4: Singing Lithuanian civilian defenders in front of the Vilnius Press Center flash victory signs at Soviet soldiers who were preparing to occupy it, 11 January 1991. Photo by Paulius Lileikis in Guntis Smidchens, (12 October 2016), "Singing Revolution: Past and Present" retrieved from https://www.fpri.org/article/2016/10/singing-revolution-past-present/

The role of media in channelizing the nationalist upsurge was manifested in the events of mass resistance against the Soviet force, when it tried to gag Baltic national radio and television stations. Since Baltic media, then known as 'popular (people's) radio' and 'popular (people's) television', could win the hearts of nationalists, people across three states thronged to streets to protect national media houses (Kaspars 2010: 63).

Notwithstanding the unorganized nature of liberation movements media glued a host of groups like Popular Front, LNNK (Latvian National Independence Movement), the Citizens Congress, the Women's League, religious movements, and environmental movements for a nationalist cause. While *Atmoda* worked as the organ of liberation front *LTF Vestnesis* was launched as a special publication for internal communication. As a result Baltic people armed only with radios and newspapers erected barricades to defend the country as well as the media which provided them first-hand experiences of liberation and national narratives of independence (Cakars 2004: 5).

Baltic media really showed its national character when Popular Fronts organized a six-hundred-kilometre human chain of two million people, famously known as the "Baltic Way", from Tallinn to Vilnius not only broadcasting the events but also publicizing and managing the movement. The rejuvenation of Baltic national identity, according to Lauristin and Vihalemm, became real during the years of transition, as intellectuals and journalists across three countries asserted the recovery of national sovereignty through metaphoric language of poems, dramas, songs, paintings and literary essays. Moreover, the institution of national songfest that could survive due to the multinational cultural character of Soviet culture also played a role in sustaining the national identity of Baltic states. The songfests emerged as the main space of cultural resistance and national awakening that could articulate the "Baltic Way" of liberation movements through popular protests like 'Singing Revolution'(Lauristin & Vihalemm 2002: 15).

Rather than disseminating the news and views, Baltic media actively participated in the construction of the public sphere that emerged during the massive popular movements in late 1980s working as the network supporting the growing political activity of people. Apart from mobilizing the resistance movements, according to Lauristin and Vihalemm, the media restored the 'national memory' of Baltic countries discussing the history of Liberation War during1918-1920, Soviet annexation and occupation, and Stalinist repressions (Lauristin and Vihalemm 2002: 26).

The Survey data of media popularity during these years show the role media played in articulating national narratives for liberation movements. Based on a survey conducted by the Department of Journalism at Tartu University in early 1990s, Lauristin and Vihalemm argue that an average Estonian read twelve newspapers and magazines regularly and the circulation of national dailies and magazines were high for ever. As the 'movements' press' replaced the old Soviet model of the 'Party press', it reflected in the emergence of a new democratic public sphere that could articulate nationalist imaginations (Lauristin and Vihalemm 2002: 23).

The Latvian experience of media popularity was not different as the media became the space for public debates on the emergence of new public sphere when the Soviet structures started to disintegrate since 1980s. Therefore scholars never hesitate to call the media as the architects of 'Latvian national renaissance' that ultimately opened the way for national independence (Brikse *et.al.* 2002: 67). According to Brikse and others, the Latvian press, instead of spreading Soviet propaganda, now articulated the narratives of national awakening and disseminated the ideas of the Latvian People's Front. Radio and television could win great public trust since they made the nationalist movements alive giving first-hand accounts of demonstrations and protests. Being true "people's media", Radio Latvia reflected the 'social and political mood of society' and gave space for public debates (Brikse et al. 2002: 69).

Lithuanian media, according to Balcytiene, also responded to the cultural and national churning bringing a host of unquestioned topics like Soviet deportations and national identity for public discussion. Moreover, the media argued that it has been invariably used ''across the Baltic states for the political breakthrough in the final years of Soviet rule. Working as network to connect the people with nationalist discourse, media gave space for democratic political dialogue that resulted in political action through singing protests and human chains across Baltic countries. The emergence of *Respublika*, an independent daily launched by Lithuanian independence movement "*Sajudis*" is the best example of such a media venture that made nationalist awakening imaginative. Though Balcytiene criticizes Baltic media for being "saturated with feelings of romanticism and nationalism" during the years of struggle for independence, she emphasizes that "the media served as a herald in the creation of the yet-unknown and entirely new public structures that emerged in connection with the massive popular movements and which were mediated through the mass media" (Balcytiene 2002: 108).

Baltic Media Transition

The hard-earned independence in the 1990s brought changes in the socio-political structure of Baltic countries which reflected in the structure and style of media also. Undergoing the transitional stage, Baltic media shifted from a controlled system to a laissez-faire model introducing professional journalism, instead of ideological propaganda and market oriented methods or party based mechanisms. However, such a transition have invited mixed response from scholars regarding the role of media as a socially responsible institution that could perform the watchdog functions especially in newly emerged democracies.

Lauristin and Vihalemm have noted that the Estonian media in the period of 1991-1994 made a rapid shift towards the liberal model that replaced the authoritarian concept of a media-state relationship with concept of a completely free media. Abolition of state ownership and subsidies for the print media led to the privatization and 'generational replacement of journalists' that resulted in the 'marketisation of journalism'. While media tried to become free of 'social commitments', it could create an 'open and neutral public space' that promoted public expression and negotiation of diverse interests and viewpoints. However, Lauristin and Vihalemm argue that the media couldn't reach up to the mark in creating a new "democratic public sphere giving "voice" to all new forces in society" as it was expected during the struggle for independence. When the new economic policies created "losers" and "winners", the media endorsed the "winners" resulting in grave imbalance in the democratic representation of "losers" in Estonian society (Lauristin and Vihalemm 2002: 30).

The independent market oriented media model developed after 1990s in Latvia also redesigned the form and contents of press, radio and electronic media. In this new scenario, according to Brikse et-al. (2002), newspapers became a 'new product' that would attract people, whereas many digests of information were published in newspaper format just as "white pages" of history. While the number of dailies went up from seven in 1990 to eighteen in 1995, changes were also brought about in the content and form of newspapers and audience as well. In a market-race with local and tabloid press, national dailies struggled to firm their existing audience and find new niches. This market-orientation of production and consumption affected the content and formats of Radio and television outlets in Latvia (Brikse et al. 2002: 72).

The transition of socio-political and economic spheres of Lithuania to an independent, democratic and market system in 1990s reflected in the media sector also. Since it enjoyed a free and uncontrolled situation contrary to the Soviet era, Lithuanian media became the space of open debates on diverse issues ranging from state policy to family affairs. Though these changes widely were welcomed by liberal intellectuals and policymakers, Balcytiene has pointed to the very shortcomings of such a market oriented media system. Instead of diversification in media ownership, contents and formats, Lithuania faced concentration and conglomeration that affected the growth of national and regional press and other media outlets. After independence, Lithuania, instead of promoting diversity in media content and format ensuring cultural and political pluralism through a democratic process of effective mobilization / participation of its citizens, went into an opposite direction. Minimizing scope for new arrivals, the national newspaper market declined to a few number of titles. Market orientation in production apart, the Lithuanian dailies, radio and electronic media showed a downward trend in the standard of analytical journalism (Balcytiene 2002: 115).

The Transitional Chaos

Once the honeymoon phase of liberation and independence was over by 20th century, Baltic intellectuals and media critics started reviving the nostalgic memories of media being the space of normative national narratives. Due to intensive commercialization of media sector, Baltic people witnessed utter chaos regarding the survival of nationalist ethos and cultural values that have been carried forward by media for centuries. In the context of recent developments in the Baltic especially Latvian media sphere, Brikse and others argue that there is a phenomenal 'crisis in traditional mass communication environment' across these countries. The growing commercialisation of news as commodity, the dramatisation and sensationalism, lack of diversity in public interest and cultural identity in contents, and the imitation of stereotypical methods to hike programme ratings are pointed out. Consequently, the traditional media that could win popular trust through orchestrating the national awakening are at stake since they lose their "reputation as trust worthy sources of information and as entities that can have a serious influence on decision-making processes" (Brikse et al. 2002: 84).

Lauristin and Vihalemm also remind the transitional stage of Baltic media that could play better socializing role in an open society though it had lost its seriousness and involvement in the political processes. Unlike in the Soviet times, 'uncontrolled and unpredictable diversity of opinions' are represented in Baltic media, whereas changes in media contents, formats, styles and language became the most powerful source of social learning. Media's role in social 'relearning and re-socialisation' is emphasized especially in the context of growing commercialization and consolidation of the media and the rapid spread of new communication technologies in Estonia. And the new trends of 'globalizing and commercializing' in Baltic media are capable to construct "the new discourses of the new society" (Lauristin and Vihalemm 2002: 40).

However, Vihalemm (2003) admits that journalistic productions across Baltic countries are recently being evaluated from the viewpoint of sales and profits instead of social or cultural values. Blaming the change in audience reception, media shifted to 'infotainment' from analysis, enlightenment, and social integration. Vihalemm points to the demise of 'culturally and socially unifying role' of Baltic media and its fall only as source for entertainment due to the diversification of outlets and the rising cost of media consumption (Vihalemm 2003: 592).

After the years of transition from controlled media system, Balcytiene notes, Lithuanian media has fallen new low in its standards of analytical journalism. In the era of neck to neck competition, major national dailies like *Lietuvos rytas* compromised their normative ethos with market oriented trends of sensationalism and commercialism. Since journalists and editors trust upon the commodity value of the media content, crime and scandal consume major space and national culture receives minimal interest (Balcytiene 2002: 117). However, Balcytiene points to the public trust media and journalists acquired since the days of national awakening based on polls that showed high confidence of Lithuanians towards media rather than any other institutions. She interprets the public trust on media either as the high politicization of the people or as their 'failure to become critical. Anyhow, the Baltic media transition in recent years has raised questions towards its continuity as a space where the national imagination of "Baltic Way" was constructed (Balcytiene 2002: 119).

Conclusion

Unlike any other national narratives the "Baltic Way" of mediated-nationalism has evolved around a continuous struggle for the survival of national character and cultural sovereignty. Notwithstanding the nation state boundaries and geographic borders, Baltic nationalism prevailed across the media in Latvia, Lithuania and Estonia in different and diverse forms. The media has been an important element in constructing and disseminating the nationalist discourses that erected a unique chain of resistance for liberation. However, the recent national discourses and media trends in Baltic states showcase a great transition from nationalist cultural ethos and norms to market-oriented commercial dealings. More studies would be needed to explore the current status of diverse media environment and its role in addressing the national imaginations of people across Baltic states.

References

Anderson, Benedict (1983, 2006), *Imagined Communities: Reflections on the Origin and Spread of Nationalism*, London: Verso.

Balcytiene, Aukse (2002), "Lithuanian Media; A Question of Change" in Vihalemm, Peeter (ed.), *Baltic Media in Transition*, Tartu: Tartu University Press.

__________ (2008), "Challenges for Professional Journalism: On tripartite identity of the Baltic media and its impact on media performance," *Informacijosmokslai*, No. 47, pp. 44-58.

__________ (2012), "Culture as a Guide in Theoretical Explanations of Baltic Media", in Daniel C. Hallin, Paolo Mancini (eds.), *Comparing Media Systems Beyond the Western World*, USA: Cambridge University Press.

Billig, Michael (1995), *Banal Nationalism*, London: Thousand Oaks.

Boiko, Martin (2002), "Baltic and Balts: On the History of Notions and the Question of Baltic Regionalism," *The World of Music*, Vol. 44, No. 3, pp. 7-19.

Brikse, Inta, et. al. (2002), "Development of the Media in Latvia in the 1990s", in Peeter Vihalemm, (ed.), *Baltic Media in Transition*, Tartu: Tartu University Press.

Cakars, Janis (2004), "The Liberation of Latvia: Media and Nonviolence", Research Report IREX Individual Advanced Research Opportunities (IARO), Latvia.

Deutsch, Karl W. (1953), *Nationalism and Social Communication: An Inquiry into the Foundations of Nationality*, Massachusetts: Technology Press.

Eisenstein, Elizabeth L. (1979), *The Printing Press as an Agent of Change: Communications and Cultural Transformations in Early-Modern Europe,* Cambridge: Cambridge University Press.

Gellner, Ernest (1983), *Nations and Nationalism*, Oxford: Basil Blackwell.

Hartman, Gary (1992), "The Origins and Growth of Baltic Nationalism as a Force for Independence", *Lithuanian Quarterly Journal of Arts and Sciences*, Vol. 38, No.3, p. 72.

Hobsbawm, Eric (1992, 1990), *Nations and Nationalism Since 1780: Programme, Myth, Reality,* Cambridge: Cambridge University Press.

Hoyer, Svennik, et. al. (eds.), (1993), *Towards a Civic Society: The Baltic Media's Long Road to Freedom*, Tartu: Baltic Association for Media Research, Nota Baltica Ltd.

Lauristin, Marju and Peeter Vihalemm (2002), "The Transformation of Estonian Society and Media: 1987-2001" in Peeter Vihalemm (ed.), *Baltic Media in Transition*, Tartu: Tartu University Press.

Kaspars, Ruklis (2010), "Baltic Media Environments: Integrated or Divided?," Vidzeme University Letonia, Retrieved from http/ revistas.ua.pt/index.php/prismacom/article/download/648/pdf.

Madianou, Mirca (2002), "Mediating the Nation: News, Audiences and Identities in Contemporary Greece," Unpublished PhD thesis, London: London School of Economics.

McLuhan, Marshall (1964), *Understanding Media*, London: Routledge and Kegan Paul.

Mihelj, Sabina (2011), "Nationalism and the media, East and West," in M. Sukosd, and K. Jakubowicz (eds.), *Nationalism, the Media and European Identity*, Budapest: Central European University Press.

Misiunas, Romuald and Rein Taagepera (1993),*The Baltic states Years of Dependence 1940-1990*, USA: University of California Press.

Sharma, Sunaina (1998), "A Study of Baltic Nationalism Since 1939," Unpublished PhD thesis, New Delhi: Jawaharlal Nehru University.

Smith, Graham (1996), *The Baltic states: The National Self-Determination of Estonia, Latvia and Lithuania*, U.S.A: St. Martin Press.

Vihalemm, Peeter (ed., 2002), *Baltic Media in Transition*, Tartu: Tartu University Press.

Vihalemm, Peeter (2003), "Changing Media in a Changing Society," *Democratizatsiya, The Journal of Post-Soviet Democratization*, 11: 4, pp. 587-600.

Chapter Five

Democratic Transition and Emergence of Multi-Party System in Lithuania

Karamala Areesh Kumar

Introduction

In 1991, Lithuania regained its independence from the former Soviet Union. Immediately after independence, Lithuania began its political transition from authoritarianism to parliamentary democracy by incorporating the norms and values of established western democracies. Lithuania introduced political institutions required for a democracy such as constitution, parliament, regular competitive elections, party system and an organised legal system. It adopted its present constitution on 25 October 1992 after which Parliamentary form of government was introduced. A unicameral legislature (*Seimas*) consisting of 141 members of which seventy-one are elected from constituencies by majority votes and seventy by proportional representation was introduced. The president is directly elected by people for a period of five years and the prime minister and other ministers are appointed by president for a four-year term subject to the approval of the parliament (*Seimas*) (Auers 2015)

In the democratization process in Lithuania, political parties play a significant role as potential actors in the establishment and consolidation of new democratic regime. The political parties are required to obtain a certain threshold for getting seats to contest elections. Under the electoral law of June 1996, the threshold for obtaining proportional seats was made five per cent (and previous concessions on the threshold rule for minority parties were abolished). According to this law, voters became entitled to record a preference for individual candidates on party lists (Law on Parties and Political Organizations of Lithuania: 2004). Hence, political parties have a great role in electing legitimate representatives of people. This study analyses the development of political parties and multi-party system in Lithuania in the broader context of post-communist democratization and democratic consolidation.

The formation of multi-party system and political parties in Lithuania is based on the country's historical background and legal framework. Political parties emerged as a result of national awakening, political movements for national independence, and efforts for creating a democratic parliamentary system. In 1991, several parties were formed during the national awakening and number of organizations re-established after regaining independence. Lithuanian constitution of 1992 introduced the legal framework for the functioning of political parties. It provides the legal definition of political party.

> a political party shall be a public legal person that its own name, has been established pursuant to this Law, and whose purpose is to meet the political interests of its members, assist in expressing the political will of the citizens of the Republic of Lithuania in enforcing State power and the right to self-government" (Law on Parties and Political Organizations of Lithuania: 2004).

Article 35 of the 1992 constitution provides citizens the right to freely unite themselves into communities, political parties and associations. However, their goals should not contradict the constitution and laws of the nation (Constitution of the Republic of Lithuania: 1992).

The operation of political parties is regulated by a number of legislations for restricting party financing. In Lithuania, the law on public finance to political parties (1999) introduced public donations to parties from 2000 onwards. State subsidies are the primary sources of finance for political parties and organizations. The parties winning at least five percent votes in parliamentary and municipal elections are eligible for the state subsidies. These laws explain the donations from trade unions, government institutions, charity and religious organizations. Donations from foreign sources are also restricted under the law of public finance to political parties. Direct subsidies were decreased and partial re-imbursement policy of campaign expenditure was introduced since 2005. Every party in Lithuania is supposed to submit declarations on their campaign accounts and expenditure within the 25 days after the elections. Any party failing to fulfil the criteria loses the subsidies allocated to that party (Law on Public Finance to Political Parties: 1999).

The disintegration of the Soviet Union led to the regaining of national independence of Lithuania and the resultant democratic transition in 1990s provided its citizens an opportunity to rebuild democracy. In this, emergence of political parties and multi-party system became crucial. Lithuania had a short period of independence in the inter-war period (1918-1940) and political parties and party systems had promoted a democratic political system then. However, during Second World War, Lithuania was forcibly taken over and united into the erstwhile Soviet Union. Democratic set up was abolished and only the Communist Party of Soviet

Union (CPSU) was allowed to function legally. This system continued until 1991. However, various political parties, which were abolished during the Soviet rule, became active once again when Soviet President Mikhail Gorbachev tried his liberal reforms of perestroika and glasnost during1988-1991. This chapter analyses various stages of party formation and the emergence and development of political parties and multi-party system in Lithuania.

Role of Political Parties in Democracy

The definition of political party or multi-party system encompasses numerous aspects. There is no all agreed definition available on political party. Several authors have studied political parties and multi-party system, and conceptualized party in various ways. Mostly, political parties are organisations of the people, managing their membership and nominating candidates for public office. They also try to have representation in both executive and legislative branches of government, thus giving stability to the political system (Maisel and Brewer 2012: 189). Sartori defined political parties as "organizations that contest political election and seek governmental office" (Sartori 1976: 64). Diamond and Gunther defined parties according to their functions. According to the authors, in established democracies, political parties perform the function of recruitment of candidates for public office, mobilization of electoral support, the structuring of policy agendas, societal representation, forming and sustaining government, bringing together sectional interests, social integration and stabilizing political process (Diamond and Gunther 2001: 20).

As per Downs' (1957) view, parties are "teams of men" seeking to maximize their electoral support for controlling government (Downs 1957: 25). According to Mac Iver, "a political party is an association organized in support of some principles of policy, which by constitutional means, it endeavours to make the determinant of government" (*cited in Kumari* 2009: 262). Epstein argues, "Party means any group, however loosely organized, seeking to elect governmental office holders under a given label" (Epstein 1967: 9). According to Janda, "Political party is an organization that sponsors candidates for political office under the organization name and ideology" (Janda et al. 2009: 189). In Dyck's view, a political party can be defined as "an organized group that nominates candidate and contest elections in order to influence the policy and personnel of government" (Dyck 2012: 190). From these definitions, it could be understood that political parties are organizations of likeminded people. They contest for elections seeking public office. Political parties organise government and influence policymaking. Political party should be a legally accepted and legitimate organization as per the prevailing law. They must have common political objective and programme. In this way, the activities of political parties are essential for proper functioning of a representative democracy. In a democratic system, political parties have several important functions and they play very important role in the process of democratization in transition countries.

The emergence of multi-party system and political parties are positive indicators of healthy process in a democratic transition. Modern representative democracy cannot operate without political parties. In democratic societies, people who share similar views and goals often join together to form political parties. They form parties to strengthen their ability and to influence the decision-making in the state. The main idea behind founding a political party is to promote a common set of values (ideology) and beliefs and develop a memorandum, which influences others based on collective beliefs and values (Thesing 1995: 190).

Political Parties perform crucial functions in democratic government system. Janda outlined four important party functions in democratic political system. These are structuring the voting choice in elections, nominating candidates for election to public office, proposing alternative programs, and coordinating with the government officials (Janda et al. 2009: 190). The foremost function of the parties in the democratic system is to act as an intermediary between society and state and between the rulers and ruled. Gunther and Diamond (2001) also identified seven types of functions of parties such as "candidate nomination, electoral mobilization, issue structuring, representing various social groups, interest aggregation, performing and sustaining governments, and social integration role". They also serve as "instruments of political education, interest articulation, political mobilization and political recruitment" (Diamond and Gunther 2001: 6-9).

The primary role of political parties in democratic countries is to encourage people to go to contest elections and participate in the electoral process. Elections are very important because they provide people the freedom to participate actively in electing their representatives (Trent et al. 2000: 73). It reflects public opinion and mass participation in decision-making. Elections can occur without democracy but democracy cannot endure without elections. The existence of multi-party system and elections broadens the concept of democracy.

Political parties play a significant role as the intermediate between citizens and government institutions in internal political environment of the country. Party organizations also help coordinate the action of public officials (Janda 2009: 191). Parties are the central intermediate structures between society and government. "A party represents a general view about the relationship between the government and society" (Sartori 1976: 170). Parties formulate and develop policies for the governing of the state. They are more effective when they are founded on a set of ideas for governance. In contemporary democracies, it is the responsibility of a single political party or a coalition of parties to organize enough elected representatives to form a government. Political parties are the prime actors in this process, and the formation of a coalition is a partisan activity. Parties from the government as well as the opposition. The party or parties that win a majority of seats in the lower house, that is the House of Representatives, form a government. The party or parties that win the second largest number of seats become the opposition (Dyck 2012: 206). The role of the opposition is to criticise government policy and prevent mismanagement of power. This role is essential for ensuring good governance and protecting the rights of citizens. Such opposition parties ultimately provide an organized alternative for the voters to support in the next election if they are not satisfied with the incumbent government performance (Ibid: 207).

Political parties are very essential for state building and establishment of democratic institutions. In the process of establishment of constitution, electoral institutions, and judicial system, political parties play a significant role. Parties played a significant role in the post-communist state. After the breakdown of communism and the Soviet Union, majority of the new European democracies had to engage in a process of state and nation building (Nqrgaard and Johannesen 1996: 12). In the period of transition, parties are very important to adopt democratic principles and market economy in the new independent state. Without a well-developed institutional capacity as well as with a domestic instability and irregularity, state remains weak, worried with internal problems, and unable to pursue efficient international policies (Ibid).

Democratic Transition in Lithuania

Democratic transition is taking place in Lithuania at various dimensions: political, economic and social. Democratic transition refers to not only the transformation of the government from authoritarianism to democracy but also transformation of the economy, and of political and social ideas including the party system. In simple terms, democratic transition means the process which ends the authoritarian regime. It further establishes a democratic regime and consolidates the same (Huntington 1968: 35). There is an absence of a precise theory which can explain the nature of democratic transition. Scholars have frequently used several explanatory variables, such as political culture, civil society, political economy, political institutions and rational choice to analyse the process of democratization. Yet they have failed to come up with a single theory that explains the democratic transition (Parajulee 2000: 3).

Huntington explained democratic transition through his theory of three waves of democratization; the first wave started in 1820, the second wave started during 1940-1962 after the Second World War, and the third wave began between 1970 and 1980. According to him, the current era of democratic transitions continues from the third wave of democratization in the history of the contemporary world.

Huntington suggested several variables that have been contributed to democracy and democratization: high level of economic growth, existence of market economy, presence of strong middle class, social polarization in the society, low level of civil violence, low levels of political polarization and extremism, and political leaders dedicated to govern the democracy effectively (Huntington 1968: 37). Transformation in Baltic states have been comparatively analysed on three levels such as:

- Transformation from authoritarian socialism to liberal democracy.
- Transformation from a centrally planned economy to market economy based on private ownership.
- Transformation from the Soviet empire to an independent statehood and adaptation to the democratic institutions (Nqrgaard and Johannesen 1996: 4).

In Lithuania, the political transition in every county was dominated by three types of political actors: hardliners, soft liners and national radicals, who actually reintroduced competitive politics into the Baltic countries (Kulik and Pshizova 2005: 121). The most important element of the post-communist democratization is the revival and reinstallation of the political parties and the multi-party system. The emergence of political parties provided a larger space to the citizens in order to express their views (Krupavicius 2005: 469).

The emergence of democracy in Lithuania has contributed to a stable government and has further created a healthy political environment feasible for the citizens. One of the far-reaching developments in the process of liberalization was the policy of reconstruction and freedom known as perestroika and glasnost initiated by Mikhail Gorbachev in 1985. Though there has been a mention of post-communist era, which showed the collapse of communism, Communist Party operated in its own capacity until the elections. The process of institutional democracy went through a series of phases without an instant change. Political leaders who represented various spheres occupied the core position in the process of transition. Two important theoretical aspects, which were responsible for the development of the institutionalised democracy, are structural constancy and "functional autonomy of political players" (Ibid: 470).

The transition period was an on-going process wherein political actors gained and attained stability. The different phases, which the transition process included, are the pre-transitional crisis confrontation, reform of system, consolidation of democracy, stable democracy or oligarchy. Firstly, the pre-transitional crisis confrontation included the Communist Party, interest groups including political parties like LCP and Sajudis. Constituent parliament dominated the phase of the reform of system. The phase of consolidation of democracy was controlled by the executive and state's bureaucracy along with a trivial influence of the interest groups, political parties and parliament. Lastly, the phase of stable democracy was functioned by executive and state's bureaucracy, interest groups, political parties and parliament. The two significant factors, which contributed to the development of the democratic process, are:

- Creation of condition that is necessary for party competition and electoral choice.
- Establishment of consultative and decisional mechanism prepared to evade accountability to popularly elected representatives (Ibid: 471).

Political parties played a vital role in the process of democratization. According to Lewis political parties did not play a major role in the institutional framework within which the critical changes of the early democratization period took place, nor were they prime movers in the initial phase of political transition (Lewis and Wightman 2003: 25). Political parties were largely absent in the early stages of changes and political transition in Eastern Europe. Party development in Eastern Europe has generally been slow and the early process of transition was clearly dominated by other forces such as social movements and umbrella organizations (Ibid). Almost all Post-Soviet states lacked enough experience of democracy and party system. In 1985, Gorbachev became president of the Soviet Union and introduced numerous liberal reforms such as Perestroika, Glasnost and New Thinking. The new thinking in the area of regional policy introduced by Gorbachev radically transformed the basis of communist rule in Eastern Europe (Ibid: 12).

Development of Party System in Pre-Soviet Lithuania

The democratic transition, development of political parties, and emergence of multi-party system in Lithuania can be better understood if one goes through the various phases in the development of its political parties. History of party system development from 19th century is relevant to understand the contextual background of the re-attainment of independence and re-establishment of multi-party system in 1990s. Various stages of development of political parties and party system could be identified in Lithuania. Krupavicius demarcates six different phases of the development of the Lithuanian political parties as follows:

- "The emergence of traditional right and left wing parties from the end of the 19thcentury until the declaration of the Lithuanian's independence in 1918, when parties were able to enter the stage of national-state politics as principal actors."
- "The period of multi-partyismfrom1918 to 1926."

- "Restricted multi-party system under the supremacy of the Lithuanian Nationalists Union (LNU), 1926-35."
- "The one party system of the LNU in the period 1935-1940."
- "Totalitarian and authoritarian rule by the Communist Party and final collapse of the competitive multi-party system in 1940-1941and from 1944-1988."
- "The establishment of *Sajudis* and the gradual revival of competitive party system after 1988" (Krupavicius 1998: 468).

Emergence of political parties and multi-party competition began at the end of the 19th century when Lithuania was under Tsarist rule of Russian Empire. This was because of the national awakening and liberation movements which emerged in Lithuania during the 19th century. The important parties emerged during this period were "the Lithuanian Social Democratic Party (LSDP) founded in 1896, the Democratic Party (LDP) in 1902 and the Lithuanian Christian Democratic Party" (LKDP) (Ibid: 463). The then newly emerged parties possessed diverse ideological standpoints. The LSDP, LKDP, National Progress, Democratic and Socialist People's parties were represented in the Lithuanian Council. The transformation of one-party system to multi-party system in Lithuania witnessed major complications and experienced a lack of stability in the political arena. The political arrangement experienced a serious cabinet crisis in 1918-1920. A working parliamentary democracy emerged only after the elections of the Constituent *Seimas* in 1920. The constitutional guarantees and legal provisions provided a space for the smooth working of the parliament (Ibid: 465).

With the emergence of new political parties, Lithuanian politics witnessed a drastic change in the power control. The external as well as internal instability in Lithuania led to the emergence of *coup d'état* led by the Nationalist Union (NU) after 1926. The democratic structure in Lithuania's neighbouring countries like Estonia, Latvia, and Weimar Germany proved to be weak and unsuccessful, which invariably contributed to the collapse of democracy in Lithuania. The primary cause, which resulted in the end of democracy, was domestic impediments. The social and economic structures failed to support the growth of democracy in Lithuania. Lithuanian society was paralysed by problems like illiteracy, low socio-economic development, and predominant dependence on agriculture (Ibid: 467).

The main factor, which adversely affected democracy, was the conservative society majorly dominated by the Roman Catholics. The democratic structure itself had a number of limitations in Lithuania. Political democracy was fragmented and unstable in Lithuania. The execution of power by the president was more controlled by the *Seimas*. The right wing Christian Democrats functioned in an unruly manner.

It objected to form a single party government in spite of having a majority in the cabinet, which further enlarged the political instability in the state. Imbalances between the centres of power, personal clashes between the political parties, and Lithuanian society's non-familiarity towards the democratic system paved a way for the authoritarian regime and resulted in the collapse of the multi-party system (Ibid). However, one of the major variations was the banning of the Communist Party. The LNU led the authoritarian regime and it sought the support of the Christian Democratic Party. In course of time, all political parties were banned except the LNU dictating the state (Ibid: 467-468).

There were four parliamentary elections from 1920 to 1926 prior to the authoritarian rule; specifically it was three parties, which dominated the parliamentary elections (Lane 2001: 21 and Krupavicius 1998: 466). They were the Christian Democratic bloc composed of the Christian Democrats (CDS), the Farmers Union and the Labour Federation further constituting the largest alliance. CDS was a reformist party, appealing both to rural and urban constituencies including professional individuals, rural labourers and small holders (Lane 2001: 21). The Christian Democrats had fought successfully for compulsory religious education in state schools, for financial support for the church from the state, and for church control over the registration of births, marriages and deaths. During the inter-war period, Christian Democrats restricted the opposition press, democratic freedom and public meetings (Eidintas et al. 1999: 52). They strengthened the influence of Catholic Church in education and the country's public life. The party support held up well until 1926. The party experienced a loss of support because of the economic recession and the high level of corruption in the government and administration. It won 59 out of 112 seats in the election of 1920, 30 out of 78 seats in 1922, 40 out of 78 seats in 1923, but only 30 out of 85 seats in 1926 (Lane 2001: 21).

The second major party was the party of rural people, more commonly called the Populists, which was liberal in orientation and on the centre left. The Populist Party merged with the Lithuanian peasants in December 1922 to form the Lithuanian Peasant Populist Union (LVLS) (O'Connor 2003: 15). Its economic and social reform programme was radical and similar to the Christian Democrats. Small landholders were among the ardent supporters of the Populist Party. The major conflict of the Populist Party with the Christian Democrats was with regard to the relation between church and state. The Populists, being anti-clerical, opposed and criticized Christian Democrats on this issue. The issue between these two blocs led to the establishment of a nationalist dictatorship in Lithuania (Lane 2001: 22).

The Social Democratic Party (SDP), a Marxist party committed to parliamentarianism and reform, drew its support mainly from the urban workers. It included radical economic and social agenda and it rejected the power of the church in politics (Lane 2001: 22 and Krupavicius 1998: 465). It remained as a minority party even during the peak of its success in 1926 winning only 17 percent of the vote. The Social Democrats supported the idea of strong government and a powerful military. Their opportunity came in 1926 (Lane 2001: 22).

The Nationalist Progress Party (NP) of Antanas Smetona and Augustinas Voldemaras was also one of the growing parties during inter-war period (O'Connor 2003: 92 and Krupavicius 1998: 466). In August 1924, the Nationalist Progress Party formed the Lithuanian Nationalist Union, a movement that was open only to ethnic Lithuanians and stressed the need for a strong army and rule by a strong leader (Idinfas et al. 1999: 51 and O'Connor 2003: 92). The Union remained a small organization without a mass following. The party held a key position in the Lithuanian State Council and claimed credit for having created the foundations of the Lithuanian state. It remained outside the parliamentary field in 1920-1926 and failed to win any seat in the constituent assembly and the first two parliaments. It considered itself as a non-parliamentary opposition to the government, criticizing the entire reforms of the Christian Democrats and the Populists and their draft laws (Idinfas et al. 1999: 51 and Krupavacius 1998: 467). The ruling party accused NP for blackmailing the *Seimas* and destroying the state.

Lithuania had experienced twenty years of independence but it failed to learn lessons from the past and, within a short period, it turned into an authoritarian regime. Lithuania was occupied by the Soviets after the signing of Molotov-Ribbentrop pact and multi-party system collapsed with the emergence of single party system, that of Lithuanian Communist Party.

Party System in Lithuania under Soviet Union

From 1940 to 1990, there was complete absence of active political parties or movements in Soviet Lithuania. During this period, Communist Party of Lithuania dominated the politics of the country. After the seizure of Lithuania, the Soviet Union started the process of demolition of the political, economic, social and cultural institutions established by the independent Lithuanian state in the inter-war period. The elite of the Lithuanian government, political parties and the senior military and police officers, business entrepreneurs and renowned personalities from cultural background were arrested and sentenced to deportation or execution (Lane 2001: 49). Political rights and freedoms were denied in Lithuania during the Soviet rule. Lithuanians were denied the rights to oppose the government policies and the Lithuanian media and culture was entirely crushed by the authoritarian regime of the Soviet Union. Sovietization policies were forcefully imposed on Lithuanian society.

Sovietization had a huge impact on all three Baltic states including Lithuania. Under the Soviet control, Lithuanian citizens suffered from certain form of legal or cultural discrimination. Soviet Union started dominating other ethnic communities in political, cultural and economic terms. In politics, an element of Sovietization led to the trend of appointing Russian citizens to leading administrative positions in national institutions. Russian culture was imposed on other minorities. Lithuanian language in official business or in schools was prohibited or restricted, public meetings were banned, and the names of the Lithuanian historical places were changed or modified (Ibid: 2). The heavily centralized economic industrialization was introduced in Lithuania during the Soviet period in order to serve Moscow's desired economic and political ends. A large number of people had been deported to Siberia and were subjected to various kinds of torture and humiliation. The centralized industrialization was the main cause of increase in unemployment and underdevelopment in Lithuanian society under Sovietization. Lithuanians lost their cultural, political and religious rights (O'Connor 2003: 129).

In Lithuania, Communist Party operated as a core political party for almost 50 years in the 20th century. On 15 June 1940, Lithuania was occupied by the Soviet Union under the leadership of Stalin. Under Stalin's regime and his successors (1940-1985), Soviet Union brought the LCP into power through the establishment of people's government. The LCP became a constituent part of what was then the All-Union Communist Party. Antanas Snieckos was appointed as the first secretary of the LCP and remained in his designation for the next three decades (Saulius 2011: 83). In 1941, LCP's Fifth Party Congress outlined the Lithuanian Sovietization programme. However, the membership of LCP stood at less than 2000. During the spring of 1941, LCP increasingly came under the direct control of NKVD, the Soviet Secret Police. During the German occupation (1941-1944), LCP suffered great loss because of execution of several members in the guerrilla warfare against the Nazis (Ibid).

From 1944 to 1953, the party was deeply involved as an ally of the Soviets in the pacification of post-war Lithuania. As a result, thousands of post-war activists were killed by anti-Soviet partisans. During this particular period the LCP was thoroughly Russified and dominated by the outsiders. In 1953, approximately one fourth of its members were ethnic Lithuanians. The situation changed after the death of Stalin. As a part of the Communist Party of the Soviet Union (CPSU), the LCP's membership during the reign of Gorbachev had 80 percent ethnic Lithuanians. However, it was a common practice to appoint an ethnic Russian in the capacity of second supervisor of the party (Saulius 2011: 180).

During the late 1950s, several prominent party members including the rector of the Vilnius University were expelled on the ground of anti-Soviet ideology. This was an attempt to establish a cultural autonomy in the Lithuanian Soviet Socialist Republic. The shift of power from Brezhnev to Gorbachev in 1985 completely changed the structure of the party. The LCP came under severe pressure because of the upheaval that seized Lithuania in reaction to the reforms and restructuring policies of Gorbachev. In the initial stage, Gorbachev's rule faced a serious resistance from the party members with regard to the policies formulated (Ibid). During the Soviet rule (1940-1985) in Lithuania, all political parties and organizations were banned. According to articles 6 and 7 of the soviet constitution (1977), the Communist Party of the Soviet Union was the legitimate political party in the union. The party was declared the leading and guiding political force of the soviet society and its political system (Krupavicius 2005: 196). Under these circumstances, Lithuanian party system had changed from dominant party system to one party system.

During the Sovietization process, large number of Russians migrated from other republics to Baltic statess. A Russian could live his or her life in non-Russian republic without ever having to learn Russian but for other communities learning Russian language was compulsory. The Russian orthodox Christianity dominated over the Catholic Christianity in the three Baltic statess. Soviet Union started closing churches and schools in the Baltic statess. It officially banned the building of the new churches, further transferring number of old churches to the Russian orthodox churches.

Baltic states remained intolerant to Sovietization policies. Lithuanians protested against the Soviet authoritarian rule and fought to restore Lithuanian independence. Lithuanian youth resorted to waging guerrilla warfare. Guerrilla war was referred to as forest brothers in all Baltic regional languages. By the spring of 1945, almost thirty thousand armed men joined to fight against the Soviets (Misiunas 1993: 81). Underground newspapers were published and distributed among the people of Lithuania in order to mobilize the citizens. The Lithuanian Environment Protection Association was established in 1960 to address the issues related to the damage inflicted by the industrialization during Sovietization. Similar movement called the Green movement was started in the same year. It has been one of the leading NGOs advocating the cause of environment protection (Saulius 2011: 107). In the 1970s and early 1980s, Lithuanian human rights group mobilized citizens to protest against human rights abuses in Soviet Lithuania (Ibid: 125).

In 1972, Romas Kalanta, a 19-year-old student, set fire to himself in a protest against the Soviet rule. This resulted in the outbreak of protest and violence by the university students and high school pupils (Lane 2001: 88). The Baltic states, specifically Lithuania, Latvia, and Estonia joined in order to overthrow the Soviet dictatorial rule. Various authors claimed that Sovietization would bring national movement, political consciousness, cultural awareness and national awakening among the Lithuanian citizens. On the other hand, Sovietization adversely affected the Lithuanian people and society, brought in discrimination in the culture, political domination, and imposition of Russian language in schools, offices and religious domination in Baltic states.

Political organizations for anti-Soviet resistance were also formed in 1940. During the Soviet rule, the Lithuanian Activists Front (LAF) became a forum against the Soviet system. After Soviet occupation in June 1940, a number of prominent Lithuanians, officials and leaders of non-communist political parties met in Berlin to establish LAF, whose avowed purpose was to restore the independence of Lithuania. The Soviet deportations of 14-17 June 1941 seriously disrupted the LAF's underground network within the country. The LAF was divided as Lithuanian front and friends of Lithuanian front. Outside the Lithuanian Activists Front, seven traditional political organizations were established such as the Christian Democratic Party, the Lithuanian Labour Party, the Social Democratic Party, the Nationalist Alliance, the Farmers Party, the Farmers Union and the Peasant Populist Union. Four new fighting groups were also established during the Soviet occupation: the Freedom Fighters Union, the Lithuanian Front, the Nationalist Party, and Movement for Unity (Ibid: 175).

Origin and Development of Multi-Party System in Post-Soviet Lithuania

The origin and development of political parties and multi-party system in Lithuania started from the Gorbachev's presidency. Gorbachev's reform policies of perestroika, glasnost and democratization changed the entire character of Lithuanian political system. The reforms mainly included the manifesto to save communism rather than a proposal to create an open society. The reforms came up with a larger agenda in order to improve the conditions of public life, which was positively received by the public (Landsbergis 2000: 374). Gorbachev experimented by de-centralizing the administration and establishing a state ruled by law that meant is a state in which the constitution had more meaning than party decrees (Eidintas et al. 1999: 195). These political and economic reforms gave the Lithuanian citizens an opportunity to form political movements and organizations such as the *Sajudis* and the Lithuanian Freedom League in 1988. Through these political organizations, Lithuanians opposed the Soviet system and demanded independent statehood. During Gorbachev's presidency, the intelligentsia played a major role in the formation of cultural and political organizations.

After the 1990 independence, democracy was reinstituted back in Lithuania with parliamentary election of 1990. Lithuania's experience of democracy is limited even though the basic elements of a democratic state have been introduced in Lithuania. After regaining its independence in 1991, free and fair elections have been the foundation of the democratic structure in Lithuania. Constitution and the issues related to human rights have been given paramount importance. Minority rights have been protected without subjecting them to any sort of discrimination. With the decline of the authoritarian regime and the revival of democracy, Lithuania has provided a larger space for the mass media in the country (Girnius 2002: 52).

Lithuania gave up its pre-war constitution and instead created a new constitution that reflected the experience of democratic countries such as the United States and France (O'Connor Kevin 2003: 170). It followed the western democracies in the process of state building, rule of law, civil society, market economy and democratic institutions. Lithuania became a member of the UN in 1991 and a member of the Conference for Security and Corporation in Europe in the same year. The country is now member of the Council of Europe and of the North Atlantic Cooperation Council. In 2004, Lithuania became member of both EU and NATO. These developments showed a sign of Lithuania's return to the family of western nations (Landsbergis 2000: 376). While supplementing all the political and economic changes, Lithuania concentrated on social change as well. Non-governmental organizations with regard to the issues related to women, business and environment were established.

With time, the collaboration of politics and a negotiated revolution transformed the one-party communist state of Lithuania into a multi-party system (Krupavicius 1998: 465). Lithuania witnessed a process of amalgamation of the political parties, which mainly comprised of two phases. The multi-party system was established in the first phase from 1988 to 1992. In the second phase of the consolidation of the political parties, the divergence among the political parties had gradually reduced and there was a wave of political dispiritedness along with the electoral volatility (Novagrockiene 2001: 142).

Between the initial stages of transition to the restoration of Lithuania's independence, i.e. the period from 1988 to 1990 witnessed series of developments. New grassroots movements emerged, laterally various political organisations were established, and the traditional political parties were restored and revived. Lithuania's independence provided a larger space to the revival of parties like the LCP. Because of numerous political activities, the Lithuanian society mobilised together, actively participating in the politics of the state. The escalating problems in the state gave birth to various other intellectual groups and organisations espousing serious causes as their agenda. The foremost priority was given to the environmental problems by the Green movement (Novagrockiene 2001: 142-143).

The initial movement of the Greens started in the 1987-1988. Followed by the Green movement, Lithuania witnessed a mass-based reform movement with the emergence of the *Sajudis. Sajudis* aimed at radically reforming the political and economic system. Similarly, a number of traditional parties such as the LDP, LNU, and LSDP were revived. The LDP, LNU, LSDP along with the Social Democrats, the Nationalists and Democrats participated in the electoral programme of 1990. Furthermore, the Christian Democrats reconstituted their party in 1990. The LKDP declared itself as the successor of the Lithuanian Christian Democratic Union in exile. Radical organizations such as the Lithuanian Youth National Union, Young Lithuania (YL), the Lithuanian Freedom League (LFL), the Christian Democratic Union (CDU), and the Lithuanian Union of Political Prisoners and Deportees (LUPPD) were established and they entered the political sphere in 1988.

The LCP entered the political mainstream as the parliamentary party. The twentieth LCP Congress, held in December 1989, adopted a new agenda rejecting completely the communist ideology. The LCP detached itself from any kind of association with the headquarters of Moscow. The LCP declared that the reestablishment of the independent Lithuanian state was the party's main agenda. In spite of having 80,000 members, the party's membership dropped to 15,000 within two years (Novagrockiene 2001: 143-144). LCP was an outcome of the Communist Party of Soviet Union (CPSU). The differences between the LCP and CPSU with regard to the restoration of the Lithuanian independence led to their division. It was in this background that the concept of political pluralism emerged in Lithuania. It also led to the decentralization of the power structure among the political parties. The Lithuanian political support was divided into three blocs supporting three different parties, the Sajudis, the LCP and the LCP (CPSU). The Sajudis and the LCP were strong defenders of the restoration of the Lithuanian independence whereas the LCP (CPSU) was against the very idea of independence (Ibid: 144). The Sajudis and the LCP proved to be strong opponents of the LCP (CPSU).

The parliamentary election of 1990 ended the first stage of the development of Lithuanian multi-party system. The end of the first stage witnessed shift of political power. The presence of voting volatility among the Lithuanians facilitated the Sajudis to gain more than 50 percent of votes. The Sajudis succeeded in attaining the majority in the parliament. During this phase, the Lithuanian state comprised of two major parties, i.e. the LCP (reformist) and the Sajudis. The disassociation of both LCP and the Sajudis from Moscow brought both the political parties to the glare of publicity.

The second stage of the emergence of the Lithuanian multi-party system was from the springs of the beginning of 1990s to summer 1992. One of the drastic changes in the political structure in Lithuania during the second phase was the fragmentation of the Sajudis. The Sajudis movement was comprised of moderates

(Bugajski 2002: 147). The right wing members among the Sajudis viewed the presence of moderates as an attempt to split the Sajudis movement. Emergence of new factions among various parties adversely affected the existence of Sajudis. The movement split into different factions opposing each other. By the time of its Third Congress in December 1991, the Sajudis had completely lost their identity. It disassociated itself from the liberal-left and the centrist forces (Ibid: 145).

According to Novagrockiene (2001), the emergence of multi-party system in Lithuania began with the entering of new parties. Fifteen new political parties and organizations were registered between 1995 and the 1996 election to *Seimas* (Novagrockiene 2001: 141-155). "The Lithuanian Polish Electoral Action (LPEA), which was founded on the basis of Polish Union, the Lithuanian Women's Party (LWP), the Economy Party (EP), the Justice Party (JP), the Socialist Party (SP), the Lithuanian Russian Union (LRU), the Lithuanian Reform Party (LRP) and the Lithuanians People's Party (LPP)" are the major newly registered parties. Placing the problems of women as a priority in its agenda, the LWP actively took part in the policymaking of the state in comparison to the other newly emerged parties (Bugajski 2002: 148).

The primary factors responsible for "the development of multi-party system in Lithuania" are, for instance, "the impact of the general logic of post-communist transition on emerging multi-partyism and on particular parties, the legal and the institutional bases of Lithuania's parties, and the relation of organisational patterns and party government in the institutionalisation of the parties" (Krupavicius 1998: 465).

The rebirth of multi-partyism in Lithuania was not a case of sudden progress; rather, it developed through different phases. Several independent organizations were crucial for the democratic transition and emergence of multi-party system. The Green Movement (1987-1988), Sajudis (1988), and Lithuanian Freedom League (LFL) were loyal supporters of Lithuanian independence and democratic movement. These organizations and movements emerged out of the extremely high understanding in the Baltic states about the necessity for a change in the political structure. These organizations emerged as a great strength for political and social movements in Lithuania during the end of the Soviet rule. They showed the utmost desire to escape from the rigours of the Soviet control and establish political freedom and independence. The Baltic states had experienced national independence during the inter-war period and claim that they were forcibly incorporated into the Soviet Union in 1940.

As a result of collective efforts of political groups which emerged during the late 1980s, independence was granted to all the three Baltic Republics in September 1991. A newly elected Lithuanian government reclaimed its independent status, which it had lost during the red army occupation in 1940. Gorbachev announced that the declaration was illegal and imposed economic sanctions on Lithuania. The Lithuanian transformation was peaceful and the intelligentsia played a specific role in the process of transformation (Janušauskienė 2001: 25).

After regaining independence, Lithuania adopted a new constitution in 1992. Various political parties emerged in Lithuania during the transition period. To attain the status of a democratic state, Lithuania introduced the rule of law, universal suffrage, a free press and business organizations. It enjoys a democratic system of government, presence of political stability, and respect for the rule of law along with the successful implementation of political rights and civil liberties. In order to ensure political, economic and national stability in the country, Lithuania joined several international organizations like United Nations (UN), the European Union (EU) and North Atlantic treaty organization (NATO). Major political forces and a strong public opinion of Lithuania supported this integration process. Aspiration for European Union membership drove the countries sweeping political, economic and administrative reforms (Goehring 2007: 416). To join the European Union, state had to fulfil the economic, political, and administrative conditions known as the Copenhagen criteria. (Svensson 2010: 59). According to Svensson (2010), Lithuania adopted the democratic institutions, rule of law, protection of human rights and minorities and market economy in order to fulfil the criteria required to join the EU(Ibid: 2). Presently, with several political organizations and parties, multi-party system is evolving in Lithuania as part of democratic transition and transformation.

Emergence of New Parties after Independence

New parties, particularly, in lithuania emerged in two phases (Krupavicius 2005: 190). The Green Party and Sajudis were founded in 1989 along with few other political groups, which later disappeared from the political field. The second phase of the new parties has started in the late 1992 and this phase is continuing. During the last two parliamentary elections of 1992 and 1996, approximately two to five new political parties were registered. With a few parties sustaining, majority of them vanished after the elections.

Table: 1 Origin of Political Parties in Lithuania

Types of parties	Process of development	Example
Historical parties	Revival	LSDP, LDP, LUHDP
Post-Sajudis parties	Disintegration	HU(LC), LUC
Ex-communist parties	Transformation	LDLP
New parties	Establishment	LLU,LWP, RP, TPP, DDVD, LRLS, LPP, etc.

Source: Krupavicius (2005: 190).

Only a limited number of new parties in Lithuania proved their ability to survive the competition with the historical, post-Sajudis and ex-communist parties. Among them the Liberals, Polish Electoral Action and the Women's Party represented in the Lithuania's *Seimas* including the local government. There are several factors responsible for the successful performance of the new parties in Lithuania. One of the primary reasons was the poor performance of the ruling party and the lack of coalescent behaviour among the ideologically similar parties on the centre-right flank of the political spectrum. However, the total number of political parties remained relatively high, with 24 political parties in 1992, 28 in 1996, and 15 in 2000. While the number of political parties in Lithuania's political stage is still quite impressive, in 2001 it reached up to approximately 40 including the unregistered parties. The period between the two parliamentary elections of 1992 and 1996 can be called the initial phase of party system consolidation (Krupavicius 2005: 191; Novagrockiene 2001: 148).

Since the 1992 parliamentary election, new parties are emerging and playing remarkable role in consolidating the Lithuanian party system. Recently Lithuanian Ministry of Justice has allowed registering the new parties. Four new parties – Courage Path Party established by Drasius Kedys, Democratic Labour and Unity Party (DDVD) led by the president Brazauskas' widow Kristina Brazauskiene, the Lithuanian Peoples Party initiated by businessperson Vladimir Romanov, and Emigrants Party – submitted their documents to the ministry for registration. These parties were supposed to take part in the general elections scheduled on 14 October 2012 if they could officially register at least 65 days before the election date. Out of 40 registered political parties in Lithuania, 28 submitted their members' signatures by 1st March and got the right to take part in the general election in the middle of October 2012 (Novagrockiene 2001).

Electoral Process in Lithuania

The post-Soviet era in Lithuania has been distinguished by a relatively stable party system and participation of parties in the electoral competition. As political parties remain as a link between the state and society, participation of political parties in the electoral process is very important in the evolving democratic system in Lithuania. Political parties help democratic government by structuring the voting choice by different kinds of mobilization and motivation. Parties involve people in active campaigning in order to get votes. Parties help inform government the interests of various sections of population while making policies. The ability of established parties to mobilize their supporters has the effect of discouraging non-party candidates from running for office and discouraging new parties from forming. Therefore, parties are one of the most important pillars of a democratic political system.

Lithuania adopted mixed electoral system in 1992 under the new constitution. The electoral law was adopted in 1992. The Lithuanian electoral system comprises of elections to the parliament, the office of the president, the councils of local governments and the European Parliament (Martinaitis 2012: 10 and Romanaite 2006: 71). The Lithuanian parliament also known as the *Seimas* consists of 141 parliamentarians. The members of the *Seimas* are elected for a four-year term. The initial name of the Lithuanian parliament was Supreme Council of Lithuania and it was later renamed as the Constitutive Assembly (*Seimas*) in 1996. Seventy-one candidates out of 141 are elected in single-member constituencies and the rest of candidates are elected under proportional representation, for a term of four years. A permanent resident of Lithuania who has attained the age of twenty-five can contest in the parliamentary elections (Ibid).

There have been seven parliamentary elections in Lithuania since independence in 1991. The parliamentary elections were held in 1992, 1996, 2000, 2004, 2008, 2012, and 2016. Presidential elections were held in 1993, 1998, 2003, 2004, 2009, and 2014 and European Parliament elections were held in 2004, 200, 9and 2014. Elections in Lithuania are considered free and fair (Goehring 2007: 430).

Legal Basis of Lithuania's Parties

The most important factor necessary for the analysis of party structure and the performance is the legal regulations of the party's activities. The laws with regard to the regulation of the political parties are introduced and formulated by political parties themselves (Lane 2001: 132). The formulation of laws by the political parties reflected the interests of few groups. In new democracies, the process of party institutionalization is based on two criterias. They are "formal or legal institutional reputations of party development, including the legal basis of party formation, and the electoral system conditions and the electoral performance" (Krupavicius 2005: 195).

Political parties started to re-emerge on Lithuanian political stage in 1988 and 1989, even though their existence lacked a certain degree of constitutional legitimacy. After the constituent elections of 1990, along with major economic, political and social reforms, several political parties also acquired required legitimacy. Between 1990 and 1992, the Supreme Council (Lithuanian parliament) was one of the institutions that could legalize parties, but it became the cradle of party politics (Krupavicius 2003: 102). In Lithuania, the constitution provides certain guarantees for "collective and individual political self-expression" such as "freedom of thought, right to privacy, the principles of equal treatment before law, right to vote, right to representation", right to criticise government, etc (Krupavicius 2005: 196).

The constitution offered a reasonable platform for discussing government policies and politics in post-communist Lithuania (Lane 2001: 132). Lithuanian constitution of 1992 has a mention about the formation of the political parties. Article 35 of the 1992 constitution state that citizens have the right to form and associate together within a community, political parties and associations only if their aims and ambitions are not contradicting the Lithuanian constitution and laws. The Article 35 also states, "the formation and activities of political parties are regulated by certain laws", if found contradictory. Article 83 of the constitution refers to political parties on a negative line stating, "the person, who is elected President of Republic, must cancel his activities in political parties and political organizations until a new electoral campaign for President of the Republic" (Krupavicius 1998: 475-476).

Despite the contradictions within the constitution with regard to the political parties, it has provided certain rights and guarantees to the citizens. It includes "freedom of thought, right to privacy, the principle of equal treatment before the law, the right to vote and to representation, the right to criticize the government and officials, etc." The political parties are bound by the constitutional law with regard to their political activities. Constitution is the only legal document to which the political parties have to abide by. Accordingly, the Soviet legal code was branded illegal due to mass movement against it. To legalize the *Sajudis*, the organization had to be registered as a social movement. According to the Articles 6 and 7 of the Lithuanian constitution, LCP was an integral part of the CPSU. It was the only legal political party, playing a constructive role in the society. These specific articles were removed from the constitution in December 1989 (Ibid: 476).

However, the *Sajudis* initiated the reconstruction of the multi-party system. In the late 1980s and 90s, few historical organizations formed their first groups stating that they were the heirs of their inter-war predecessors. These organizations included the Democratic, the Christian Democratic, the Social Democratic parties, Nationalists Union and the Young Lithuanian. In April 1989, the *Sajudis* voted for a proposal, which would transform the LCP into an autonomous political party. The motion anticipated that "all other parties should be legalized" and they should "receive equal treatment under the law". The formation of these political parties happened at a great speed. Major changes with regard to the regulation of the political parties were made by the Constituent parliament in September 1990 by adopting "Law on political parties and political organizations". These laws explained the process of party formation and activities pertaining to the political parties. It also provided the citizens of Lithuania with the "right to form and participate in the political parties". The right to membership was not provided to the military and police personnel, staff of national security agencies and judicial officials during their period of service. The five basic components required for party formation and registration includes "to have, at least, 400 founding members; to pass a party statute and basic programme; to elect leadership; to form party institutions at a conference or congress of the founding members or their delegates; to register the political party with the Ministry of Justice" (Ibid).

Party registration process in Lithuania was considered stringent. Before registering, every political party had to present the list of founders with names and signatures. It also had to provide the address proofs of the citizens, personal codes, professions, confirmation of the citizens as to he/she is not a member of any other party. The registration process also requires the submission of "a protocol of the founding conference, party statute and even designs of party symbols" (Krupavicius 2005: 197). These laws also provided strict rules regarding the financial sources of the political parties. Membership fees, profits from publishing and private donations were the legal financial sources of the political parties. Except for few parliamentary parties, the use of public funds was prohibited. These laws entirely "ignored the allocation of material and financial resources for electoral campaigns". Separate laws were created in order regulate the finances provided to the campaigns. According to these laws, the political parties have to open special accounts for electoral campaigns. Maximum levels of electoral expenses have been set up in order to maintain the "equal opportunities in competition for votes". These laws have not been effectively implemented due to the difficulties in regulating the finances of the political parties (Krupavicius 1998: 477).

Major Political Parties in Lithuania

Since the regaining of independence in 1991, Lithuanian Democratic Labour Party (LDLP), Lithuanian Social Democratic Party (LSDP), Homeland Union-Lithuanian Christian Democrats (TS-LKD), Liberal and Centre Union (LCS), Liberals Movement of Republic of Lithuania (LRLS), New Democracy- Women's Party (ND-WP), Lithuanian Democratic Party (LDP), New Union- Social Liberals (NU-SL), National Resurrection Party (TPP), Lithuanian Christian Democratic Party (LKDP), the Lithuanian National Union (LNU), Order and Justice (TT), Labour Party (DP), and Lithuania Peasant Popular Union (LPPU) are the major political parties participating in the democratic process of Lithuania. Apart from the major political parties, the Union of the Russians and Electoral Action of Poles (AWPL) are the two major influencing ethnic parties in the Lithuanian political system.

Since the 1919 initial independence, Lithuania had experienced vicissitudes in the democratic transition and party system. After the First World War, Lithuania declared its independence; during this period, Lithuania had experienced two-party system with the bloc politics of Social Democrats, Christian Democrats and Nationalists until 1926. In 1926, multi-party system was established in Lithuania with the emergence of new political organizations. By the end of 1930s, Lithuania turned into the dominant party system. After the soviet occupation, Lithuania experienced single party system rule from 1940 to 1985. Gorbachev's reforms gave an opportunity to rebuild multi-party system in Lithuania. In the initial period of independence, Lithuanian political elites tried to build two-party system based on ideological differences, but the attempt failed. After the establishment of traditional parties, new movements and new parties, Lithuania adopted the multi-party system to govern the state.

Conclusion

For the democratic consolidation of transitional state, political parties are very important. According to this perspective, they are very essential to make distinction between democracy and authoritarianism. The emergence of parties and multi-party system are positive indicators of healthy process of democratic transition. The development of political parties and stability of the multi-party system are necessary for the consolidation of democracy in Lithuania.

However, the evolution of multi-party system in Lithuania is found different. Though there are signs showing instability and fragmentation in the political landscape, it is not at the detriment of democratization and evolution of democratic political system. Lithuanian parties have advanced well in the process of institutionalization and are "successfully performing the functions of the intermediary structures in consolidating democracy". In fact, satisfaction with the economic, political and institutional performance is increasing among the Lithuanian citizens. The number of parties functioning in Lithuania is consistently growing. Rapid development of political parties and stability of multi-party system are essential for the party's development in Lithuania. The parties must open their doors to the non-elites also. This strategy will help in broadening the parties' popular base at the local level, making them effective channels.

References

Bielinis (2011), "The Labour Party Case Can Become an Election Sensation", *Lithuania Tribune*, retrieved from http://www.lithuaniatribune.com/2011/10/28/the-labour-party-case-can-become-an-election-sensation/.

Bugajski, Janusz (2002), *Political Parties of Eastern Europe: A Guide to Politics in the Post-Communist Era*, New York: The Centre for Strategic and Institutional Studies.

Central Election Commission of Lithuania (2008), Elections to the Seimas 2008 [Online: web] retrieved 10 June 2012, retrieved from http://www.vrk.lt/en/pirmas-puslapis/previous-elections/elections-to-the-seimas-2008/.

Central Election Commission of Lithuania (2009), European Parliament Election [Online: web] retrieved 10 June 2012, retrieved from http://www.vrk.lt/en/pirmas-puslapis/previous-elections/european-parliament-elections-2009/.

Constitution of the Republic of Lithuania (1992), constitution of republic of Lithuania, retrieved from http://www.litlex.lt/Litlex/Eng/Frames/Laws/Documents/CONSTITU.HTM.

Diamond, Larry Jay and Gunther Richard (2001), *Political Parties and Democracy*, Mary Land: John Hopkins University Press.

Downs, Anthony (1957), *An Economic Theory of Democracy*, New York: Harper and Row.

Dyck, Ran (2012), *Canadian Politics*, fifth edition, Toronto: Nelson Education Limited.

Epstein, Leon D. (1967), *Political Parties in Western Ddemocracies*, London: Pall Mall Press.

Girnius, KestutisK. (2002), "Democracy in Lithuania", in Moly Kaldor and Ivan Vejvoda (eds.), *Democratization in Central and Eastern Europe*, New York: Continuum.

Goehring, Jeanntee (2007), *Nations in transit 2007: democratization from Central Europe to Eurasia*, New York: Freedom House.

Huntington, Samuel (1968), *Political Order in Changing Societies*, New Haven: Yale University Press.

Eidintas, Alfonsas,Vytautas Žalys, and Alfred Erich Senn (September 1999), *Lithuania in European Politics: The Years of the First Republic, 1918–1940* (Paperback ed.), New York: St. Martin's Press.

Janda, Kenneth, Jeffrey M. Berry, Jerry Goldman, and Deborah Schildkraut (2009), *The Challenge of Democracy, Essentials: American Government in Global Politics*, Boston: Words worth.

Janušauskienė, Diana (2011), *Post-Communist Democratization in Lithuania: Elites, Parties and Youth Political Organizations*: 1998-2001, Amsterdam: Editions Rodopi B.V.

Krupavicius, Algis(1998), "The Post-Communist Transition and Institutionalization of Lithuania's Parties", *Political Studies*, XLVI: 465-491.

__________ (2003), "The left-wing parties in Lithuania: 1920-2002", in Leftwish Curry Jane and Joan Barth Urban (eds.), *The left transformed in post- communist societies: the case of East-Central Europe, Russia and Ukraine*, Maryland: Roman and Little Field Publications.

__________ (2005), "Political parties and multiparty system in the Baltic countries: 1990-2001", in Kulik Anatoly and Pshzova Susanna (eds.), *Political parties in post-soviet space: Russia, Belarus, Ukraine, Moladova and the Baltic states*, London: Praeger.

__________ (2008), "Lithuania", *European Journal of Political Research*, 47: 1048-1059.

Kulik Anatoly and Pshizova Susanna (2005), *Political Parties in Post-Soviet Space: Russia, Belarus, Ukraine, Moldova and the Baltic states*, London: Praeger.

Kumari, Pushpa (2009), "The Changing Nature of the Party System", in NeeraChandoke and Praveen Priyadarshi (eds.), *Contemporary India: Economy, Society and Politics*, New Delhi: Dorling Kindersley (India) Pvt. Ltd.

Landsbergis, Vytautas (2000), *Lithuania: Independent Again*, Cardiff: University of Wales Press.

Lane, Thomas (2001), *Lithuania: Stepping Westward*, London and New York, Routledge.

Law on Parties and Political Organizations of Lithuania (2004), Republic of Lithuania, 23 March 2004, no. IX-2072, Vilnius: (online: web) retrieved on 20 January 2012, retrieved from http://www.litlex.lt/Litlex/eng/Frames/Laws/Laws.htm//.

Law on Public finance to political parties (1999), Republic of Lithuania Law on Funding of, and Control over Funding of, Political Parties and Political Campaigns, retrieved from http://legislationline.org/topics/subtopic/16/topic/1/country/17.

Maisel, Lovis Sandy and Mark D. Brewer (2012), *Political Parties and Election in America: The Electoral Process*, Maryland: Roman & Little Field Publishers.

Lewis, Paul and Wightman Gordon (2003), "The Emergence of Multi-Party System in East-Central Europe", in Pridham Geoffrey and VanhanenTatu (eds.), *Democratizationin Eastern Europe: Domestic and International Perspective*, New York: Routledge, 151-190.

Martinaitis, Zilvinas (2012), "Explaining Electoral Reforms in Lithuania", *Journal of Baltic Studies*, 1: 1-12.

Matteo, Bonotti (2011),"Conceptualizing political parties: A Normative Framework", *Journal of Politics*, 31(1): 19-26.

Misiunas, Romuald J. and Rien Taagepera (1993), *Baltic states: Years of Dependence, 1940-1990*, Berkeley: California University Press.

Mullett, Adam (2010), "Peasants Union Bolster Coalition, But Weakness Remains", *Baltic Reports* retrieved from http://balticreports.com/?s=lithuanian+peasant+popular +union/html.

Novagrockiene, Jurat (2001), "The Development and Consolidation of Lithuanian Political Party system", *Journal of Baltic Studies*, 32 (2): 141-155.

O'Connor, Kevin (2003), *The History of the Baltic states*, Greenwood Press: London.

Nqrgaard, Ole and Johannesen Lars (1996), *The Baltic states After Independence*, London: Edward Elgar Publishing.

Parajulee, Ramjee P. (2000), *the Democratic Transition In Nepal*, Maryland: Roman & Little Field Publications.

Romanaite, Aine (2006), "The Development of Lithuanian Party System from Stability to Perturbation", in Mulders, S. (ed.), *Post-Communist EU Member State: Parties and Party System*, London: Ashgate publishing.

Saulius, Suziedelis (2011), *Historical Dictionary of Lithuania*, Maryland: Scarecrow Press.

Sartori, Giovanni (1976), *Parties and Party System: A framework for Analysis* (vol. 1), New York: Cambridge University Press.

Svensson, Jenny (2010), "Governance through Mediation: EU Twinning in Lithuania", in Bengt Jacobsson (ed.), *The European Union and the Baltic states*, London: Routledge.

Thesing, Josef (1995), *Political Parties in Democracy*, Sankt: Augustin.

Trent, Judith S. and Robert V. Priedenberg (2000), *Political Campaign Communication: Principles and Practices*, New York: Roman and Little Field Publication.

Chapter Six

Political Economy of Neoliberal Reforms in Baltic States: The Case of Estonia

V. Lenin Kumar

Estonia, one of the Baltic republics[1] of the former Soviet Union, regained independence in 1991. In the post-independence period the country faced several new challenges such as political instability, economic decline and chaotic social situation caused by the Soviet disintegration. As a result, Estonia has been undergoing multidimensional transition: political, economic, social, cultural, and de-Sovietisation processes. Institutional restructuring, democratization of political system and market-oriented economic reforms have assumed key roles in this whole process. Estonia embraced neoliberal economic reforms as a crucial element in the post-Soviet nation building with a view to transform their economy into a market economy, distanced from Russia, and integrated with Europe.

Liberalisation of Economy

Liberalisation of economy generally means liberating the economy and market from the state's control. The shock therapy economic model demands immediate trade liberalisation and price liberalisation on the part of the government to complete the successful neoliberal transition. The government must withdraw its role from all parts of economic activity. This chapter analyses neoliberal economic reforms and policies pursued by various governments in Estonia. Estonia followed the radical shock therapy economy model and implemented trade and price liberalisation before disintegration of Soviet Union. During the Soviet period, market price of goods and commodities was controlled, managed and fixed by the government and trade was strictly restricted by the government. Under the neoliberal logic, the market decides prices and value; government interferences only help few people monopolise the market. Along the same lines, Estonian government liberalised the prices from the government control except few basic commodities (Lainela 2002: 32). Estonia transformed itself from being a former Soviet Union country to most liberal economy in the world, but the journey to achieve this remarkable feat made Estonia go through several hurdles. Despite warnings from international organisations, fear of economic crisis, and the considerably small economy, Estonia vigorously pursued neoliberal economic model. Although in the first decade of the transition Estonia witnessed deep political instability and short term economic crisis, it has successfully overcome the shortcomings and joined elite economic organisation, the Organisation of Economic Cooperation and Development (OECD) in 2010. In the year 2015, World Bank ranked Estonia 17th out of 189 countries in doing Business (A Dynamic Economy, http://estonia.eu/). Regardless of much unemployment, increasing inequalities and other social consequences, policymakers in Estonia pursued neoliberal economy better than the rest of the Baltic countries and former Soviet Union countries.

Neoliberal Economic Reforms in Estonia

The crux of the politics of Estonian elite constituted in that they wanted to shift their politics and economics from East to West. The Estonian political leaders chose the economic path of the country long before the collapse of Soviet Union. The political institutions and constitution is liberal and most of the reforms followed the Western model. The Estonian political leaders and political elites chose the neoliberal trajectory. Mart Laar, the first elected Prime Minister of Estonia clearly stated about how he was inspired by Ronald Reagan and Margaret Thatcher's policies and their anti-Soviet stand. Mrs Thatcher was the first person who openly implemented neoliberal policies in the United Kingdom (UK) and she came to be followed by Reagan in the United States (Subrenat 2004: 226).

Almost every political party in Estonia followed the same set of economic policies. Lennart Meri, the first elected president of Estonia, in his address to the United Nations General Assembly in 1993 clearly indicated that Estonia's future economic policy would be based on free market, stating that "free market and democracy are interconnected" (Meri 1993 at the UN). The same year Meri, in his address at Kuwait city, went a step further and assured that Estonia wanted to integrate with the world economy within two years of regaining independence from the Soviet Union. Estonia invited more than 30 countries to invest and buy their state owned enterprises (Meri 1993 at Kuwait City).

Estonian neoliberal development can be divided into three phases. The first phase spans from 1991 to 2000. The second phase extends from 2000 to 2007 and third phase begins from 2008 continuing till now. The first phase of neoliberal reforms faced several problems that included both economic chaos as well as political instability. While the second phase of economic transition brought political stability and growth in the Estonia's economy, it was in the third and the final phase that the

Estonian economy and society faced massive economic crisis and social unrest with increase in unemployment and cut in the welfare policies.

To complete the successful economic transition from socialist economic model to neoliberal model the Estonian government primarily focused on six basic issues: namely, deregulation of price, reform of property rights, enterprise reforms, privatisations, macroeconomic stability and liberalisation of trade. Neoliberal economic model's main agenda is accumulation of private property for individuals. Previously the entire economy used to be run under the control of the state. In order to liberate it from the clutches of the state, privatisation is a primary and important step, which the Estonian government took right at the outset. Privatisation of state-owned enterprises and land is a primary requirement to have a transition from a socialist economy to a capitalist market economy. Prices, freed from the constraint of the state control, move to balance market levels. Markets, once introduced, become the basis for allocation of resource and radically change the role of the government. The role of the government is reduced to laying the ground rules for the evolution of a market system from production of goods to services.

De-Controlling of Prices

The Estonian government started the price liberalisation process before its independence. The price liberalisation process started in 1989 and almost completed in 1992. In July 1991, the Estonian government eliminated the state pricing system; and by end of 1991 only 10 percent of the goods and services were fixed by the government (Meyers et al. 1992: 5). In 1992, rationing of goods was disbanded and providing subsidies for ration was stopped by the government. The Estonian government did not control the prices of the commodities produced by the private companies.

Trade Liberalisation

Establishing the trade relations with foreign countries became one of the most important tasks of the Estonian government. It was viewed by the Estonian government as a way to escape from their past. It was hoped that trade would help them in the de-Sovietisation process too. Estonia has become a leader among the Baltic states in terms of liberalising foreign trade and removing all the tariffs. Estonia is one of the few countries that do not have any import protection on agriculture as well, even while other two Baltic states do have some sort of tariffs on agricultural imports.

Estonia is considered the most liberal trade friendly country within the European countries (Lainela 2002: 33). Estonia went into action as soon as they got independence from the Soviet Union removing trade tariffs from most of the goods.

In the year 1991, around 200 goods were under the quota protection. However, within two years, only five goods were left under the tariffs. Further, by the year 1997, the government had abolished all the trade tariffs (Feldmann 2001: 544). Before 1991, only 3 percent of trade was with non-Soviet countries (Feldmann 2001: 542). The important impetus behind trade liberalisation was the fact that unlike other Western countries, former Soviet Union countries did not have traditional big industrialist or capitalist class. Thus, most of the investment in Estonia after independence came from foreign companies.

Trade liberalization was in fact thus a mode to attract foreign investment. In the beginning of 1994, the FDI (foreign direct investment) amounted 4 percent in overall GDP (World Bank 2015). In 1993 after several decades, Estonia signed its first free trade agreement with other Baltic states. Before the free trade agreement, the government abolished most of the trade restrictions. In the pre-independence era, Estonia's economy revolved around Russia and other Former Soviet Union countries. Since the disintegration of the Soviet Union many countries got independence, all of which have chosen the same set of liberal polices leading to competition among these new countries. As a result, Estonia chose more radical step to attract more foreign investors. Currently Estonia is considered one of the most investor friendly countries in the world. In 2015, World Bank and Heritage Foundation ranked Estonia 8th out of 178 countries making it one of the freest economies in the world (A Dynamic Economy, http://estonia.eu/).

Privatisation and Liberalisation of Economy

In Estonia, state owned enterprises were sold to foreign owners. As very few people had sufficient money to buy these state enterprises, most of the state owned enterprises were sold to Multinational Corporations and Western country corporations. The first and foremost advice for these countries, given by IMF and World Bank, was to open their internal market for the foreign investors and to make laws in favour of privatisation. "Shock therapy" was nothing but another term for neoliberal policies advocated by the IMF, World Bank and the Western capitalist countries. The new liberal regimes went on to implement the neoliberal policies in their entirety and created the legal frame within which they made their laws for privatisation.

Even before the disintegration of the Soviet Union, Estonia established around 150 joint enterprises with other countries (Brown 1993: 494). Thus after the disintegration, Estonian policymakers started implementing the neoliberal policies with the help of IMF and Western Europe countries. The first measure they took was regarding property (Gillies et al. 2002). They introduced the Property Reform Act to free property from the state. This was necessary so that the privatisation process could be done with a proper legal base.

Among the Baltic states, Estonia has the record of having the best privatization record. Around 50 per cent of the state owned enterprises including agricultural enterprises in Estonia had been privatized by business units by 1994 through auctions and tenders, which were used to attract foreign investment. The process began in 1991 with the law of the property reforms while the country was still a part of the Soviet Union. The process of further privatization began after the country attained independence, and it attained full pace in 1993 with laws like land reforms, law on real estate, bankruptcy law, and securities law that came into force along with the adoption of the Privatisation Law in June 1993, which founded the Private Sector Development *Department* in Estonia. The state owned properties in the process were bought by either private foreign enterprises or domestic purchasers with foreign partners (Lopez et al. 2002).

The primary objective of the foreign policy of Estonia was to build a strong relationship with the Western countries so that they could create a strong market economy based on the Western European model. For this reason, they signed numerous FTAs (Free Trade Agreements). Estonia signed such an agreement with EU on 1 January 1995. Estonia also signed the Europe agreement in 1994-95 (association agreement). After signing such agreements and laying the foundation for a market economy, Estonia applied for European Union membership in 1995 (Feldmann and Sally 2001: 21). Estonia applied for the membership of other international organizations like the IMF on 9 September 1991; also the World Bank and European Bank for Reconstruction and Development; and was admitted to the United Nations on 17 September 1991 shortly afterwards. At the same time, the Western countries and the US appreciated Estonia's move towards neoliberalism and to encourage further this process they gave financial aid to Estonia making it to be the first country, among the former Soviet countries, to receive financial aid from the Western countries.

As it is clear from the discussion so far, Estonian economic policies came to be based on certain fundamental features, which formed the principles of neoliberalism. Firstly, the basis for the policies is the overarching goal of creating a market-based economy. Secondly, the achievement of this basic objective required the establishment of a set of code of laws and institutions that would ensure respect of private property and maintain the sanctity of contracts. Thirdly, the integration of the new economy with the world economy was essential. The creation of a market economy required that all barriers to trade and tariff be removed. It was, therefore, the re-establishment of the Estonian ports as significant centres became necessary. Further, all of this meant that the new Estonian government and Western countries would have to try to avoid Russian influence and would have to avoid dependence on Russia. Finally, these requirements implied that Estonia would have to come out of the Rouble zone because they needed to get more foreign investment. All of the above objectives were systematically pursued and carried out. The above principles were set as the 'seven point agenda' by Estonia (Gillies et al. 2002: 178) and moved towards implementing this agenda through rapid legislations during 1990, 1991, and the first half of 1992. Estonia seemed to be in a hurry to carry out the liberal economic reforms so that they could get hold of more foreign investors for selling their state enterprises.

During the process of privatisation, Estonia faced hurdles in the early stages but they overcame these hurdles and successfully implemented the privatisation policies unlike other former Soviet Union countries. The reasons for the same are as follows: Firstly, while dealing with state firms, about 300 bankruptcy proceedings have taken place by the termination of soft credits to enterprises and the active implementation of the bankruptcy law (Lopez et al. 2002). Prices have been liberalized by a currency board system that links money creation to hard currency reserves keeping inflation at modest levels, and it has opened the trade regime subsequently encouraging foreign investment. Secondly, all the political parties in Estonia favoured the privatisation process. Political leaders persuaded the people to bear the ad-hoc yet arduous adjustments. Lastly, geographically Estonia is a small country, and its size acts as an important aspect in its ability to gain quick charge of her economy. Further, Estonia's most important standing characteristic compared to other Baltic states is that geographically she is far and distant from Russia. Estonia has used Foreign Direct Investment as one major tool to break away from Soviet Union and restructure.

Once the Estonian government changed the rules and regulations for the investor friendly environment, the FDI flow to Estonia was more than it was in any former Soviet Union countries according to the EU estimation. It must be observed that the foreign trade and FDI in Estonia have grown from 82 million dollars to 12.664 billion dollars between 1992 and 2006 (Juliussen 2008: 2). After the economic crisis of 2008, these investments fell to 1569 million dollars in 2012 and 553 million dollars in 2013 (https://en.portal.santandertrade.com). The FDI situation in Estonia has shown improvement in 2014 whereby 983 million dollars have made inroads to its economy and as of now, Estonia has received investments at the worth of 15.6 billion euro by the 2013 estimates. Out of these investments, 16 percent went into real estate activities, 15 percent into trade in wholesale and retail, 14 percent into manufacturing and 8 percent into professional, scientific and technical activities. Swedish companies have made 27 per cent of these investments, while Finnish, Dutch, and Norwegian companies have made 21, 10 and 6 percentages of investment respectively (*Estonian Investments* and Trade *Agency*: www.*investinestonia*.com).

Voucher Privatisation

Voucher Privatisation is one kind of privatisation experiment process in former Soviet Union. Vouchers are transferable shares in privatised firms, in investment fund companies, residential housing and land. Each resident receives national capital voucher once he or she is over the age of 18, along with each voucher, every individual is also given denomination at 300 kroons.[2] A second instrument, the compensation voucher, is issued for a person whose property was expropriated illegally and expelled. People who were expelled during the Soviet era also received compensation vouchers. These vouchers doubled for the total cost of the property at the time it was confiscated. An unsettled problem in the Estonian privatisation program is that the face value of the vouchers outstanding far exceeds the likely value of assets being sold. Moreover, even more vouchers are being created as restitution proceeds slowly.

According to estimates by the Ministry of Finance, about 10.5 billion crowns worth of vouchers have been promulgated: while 8 billion crowns in "national capital" vouchers have been allotted to all citizens, around 2.5 billion crowns in "compensation" vouchers have been given out for injustices suffered during the Soviet period (Nellis 1996: 3). The ministry calculates that 70 percent of about 1.2 billion crowns of vouchers swapped by the public for housing has been privatized. Another 1.8 billion crowns of vouchers have been exchanged by people in privatisation transactions. Out of this, only about 100 million crowns of vouchers were used in public offerings in two large combinations. A rough calculation of the value for the remaining vouchers is about 7.1 billion crowns, or approximately US$630 million. The minority percentages held back from all the firms remaining to be sold are unlikely to be large enough to absorb this outstanding stock of vouchers (though the problem is eased if the trading of vouchers allows their price to fall to clear the market). Citizens may use their vouchers in a variety of ways like by simply selling them to any bidder, or exchange them for shares in companies or in investment funds, buy the housing, purchase land, or buy bonds from a Compensation Fund. In November 1995, it was announced that vouchers might be used at face value for up to 50 percent of instalment payments for privatized companies (Nellis 1996: 3).

The Legal Measures for Privatisation

Mart Laar's statement that "Radical economic reforms cannot be implemented without laws regulating the economic space" (Laar 2007: 7) clearly underlines the importance of and the intention behind the legal measures to have successful economic transition. Estonian government had systematic approach for the successful privatisation process. Various Estonian Governments irrespective of political parties brought various legal measures to complete the privatisation process in Estonia.

The following legal measures had to be taken to create the market economy. Firstly, legislation was drafted for cutting all state subsidies. Secondly, measures were enacted for the rapid development of an entrepreneurial small business sector based on private ownership. Thirdly, controls on prices and wages were removed. Fourthly, new regulations for bank were passed. Fifthly, the principles were published regarding governing ownership. The Estonian government first introduced an ownership act in 1991; the primary purpose of this act is to change the legal framework for future market economy. It is clearly written in the law that protection of the integrity of property and free enterprise and security from violation of ownership rights and smoothening of the process of move towards market economy form the basis of the ownership reform. On the way to ownership reform, while returning property to its rightful owner, or while providing compensation to a former owner, there will not be any bias against the interests which are protected by law (Republic of Estonia Principles of Ownership Reform Act 1991).

Privatisation of small and medium sized firms was begun after the creation of a privatisation agency. Measures were executed to encourage foreign direct investment. Further, all tariffs were removed. Finally, and crucially, the new government took measures to control inflation. These are some of the important steps taken by Estonia, and the help of foreign advisories in this process was crucial.

Estonia has led the Baltic states in the path to reforms. As soon as the Soviet law changed in 1987 permitting state enterprises to seek western partnership and supplies, Estonia was probably the first to immediately act and establish over 150 enterprises jointly with western partnership. After changing their economic policies, it is vital to remember, Estonia faced extreme economic instability. An instance of this is that economic decline that continued throughout 1991 and 1992, with some estimates of a decline in GDP (Brown 1993: 494) between 35 percent and 50 percent. Estonia began their market-oriented economic policies with privatisation. In the initial years itself almost 40,000 of 45,000 (Purju 1996) businesses were owned by private entities. Nevertheless, at the same time the country faced serious inflation between January 1991 and 1992. In January, consumer prices rose by 629 percent (Brown 1993: 494), while the rise between February 1991 and February 1992 was a whopping 1,015 percent; and in March 1992 the inflation rate was around 1,169 percent (Brown 1993: 494).

After the collapse of the Soviet Union, Estonia turned into one of the highly liberal trade regimes, particularly in terms of its relationship towards the West. To create a market-based economy, Estonia needed strong institutions and it was to this end that they created a separate agency for privatisation. After establishing this agency, it started the privatisation process, and carried it out over the period between 1991 and 2000. The Estonian privatisation agency contracted 575 agreements, which amounted to 8.3 billion EEK[3] (Purju 1996). Almost every privatisation came through foreign direct investment, and at the end of 2000, one decade after the economic reforms, the economy was completely dependent on FDI, with more than 44.5 billion EEK of foreign direct investment, an amount that exceeded several times the amount accruing from direct privatisation.

The law on cooperatives passed by the Estonian parliament established the legal regime for the cooperatives in August 1992 (Purju1996). The number of non-agricultural cooperatives was increased, and the official number of registered enterprises was 4288 (Purju 1996) in August 1992. After the change of law came in 1987 for the establishment of joint ventures, this form of alloyed ownership between a foreign company and a domestic state cooperative increased speedily during the following years. There were 11 joint ventures in 1988, but after the collapse of Soviet Union, the numbers of joint ventures increased rapidly because of the privatisation policies (Purju 1996). Edgar Savisaar was the first Prime Minister of Estonia after the collapse of Soviet Union. He announced that his government primary goal was Estonia's transition to a market economy.

Estonia made all possible ways to attract the FDI like giving tax relaxation and undervaluing their currency, and all these steps led Estonia to become one of the highly liberal countries in whole of Eastern and Central Europe (OECD Reviews of foreign direct investment in Estonia 2001). Total direct foreign investment reached 700 million between 1991 and 1996, which made Estonia achieve one of the highest levels of per capita foreign investment in Central and Eastern Europe. In the year of 1996, the US share of FDI in Estonia was 27.8 percent (Country studies, US 2010). Estonia's parliament made a law for foreign investment and it was passed; main object of this law was to give guarantee of equal treatment to foreign investor as government entities to ensure free refurbishment of profits.

The 'Law on Ownership' as approved in June 1990 came to be the first important law authorised by the parliament during this period of transition (Purju 1996: 6). The prime objective of this law was to change the ownership from state to individuals because the basic principle of the privatisation is ownership by individuals or group of individuals. Therefore, the motivation behind this law was to take the state's hands out of the properties. In the same year, the parliament passed 'The Law on Small Scale Privatisation' as prepared by the government. The Department of State Property was founded in October 1990. Creating this institution had significant importance, as the primary objective of this department became to ensure privatisation in small-scale sector and the supervision of the reimbursement process. The Law was adopted by the Supreme Council on 13th of June 1991 (Mygind 2000: 7) according to which the use of vouchers became the main device for privatisation. At the same year in the month of October, the parliament passed one of the important laws regarding land reforms. According to this Law, the land from state ownership came to be converted to private ownership.

At the beginning of 1991, the total number of privatized small-scale units was estimated to be 1200 service facilities, 500 shops and booths, and 80 catering facilities. In April 1992, the law on the privatisation of Dwelling was adopted to regulate the privatisation process (Purju 1996: 17). The 'privatisation law' adopted by parliament in June 1993 (Jeffries 2004: 166) sought to juridical equalize privatisation at both small scale and large-scale levels. The main goal of the Law was to provide an overarching legal and institutional framework for privatisation at the two levels of small scale and large scale at the same time; previously these two were treated separately. In Estonia the process of privatisation came to be done by creating firstly a firm legal base because while doing mass privatisation the state wanted proper institutions. Based on this understanding the privatisation law was adopted in Estonian parliament. It was the department of state property that organised the small-scale privatisation utilizing the methods of auctioning, selling of shares, or competition of business tender (Savas 1992). By April 1992, seven large enterprises were already privatized.

Estonia had very little knowledge about the privatisation processes. Thus, they called multinational experts in the form of multinational team of experts from Germany, the US, Sweden and Canada, to manage the privatisation of the medium and large business sector of the economy. The method of privatisation, as modified for use in Estonia was based primarily on the principle of selling firms to the highest bidder, regardless of their nationality. By mid-1996, Estonia had sold the 450 state owned enterprises (Jeffries 2004: 166) in the way to privatisation and the government earned around $ 227 million. Sector wise, 70 percent of the services and 90 percent of the manufacturing were privatized from 1991 to 1995. Private sector shares, the major part of the GDP, were of around 70 percent (Jeffries 2004: 166).

The Estonian industry is the major sufferer of this transition because most of the Estonian economy sustained on the industrial sector. The selling of these state owned enterprises led to more unemployment in the Estonian society. The major task of the privatisation programme in Estonia is based on selling these big industries to foreign investors in the auction. The Estonian government was further interested in building joint venture with foreign companies and by January 1991, 232 joint ventures had been registered in Estonia, which by October 1991increased to 313. Among the other countries, Finland led the joint ventures by having 159 such joint ventures with Estonia, which is higher than with any other Western country (Country studies US 2010). For getting more foreign investment, Estonia needed proper legal based framework. For that purpose, Estonia passed a new foreign investment law offering tax breaks and import-export incentives to foreign investors. Government of Estonia gave more tax relaxation for the foreign investor like two years of tax exemptions.

Estonia is the first former Soviet country to allow the foreigner to buy land in Estonia, with some rules. In 1993, Estonian government allowed the foreigner to buy the land, but only through the purchase of privatized share enterprises (Jeffries 2004: 163). At the same time, the government put some rules for the joint ventures such as a non-Estonian cannot own more than 50 percent of the equity in joint ventures without government permission.

Some key institutions were created by the Estonian government to manage the whole privatisation programme. The governments first setup the privatisation of Estonian enterprises to begin dealing with the direct sale of large-scale enterprises to foreign and domestic investors. Despite having serious reservations about this move, this programme brought on track back by 1993. In the summer of 1993, the Estonian government merged its two major privatisation institutions into one and created the new institution called Estonian Privatisation Agency (Smith 2001: 129). The sale of state property in exchange of Estonian Kroon during 1991-92 by the government was considerably high. The government sold 676 properties for a total of EKR 64.3 million by October 1993. Another 236 small enterprises had been sold for a total of EKR 169 million. When the government started the process of selling the large state owned enterprises, a total of EKR 117.8 million had been garnered from the sale of the first phase of thirty large-scale enterprises (Country Studies US 2010).

Three major property reform tasks remained in the year of 1993. In the very first, mostly unprofitable state enterprises were yet to be sold off. Secondly, the issue of providing compensation for remnants of pre-war property claimants remained unsettled. Lastly, the major and very important part of privatization that remained was of housing sector. To solve these three problems, the Riigikogu, that is the Estonian unicameral parliament, passed a law on privatisation in June 1993 (Smith 2001: 129).

Estonia's Membership in International Organisations

After the independence, Estonia wanted to establish ties with international organisations to break the isolation and wanted to integrate Estonian economy at par with the world level. In addition, the transition from state owned form of economy to market economy needed more experience and guidelines. The Estonian transition for that matter was helped out by the Western countries. The major part of the economic advice and assistance for this was given by IMF (International Monetary Fund) and World Bank. In the processes of transitioning to market economy, they got considerable money from both these institutions. The Estonian parliament gave approval to join the IMF in April 1992. Once Estonia joined the IMF, it started receiving loans to reconstruct its economy (IMF and Estonia, https://www.eestipank). In the same year, Estonia joined the World Bank. These two international organisations pressed Estonia to speed up its privatisation and liberalisation process.

In August 1992, Estonia signed its first memorandum with the I.M.F to secure $40 million stabilization loan from the I.M.F (Jeffries 2004: 164) and $30 million from the World Bank (Country studies US 2010).However, these loans were given with certain terms and conditions. These memorandums, for example, obligated the Estonian government to balance its budget, to restrict wage increases, speedup the privatisation process of the state enterprises, and to maintain a stringent monetary policy. In 1995, Estonia applied for WTO membership and started the negotiations. Estonia implemented the most radical liberalisation policies to get its membership. Naturally, it has evolved as a Most Favoured Nation (MFN). Because of these developments, Estonia got the WTO membership in 1999. Estonia was the third former Soviet state to join the WTO (Feldmann and Sally 2001: 18). It is important to keep in mind that the membership of WTO was given only after the process of privatisation was successfully launched and substantially carried out. The membership of European Union was a long waited aspiration and it was a long time goal for Estonia to join the Western European community.

The process for applying for EU membership started in 1992, when agreement between the Republic of Estonia and the European Economic Community on Trade, Commercial and Economic Cooperation was signed. In 1992, Estonia also had become a member of the European Bank to rebuild its economy after the huge inflation and instability in the country. After the membership, Estonia received total of $46 million in loan for improving its infrastructure (Country studies US 2010). The first free trade agreement was signed between Estonia and EU in 1994. After prolonged negotiations, Estonia finally became member of EU in May 2004. Before the EU membership, Estonia agreed to all the conditionalities to be a member. By the time Estonia achieved the membership, it became one of the most liberal countries in the entire Europe.

Estonia became member of OECD in 2010, the exclusive organisation for developed countries. Before the membership, Estonia agreed to all the conditions of the OECD guidelines, namely liberalisation of the capital being one of the key conditions of OECD (OECD 2010). There were nine important basic principles of the OECD most of which revolved around free trade, less restrictions, and liberalising capital. The Estonian economy was completely integrated with international economy and liberated from its government.

Currency Board Reforms and Reopening Stock Exchange Market

To create a market-based economy Estonia needed its own currency since trade dependence on Russia would come in the way of a reorientation of foreign and economic ties towards the Western countries. Price liberalization was required for the implementation of the new currency, which started in late 1989. Changes in prices as sponsored by enterprises came to be allowed by this reform of the government. Control was maintained over price framework at the wholesale and retail levels for a broad range of goods. At first, prices of goods like paper products, furniture and vegetables were decontrolled. In October 1990, prices of food were raised and later subsidies were reduced on energy, telecommunication and transport. In July 1991, prices of goods like milk, meat and several other consumer goods came to be deregulated. At the end of 1991, prices of 10% of the consumer basket remained under government price fixing procedure while 30% were under some other administrative regulation. All other prices were more or less free and their movement reflected supply and demand conditions on the market. Further deregulation took place within the framework of the stabilization package. By the end of 1992, the price liberalization process was virtually completed.

The Estonian policymakers, therefore, adopted Western suggestions completely and they in turn saw the introduction of the new currency as a symbol of their 'independence' and new identity. Estonia was, therefore, the first former Soviet country to come out of the Rouble zone. The idea to establish currency process started before the Estonian independence, during the perestroika period. Edgar Savisaar along with others planned to establish new currency for Estonia. Before establishing new currency, Estonian government planned to have economic independence from Soviet Union by establishing the new Estonian Bank in 1990 (Erixon 2010: 16).

In April 1990, over a year before the Soviet Union's disintegration, the Estonian Supreme Soviet passed a resolution on the introduction of a national currency (Feldmann 2013: 356). The Estonian Supreme Soviet passed a resolution on the introduction of a national currency (Taagepera 1991). When Estonia regained independence in 1991, it was still part of the rouble zone and embedded within the Soviet economic system (Feldmann 2013: 356). The Estonian currency board was established in 1992 during the steep period of economic crisis. Unlike the traditional central banks where the political interference happens, the purpose of the currency board is to function irrespective of any government's policies. The board is autonomous and unlike the central banks, the currency board does not regulate the commercial banks. The primary goal of the currency board is to attract more foreign currencies and keep the inflation rate under control and finally to continue the process of privatisation and liberalisation without any political interferences (Erixon 2010: 18).

During this transition, the Estonian economy faced crises due to price liberalization and deregulation of the state enterprises. The Estonian government approached the IMF regarding the new currency, and IMF rejected the idea of the Kroon because of the instability of the economy and the small population of the Estonia. Still the Estonian government wanted their new currency because for them the introduction of the new currency meant getting political and economic freedom from Russia.

On 20 June 1992, the Estonian government under the interim Prime Minister *TiitVähi* introduced the Kroon. It was valued more than the Rouble (10 RR= 1EK), and was tied to the Dutch mark at a rate of 8 EK= 1 DM (Gillies et al. 2002: 179). The Kroon was deliberately undervalued by 15 percent (Brown 1993: 496) in order to attract more foreign investments. Estonia desperately needed foreign investment in their country for the privatisation process. In 1991, all the countries of Soviet Union were separated, and so there was competition between these countries to attract foreign investors and to get membership from the IMF, WTO and EU. It was for this reason that the Estonian government adopted the method of undervaluing the currency and offering tax relaxation. Estonia tried to take the lead and took all the measures required to get membership in the IMF and EU. For example, when Estonia first applied for membership in the IMF, the IMF's response was the need to see a program for speedy privatisation and liberalization to grant membership to Estonia. To achieve this, the policymakers in Estonia established the legal and institutional framework for the rapid marketisation of economy.

The introduction of the Kroon is the one of the major reform in this process. After the initial stage, Estonia started showing the recovery with the help of the currency board. In 2000, the GDP grew to 6.5 percent. The sufficient reserves totalling 680 million Deutsche Marks is another reason for not having a run on the currency. Inflation was only 3.1 percent in 1999. The currency board has proven to be very successful in stemming inflation (Sandholtz and Koetzle 2000: 31-50). The currency board and the kroon came to be viewed as a symbol of the successful transformation of the Estonian economy, which contributed to a stable economic and business environment. It must be noted here that Estonia is the first Former Soviet Union country to establish currency board (Feldmann 2013: 357).

Estonia entered the Euro-zone 2011 whereby January 1st onwards Euro became official currency of Estonia. The long political ambitious of moving towards West was somewhere accomplished with this move to Euro-zone. The Estonian government planned to reopen Tallinn stock exchange, which was active in early 20th century but closed down in 1941. In May 1996, Tallinn stock exchange was reopened. In the earlier days, the stock exchange saw a decline and crisis. In 1998, the Russian economic crisis had a major impact on the Estonian stock exchange; but again since 2000 to 2008 it has run without any glitches (Baltic Capital Markets Forum 2016).

Tax Reforms

One of the prime agenda of the neoliberal policies in general is to implement flat taxes meaning implementing same tax for big corporates and small petty producers. In the year 1994, Estonia was one of the first countries to implement the flat tax reforms (Hinst 2011), where income and corporate tax rates of 26 percent, and non-wages labour costs to finance health and pension at 33% tax was introduced (Funke 2002: 102). As a part of the liberal market economic transition, Estonia reduced the corporate income tax from 35 percent to 26 percent in 1994 (Purju 2010: 1), but at the same time the Value Added Tax (VAT) was increased from 10 percent to 18 percent. In the beginning years, to meet the transition needs, the VAT was increased to manage the 2008 economic crisis (Purju 2010: 1). The Estonian Government increased the VAT to 20 percent (A Dynamic Economy, http://estonia.eu/). The reason for decrease in the corporate tax is to attract more foreign investors. This is not just in the case of Estonia, in fact, this flat tax concept was followed in Eastern and Central European countries. These tax reforms are one of the strong reasons behind the privatisation and macroeconomic stability.

The Income Tax Act of Estonia has been in force since 1, January 2000. The main principles of the Income Tax Act concerning the profit distributions are taxation of the distribution, and not on the accumulation of the income, or application of the tax exemption on the profits reinvested within the company (Oro 2000), but the taxes are 20 percent for finance. Moreover, in the case of social insurance like pension, both workers and disabled persons are included in the social insurance and health insurance, with employer tax at 13 percent. The Government has reduced the corporate income tax and increased the workers contribution to around 2 percent (Purju 2010: 1). It must be noted here that the Estonian income tax system is considered one of the simplest tax regimes in the world, with its flat rate of 20 percent. Deferral of taxation shifts the time of taxation from the moment of earning the profits to that of their distribution. Undistributed profits are not subject to income taxation, regardless of whether these are reinvested or merely retained (Republic ofEstonia – US Department of States 2017). The government introduced flat tax reform of 20 percent from 2015 onwards.

During the Soviet period, health and pension social security measures never had a separate tax. After 1991, Estonia elected a path of liberal economic policies with the advice of World Bank, and a part of the neoliberal policy includes regulation of taxes and implementation of new taxes. However, in Estonia the neoliberal model of tax reforms only helped corporates to grow and increased the workers' contribution for health and pension by way of tax; hence, it is evident that the government tried to reduce its role as social security provider. Along with flat tax, to attract corporate investments, the Estonian government made tax free the reinvested corporate profits.

Banking Laws and Banking Crisis

Establishing a new and independent bank was necessary for Estonia. In the new constitution, article 111 gave the sole right to the Eesti Pank to issue the new currency and the most important duty of this bank was to stabilize the new national currency Kroon. Article 112 gave guiding principle to Eesti Pank to operate and work as per its governing law; and its activity must be reported to the parliament. In continuity with these articles, the parliament adopted law on Eesti Pank in 1993 (Drevina et al. 2007: 12).

After getting full authority from the monetary reform committee, the Central Bank of Estonia gave more licenses to private banks. In 1993, there were 21 banks in Estonia including one foreign owned bank. The government's share in the whole of banking asset was reduced to around 25.7 percent. In 1994, around 22 banks including one foreign owned bank had state assets of 28.1 percent. In 1995, government's share in 18 banks and the four foreign owned banks was reduced dramatically to a very low 9.7 percent. In the next year, number of banks was also reduced to 15 that included three foreign banks. However, government's share was cut further down to 6.6 percent. Whereas in 1997, there were around 12 banks including three foreign banks where the state's assets were reduced to 0.0 percent shares (Barisitz 2002: 87); and some of the banks merged while some of them were liquidated.

Within one year of the new banking system, problems emerged, as in 1993 when Eesti Pank announced a stabilization period; new banking licenses were stopped due to some crisis (Sõrg and Vensel 2002: 44). There were strong reasons behind this government action because in the beginning of the new banking reforms, there was serious planning and management problems. In the early reforms, the government increased the minimum limit for the capital requirements from 5 million EEK to 6 million EEK. Because of these criteria, the small banks could not offer to touch the minimum requirements. In early 1993, around eight small credit institutions were liquidated, as they did not meet the minimum requirement. Thus, the total number of Estonian credit institutions was reduced from a maximum of 42 at the end of 1992 to 21 at the end of 1993 (Barisitz 2002: 92).

Within a short time, Estonia faced two financial crises. One crisis occurred in the beginning of the transition period, and the other was during the 1998 Russian and Asian financial crisis. The first crisis was common to all the transition countries because when the government decides to go for full liberalization process they faced some serious management and financial problems. When Estonian government started the "Shock Therapy" economic process, speedy reforms took place in all sectors. The first and foremost advice on reform was to liberalize the monetary and banking sector (Drevina et al. 2007: 11). Poor management and lack of planning and inability to handle the FDI in banking sector led to the first banking crisis in Estonia from 1992 to 1994 (Sõrgand and Vensel 2002: 47).

The second crisis was related to the international financial crisis. When the Estonian markets were dominated by the multinational and foreign companies, they withdrew their investment from Estonian market leading to a very young stock market facing an immediate crisis (Sõrg and Vensel 2002: 46). In comparison to other Baltic states, Estonia has managed to come out of the crisis with the help of Finland and other Western European countries. In spite of some success in the beginning of the transition period, there was some threat to internal economic stability because Estonian banking sector was deeply involved in the privatisation process. as and when the banks get liquidated, governments are required to save the private banks where they have to spend ultimately common person's tax.

In order to liberalize the economy and control the economic and currency regulation transition, Estonia needed strong banking reforms and regulation. The Bank of Estonia was established at the end of 1989. The main job of the bank was to create the entire banking system, ensure economic sovereignty and restore normal and smooth performance of the market economy. The banking law introduced in 1993 came operational in 1994 and the banking act was again amended in 2003 along with the rules and regulations of European Union banking policies. They already had a little experience in running the central bank between the First World War and Second World War. The bank was re-established after the collapse of the Soviet Union. Bringing back the Estonian Central Bank was very significant in the whole liberalization process. Before launching a new currency Kroon, they needed their own strong banking and monetary system to strengthen the macroeconomic system. Estonian Central bank is called Eesti Pank, and was established on 24th February 1919, after they got independence from Russia. However, this bank did not last long. After the break out of the Second World War, in 1940, Estonia was taken over of by the Soviet Union, and the Eesti Pank was nationalized (Drevina et al. 2007: 10).

During the perestroika period in December 1989, the Supreme Soviet of Soviet Socialist Republic passed a resolution to re-establish the EestiPank (Drevina et al. 2007: 10). Estonian Central Bank officially started to function after the disintegration of USSR, that is, around 1991. It took nearly two years to work as a separate bank before they got autonomy, but Eesti Pank had to stay with the USSR central bank. On 1 July 1991, the monetary reform committee gave authorization to Eesti Pank to give foreign exchange licenses to private banks (Drevina et al. 2007: 11).

Conclusion

"Liberalize, then negotiate, but don't negotiate and then liberalize" was slogan put forward by Mart Laar (Feldmann and Sally 2001: 14) who implemented neoliberal reforms in Estonia. Privatisation is one of the essential conditions for the establishment of the market. Therefore, the motivation for privatisation is clear in the case of Estonia. The political economy of neoliberalism involved the advice and guidelines of the international organisations to all the newly independent countries to withdraw the state's hands from all sectors. The role of the state in neoliberalism is to protect the market, and so it should make comprehensive laws for privatisation and withdraw all subsidies from agriculture, industry and service sectors. In the case of Estonia, the policymakers first attempted to change property relations. Then the government made particular institutions to control and regulate the privatisation process such as the state property department. Privatisation enterprises were created for the process of liberalization and creation of the market-oriented economy.

There are certain clear laws for privatisation that highlight the impact of neoliberalism (Sanguinetty and Mastrapa 2014). An example of this is the privatisation agency did exactly what the market and the Western countries wanted it to do. They followed exactly the Western model of privatisation, as these countries had no institutional experience. Almost 90 percent of the state owned enterprises were sold to foreign companies and there were no concrete measures for controlling the entry of FDI. In the economy, almost two third of the GDP came from the privatisation process, i.e., the government got revenue from selling the state enterprises. Thus, the country was completely dependent on foreign capital. Most of the economic expansion happened only in the service sector. The country, therefore, lost self-reliance just a few years after independence (Thorhallsson and Kattel 2013).

The political elites also played a key role in this transition process. In this period, there was no strong and single government in the parliament. As a result, there was great instability at the political level. For example, within nine years there were seven governments. The fact that despite this the process of privatisation happened itself shows that the motivation of pursuing the neoliberal policies was shared by all the parties. There were serious scandals and corruption in the period of economic transition. As the government was selling the state enterprises the level of corruption increased, especially in the time of auctioning. The foreign companies controlled and dominated the whole process of economic transition. Political objectives behind this process of privatisation was to create vested interest groups which, after ownership of resources passed to private hands, would oppose going back to a planned economy. The political elites in Estonia changed the property rights by way of making laws, so that multinational companies holding most of the shares would in the face of potential opposition from the state or from any other political group could always threaten to pull out from the economy, thus posing a permanent obstacle to the restoration of a planned economy (Hoag and Kasoff 1999).

The entire policy regime was created under the guidance of the IMF and the World Bank. Their 'technical advisors' were countries appointed by the policymakers who could control and manage the entire privatisation process. The privatisation of large-scale enterprises, for instance, was done with the help of Sweden, Finland and Germany. The argument given for privatisation is that it is intended to improve the working of the economy. Scholars from Western countries argued that the privatisation process would bring new technology to these countries in transition because the market is based on best service and best technology, with healthy competition leading to better economic conditions. These are some of basic arguments for privatisation worldwide. However, these scholars conveniently forget to point out the fundamentally harmful nature of privatisation (Purju 1996).

One of the key principles of privatisation is profit making and maximization of profit. For profit maximization, individuals or groups will bring new technology and methods of production, but the condition of workers' rights and employment will deteriorate, because the major objective of the individuals or groups is to make maximum profit. For that matter, they will necessarily reduce the number of the workers in establishment, as has happened in all the countries in transition. In the absence of local competition, the privatisation process will only help the foreign companies, and the entire argument of competence, technology and better management will happen only if there is substantial local investment. The former Soviet Union countries, of course, it would be recalled, only had state owned enterprises. Nevertheless, in the neoliberal economy, the state cannot hold any asset apart from those that are necessary for shielding the market. Therefore, the argument of pro-neoliberal scholars may apply in the traditional liberal countries like the US, but an advocacy of privatisation in the former Soviet countries led to seriously negative consequences.

Notes

1. Latvia, Lithuania and Estonia together are known as Baltic states. These three countries were provinces of Russian empire until 1918. They achieved independence during First World War and remained as sovereign states during the interwar period, 1919-1939 and for the initial months of 1940. However, the Second World War geopolitics changed their destiny. They were incorporated into Soviet Union in 1940 and remained under Soviet occupation until 1991 when the Soviet Union was disintegrated.

2. The kroon (sign: kr) was the official currency of Estonia for two periods in history: 1928-1940 and 1992-2011. It is also often called *crown*.
3. EEK is the Estonian kroon.

References

A Dynamic Economy, retrieved from http://estonia.eu/about-estonia/economy-a-it/a-dynamic-economy.html.

Baltic Capital Market Forum (2016), retrieved from http://www.nasdaqbaltic.com/files/baltic/Baltic_Capital_Markets_Forum/FilipGorczyca.pdf.

Barisitz, Stephan, (2002), Banking in the Baltics – the Development of the Banking Systems of Estonia, Latvia and Lithuania since Independence retrieved from http://www.suomenpankki.fi/pdf/65297.pdf.

Brown, William S. (1993), "Economic Transition in Estonia," *Journal of Economic Issues*, 27(2), 493-503

Country studies US (2010), retrieved from http://countrystudies.us/estonia/

Drevina, Kristine, Kestutis *Laurinavicius*, and Andres *Tupits* (2007), *Legal and Institutional aspects of the currency changeover following the restoration of the independence of the Baltic states*, Frankfurt:European Central Bank.

Erixon, Fredrik (2010), Baltic Economic Reforms: A Crisis Review of Baltic Economic Policy, European Centre for International Political Economy.

Estonian investment agency economy, (2015), retrieved from http://www.investinestonia.com/en/about-estonia/economy-at-a-glance

Estonian Investments and Trade *Agency*: www.investinestonia.com.

Feldman, M. (2013), "Varieties of capitalism and the Estonian economy: Institutions, growth and crisis in a liberal market economy", *Communist and Post-Communist Studies*, 46(4): 493-501.

Feldmann, M. (2001), "The Fast Track from the Soviet Union to the World Economy: External Liberalization in Estonia and Latvia", *Government & Opposition Government and Opposition*, 36(4), 537-558.

Feldmann, Magnus (2013), From the ruble zone to the euro zone: the political economy of Estonian macroeconomic policy, *Post-Soviet Affairs*, 29 (4), 354-370.

Feldmann, Magnus and Sally, Razeen (2001), From the Soviet Union to the European Union: The political economy of Estonian trade policy reforms, 1991-2000, Bank of Finland Institute for Economies in Transition (BOFIT), https://helda.helsinki.fi/bof/bitstream/handle/123456789/12586/98281.pdf?sequence=1

*Foreign direct investment, net inflows (BoP, current US), retrieved from http://data.un.org/Data.aspx?d=WDI&f=Indicator_Code:BX.KLT.DINV.CD.WD

Funke, Michael, (2002), "Determining the taxation and investment impacts of Estonia's

2000 income tax reform", *Finnish Economic Papers*, 15(2):102-109.

Gilles, James, Leimann, Jaak and Peterson, Rein (2002), "Making a Successful Transition from a command to a market to a Market Economy: The lessons from Estonia", *Corporate Governance*, 10 (3).

Hinst, Daniel (2011),*Flat Tax Reforms in Estonia and Slovakia*, Zagreb: Centre for Public Policy and Economic Research.

Hoag, J., & Kasoff, M. (1999), "Estonia in Transition", *Journal of Economic Issues, 33(4): 919-931.*

IMF and Estonia, retrieved from http://www.eestipank.ee/en/eesti-pank/imf-and-estonia

Jeffries, I. (1993), *Socialist economies and the transition to the market*: A guide. London: Routledge.

Jeffries, I. (2002), *Eastern Europe at the turn of the twenty-first century: A guide to the economies in transition,* London: Routledge.

Jeffries, I. (2004), *The Countries of the Former Soviet Union at the Turn of the Twenty First Centuries,* New York, Routledge.

Juliussen, Siren Skramesto, (2008), "Foreign Direct Investment in Estonia Local Outcomes of Global Processes", retrieved from http://org.uib.no/fdi/content/files/Siren%20 Juliussen.pdf.

Laar, Mart (2007), The Estonian Economic Miracle, retrieved from http://www.heritage.org/report/the-estonian-economic-miracle

Lainela, Seija and Sutela, Pekka (2002), Introducing New Currencies in the Baltic Countries, Review of Economies in Transition, Institute for Economies in Transition, Bank of Finland.

Lopez, Darman, Hubbard, Erin and Koetzle, John (2002), Privatization in Estonia, retrieved from http://econc10.bu.edu/economic_systems/Economics/Transit/Privatization/privat_estonia.htm

Meri, Lennart (1993), Address By Mr. Lennart Meri President Of The Republic Of Estonia At The 11th Plenary Meeting Of The Forty-Eighth Session Of The United Nations General Assembly 30 September 1993 New York.

Meri, Lennart (1993), Address of H.E. Lennart Meri, President of the Republic of Estonia Kuwait City, 5 December 1993.

Mygind, Niels (2000), "Privatisation, governance and restructuring of enterprises in the Baltics", working paper, OECD.

Nellis, John (1996), Finding Real Owners – Lessons from Estonia's Privatization Program, World Bank, Note no. 66.

OECD (2010), retrieved from http://www.oecd.org/estonia/estoniasaccessiontotheoecd.htm

OECD report (2012), Economic Surveys Estonia

OECD Reviews of foreign direct investment in Estonia, 2001, retrieved from http://www.oecd.org/investment/investmentfordevelopment/oecdreviewsofforeigndirectinvestment estonia.htm

Oro, Lemmi, (2000), Corporate income tax policy in Estonia, retrieved from http://www.oecd.org/dataoecd/11/62/1903051.pdf

Purju, A. (1995), "Voucher privatisation in Estonia", *Communist Economies and Economic Transformation,* 7(3), 385-408.

Purju, Alari (1996), The political Economy of Privatization in Estonia, retrieved from http://siteresources.worldbank.org/INTDECINEQ/Resources/SAIS_Privatisation_in_Estonia.pdf

Republic of Estonia – US Department of States (2017), https://travel.state.gov/content/passports/en/country/estonia.html.

Republic of Estonia Principles of Ownership Reform Act, 1991 (1991), https://www.riigiteataja.ee/en/eli/514112013010/consolide

Sandholtz, W., and W. Koetzle (2000), "Accounting for Corruption: Economic Structure, Democracy, and Trade," *International Studies Quarterly*, 44: 31-50.

Sanguinetty, Jorge A. and Tania Mastrapa (September 2014), "Lessons learned from 20 years of Privatization: Albania, Estonia and Russia", retrieved from http://www.ascecuba.org/c/wp-content/uploads/2014/09/v20-sanguinetty mastrapa.pdf.

Savas, E.S. (Nov-Dec. 1992), "Privatization in Post-Socialist Countries," *Public Administration Review*, 52(6):573-581

Seven,Bulent (2002), Legal Aspects of Privatisation: A Comparative Study of European Implementations, USA,Dissertation.com.

Smith, J, David, (2001), *Estonia Independence and European integration*, London, Routledge

Sõrg, Mart, and Vello Vensel, (2002), "Development of the Banking System under the Estonian Currency Board", *International Advances in Economic Research*, 8 (1): 35-48.

Subrenat, J. ed. (2004), *Estonia: Identity and independence*. Amsterdam, Rodopi.

Taagepera, R. (1991), "Building Democracy in Estonia", *Political Science & Politics*, 24 (03): 478-481.

Thorhallsson, B., and Kattel, R. (2013), "Neo-Liberal Small States and Economic Crisis: Lessons for Democratic Corporatism", *Journal of Baltic Studies*, 44(1): 83-103.

Chapter Seven

The Impact of Language Politics on Education in Baltic States: The Case of the Russian Speaking Minorities

Zakali Ayemi

The post-independent Baltic states introduced several policy reforms affecting the rights of the minorities. However, one of the most critical reforms was the language reform, which was translated even to education affecting the huge monolingual Russian minorities. With the changing demands of the society and globalisation, the language policies are relaxed to a certain extent. Today, bilingualism in education is promoted all over the Baltic states, though constraints and resistance exist. This chapter analyses politicisation of language in the nation building process of the Baltic states and its impact on education of the Russian minorities.

Language is one of the greatest yet elusive means of exclusion and marginalization both within education and in the developmental process of the nation (Tamim 2014: 280-299). Language and education together are indispensable in the nation building process or nation formation, without which a channel for communication not only between different nations but also in the attainment of civic integration within one nation state is impossible. Additionally, language assists one's ability to acquire knowledge and participate or engage with the social world by providing a source of control over resources, outlining knowable and achievable, delineating freedom to choose and widening prospects to valued goals. As per Cummins, by considering education as a process of knowledge construction, self-actualization, widening participation and decreasing vulnerability, languages within education could be an important 'intervening variable', which affects the extent of transformative educational outcomes in multilingual contexts (Tamim 2014: 280-299). In multi-ethnic Baltic states, language politics is particularly interesting because of their past legacy of being under the occupation of the Polish, the Germans, and the Russians. However, the most critical one being under the Soviet rule wherein intense

Russification of the society, culture, and education was carried out. In the nation building process of the Baltic states, the language question plays a very crucial role because of the use of language in identifying one's national identity.

Language was considered as the basis for fighting of the independence of the Baltic states (Dundua 2014: 171-183). Under the Soviet rule, the Baltic states had to use Russian as the official language undermining their native languages. However, on the onset of independence, the native languages were reinstated as the official language and the medium of instruction. However, currently due to a large number of Russian speakers especially in Latvia and Estonia, the issue of using native language as a medium of instruction in the education sector has become problematic. Firstly, the resistance from the Russian minority and secondly the abrupt change in the medium of instruction in education, which is negatively affecting the learning process of children, are issues now.

As per the study conducted by international Save the Children Alliance (2009), language barriers keep away many children from progressing academically as they learn based on linking new knowledge to what is already familiar to them. Teaching in a language unfamiliar to them excludes children from attaining quality education, gaining skills and competence. Furthermore, marginalization of linguistic communities from attaining education due to their inability to understand the language of instruction contributes to political instability and conflict, and reduces the prospect of economic growth of countries as they move towards globalisation. Additionally, education is central to nurturing mutual understanding within a democratic context, managing cultural and linguistic diversity for the process of development in the multilingual Baltic states.

Language and Nation Building Process in the Baltic States

Language legislation is a fundamental element of nation's political development as it forms a direct link between politics and national identity. It is a means to nation building and ethnic containment (Jarve 2003). Language in the Baltic states is highly politicised and volatile being linked to nationalism. The Russification of the Baltic states along with the establishment of Russian language as the official language caused tensions in the Baltic states, which later became the reason behind the fight in the process of nation building. As the Baltic states gained independence, the native languages were reinstated and language reforms took place, which is now threatening the existence of minority languages. Progress to democratisation and participation in the international arena is making the issue of language in the Baltic states even more prominent. The Baltic states, however, are eventually undertaking numerous language reforms to contain the issue of language both in the administrative affairs and in education.

Language under the Imperial Russia and the Soviet Union

The Baltic states were under the Russian occupation twice. Firstly, in the nineteenth century under the Imperial rule wherein Russification was carried on as people started resisting the Tsarist rule. Lithuania was the first country to experience strict political control and cultural suppression by affirming Russian as the official language. Education came under the direct control of the Imperial and the use of Russian language became compulsory in the schools. Eventually, these policies were implemented in Estonia and Latvia too.

During 1918-1940, the Baltic states enjoyed momentary independence. However, under the second occupation, then by the Soviet Union, stringent policies were implemented. Internationalism, the new face of Russification turned an instrument to form one common Soviet people by undermining the culture of the Baltic states and further suppressing their rights. Russian once again was declared as the official language and made to use in all official matters in the Baltic states. Most of the major institutions used Russian as the official language, and the notable cultural, scholarly, and scientific works were produced in Russian. The Baltic education system was carried out in Russian and people were forced to become bilingual by studying Russian courses. Teachers were trained as per the Soviet directives clearly indicating Russian interests. Additionally, to add to their woes huge population transfers took place from Russia to the Baltic states affecting the ethnic composition especially in Estonia and Latvia. The massive ethnic composition change in Latvia and Estonia was due to the presence of industries while in Lithuania not much change was experienced as it was less industrialized. These policies engraved negative perception towards the Russian minority to date. The presence of Russian minority is reflected as a recapitulation of the humiliating half a century of Russian domination. After independence, the Baltic states sought to impede the influence of the Russian minority. However, interactions with various international organizations (especially the European Union) made them relax their attitude and treatment towards the Russian minority (Tulun 2012).

To protect and preserve the culture and language, parallel Language Acts were adopted in the late 1980s in the Baltic states befitting the basis of their movement for nation building. The Estonian Language Act 1989 declared Estonian as the official language but acknowledging the importance of the Russian language. The medium of education was to be taught in Estonian across its territory; however, Russian was used in regions with the high Russian speaking population. The 1989 Language Act was a ground breaking step towards nation building. It not only established a parity of Estonian with Russian but also the first legislative step trying the Russian language and monolingual Russian-speakers in Estonia.

Next, Lithuania adopted its Language Act 1989, and as per the decree, Lithuanian was declared the official language. However, unlike Estonia, the government supported the non-native speakers to learn the language. Proper facilities and training were provided to students and teachers, and special courses provided in education institutes where the medium of instruction was not Lithuanian. The Latvian Language Act 1989 constituted similar provisions by declaring Latvian as official language; however, it was amended in 1992 with explicit reference to Russian. The monolingual Russian speakers were not permitted to hold administrative posts unless they learn Latvian (Jarve 2003). The Language Acts delimited the rising importance of Russian in public sphere and protected the rights of the natives through promotion of their native languages.

National identity on the foundation of language became very prominent during post-Soviet period. The Baltic states formulated policies based on their experiences of the past. As per Renal'd Simonian (2004), Estonia and Latvia were so fixated of the past that these two states desired to build a mono-ethnic state with an aim of the supremacy of the titular[1] majorities (Simonian 2004: 67-88). In the complex process of nation building, language became vital to be naturalized or integrated into the states. This, in turn, became a huge issue for the Russian ethnic group members, as they could not speak the native languages (Dundua 2014: 171-183).

New language laws were passed giving more importance to the native languages with several amendments in the Language Act (in Latvia in 1992, while in Estonia and Lithuania during 1995-1999). For instance, the language in the Baltic states was used as a citizenship mechanism to exclude the Russian minority and bar them from exerting political power (Tulun 2012). Citizenships in Latvia and Estonia became possible through naturalisation creating conditions for the Russian minority to emigrate. No serious efforts were put in for the non-native speakers to learn Latvian or Estonian. While on the other hand, the case of Lithuania was different, as the state did not have any sizeable Russian minority; it did not impose any requirements nor was naturalization process placed. Language was less politicised in Lithuania, the government passed a law to teach everyone the native language in secondary school despite their ethnic origin (Dundua 2014: 171-183).

Table 2: Change in Ethnic Composition from 1923 to 2011

Country	Ethnicity	1923-1934 (in %)	1989 (in %)	2000-2001 (in %)	2011 (in %)
Estonia	Estonian	92. 4	61.5	67.9	70
	Russian	3.9	30.3	25.6	25
	Others	3.7	8.2	6.5	5

Latvia	Latvian	73.4	52.0	57.7	62.1
	Russian	10.6	34.0	29.6	26.9
	Others	16.0	14.0	12.7	11
Lithuania	Lithuanian	84.2	79.6	83.4	84.2
	Russian	3.2	9.4	6.3	5.8
	Others	10.1	4.0	3.5	3.4
	Polish	3.2	7.0	6.7	6.6

Sources: (Hogan-Brun 2007: 556; Statistical Office of Estonia, Central Statistical Bureau of Latvia, and Statistics Lithuania, 2015)

From the table 1, it can be inferred that 1923-24 to 1989, there was a drastic decline of the native ethnicities in Estonia and Latvia while moderate in Lithuania. However, after independence of the Baltic states and reinstating of the native languages as the official language, the native ethnic composition in each of the Baltic states has significantly increased from 1989 to 2011.

Contemporary State of Language and Education in the Baltic States

After tumultuous struggle with the language issues, currently, the Baltic states are undertaking special efforts and steps to accommodate multilingual policies especially in the field of education. The educational policies throughout the Baltic states support cultural and linguistic diversity; however, policies are more liberal in Lithuania followed by Estonia and then Latvia. Positive steps are established moving from a monolingualism or bilingualism with Russian to a bilingualism or trilingualism by learning the native language. State exams are introduced to certify professional linguistic competence as well as part of naturalisation requirement. Successful execution of the emerging language laws is examined nationally by language inspectors. As cited by Hogan-Brun (2007), the improvements, as shown in table 2, have been noticed in the titular language situation across the Baltics.

Table 3: Rise in total percentage of the population speaking titular language

Titular language	1989 (%)	2000 (%)
Latvia	62	82
Estonia	67	80
Lithuania	85	94

Source: Hogan-Brun (2007)

The attitude of the minorities towards titular language is changing as native language plays an important part in attaining citizenship and also getting employment. At the same time, the host countries are becoming more open towards the culture and language of the minorities (Hogan-Brun 2007: 553-570).

As mentioned earlier, teaching in a language familiar to the children is vital for them to better understand the subject and gain skills and competence. Decentralisation of education is taking place along with the implementation of policies to cater to the hybrid school population. In spite of the medium of instructions to be carried out in native languages, the regions having huge minority communities are allowed to carry out instructions in the first language with the titular language as a compulsory subject. The students are to take the exam in titular language along with general language proficiency certifications for employment and pursuing further education. Now, the parents send their children to schools teaching in the titular language due to the better prospects of titular languages in finding employment (Hogan-Brun and Ramoniene 2004: 62-77).

Further reforms are implemented to update education as per the changing needs of the society and demands of the global market. Lithuania's Ministry of Education and Science introduced "Development of Bilingualism" project in September 2001 to provide open multicultural education, wherein identity of all students is valued, and the curriculum content enriches their bilingual development. In Latvia, the first step to reform educational system was taken in 1995, however, changes are made. The new Education Law of the Republic of Latvia envisages teaching of two subjects at primary level in the state language while three subjects in non-main stream schools at the secondary level. To further develop the position of the Latvian, in 1998 the Law on Education and General Education approved models for bilingual education in Russian-medium schools wherein 60 percent of the curriculum to be taught in the official language in all state education establishments at upper secondary school level (Hogan-Brun and Ramoniene 2004).

In Estonia, there is no official decree supporting bilingual education, though such approaches are being practised through promotion of early and late immersion programmes. Like in Latvia, to promote learning of Estonian in minority language-medium schools, the state and the local governments are being instructed to promote an eventual transition to teach in the titular language of up to 60 percent in total at the secondary level (Hogan-Brun 2007: 553-570). Some of these language reforms in education have not been successfully implemented due to the resistance from the Russian minority as learning a new titular language would be a challenge for the children and affect their future prospects of getting employed. Additionally, lack of proper planning and use of resources has hampered these policies to be materialised.

Conclusion

Language is not only the main tool of communication, but is also closely related to national identity. The language factor determines the process of nation-forming and facilitates its further formation as in the case of the Baltic states. Due to the

Soviet Union's past treatment of the Baltic states, a deep feeling of abhorrence is ingrained towards the Russian minority especially in Latvia and Estonia. After the independence of the Baltic states, several policy reforms have been implemented in official, administrative and education arenas impacting the minorities in retaining their rights. Language reforms were passed making native language as the official language and politicizing it to the extent of excluding the Russian minority and barring them of their rights. The Russians had to naturalise themselves and learn titular language to reside in Latvia and Estonia. Language reforms in education also took place, and the medium of instruction in the major educational institutions were replaced by titular language instead of Russian. These language reforms are highly resisted by the minorities, as many of them, being monolingual, found the process of education in a new language affecting the learning process of the children and barring them of employment opportunities.

Nevertheless, with the changing demands of the society and the interaction of the Baltic states with international organizations such as the European Union, the language policies are loosening. For instance, bilingual education system wherein both the titular and minority language are taught, was promoted. Bilingual education system is also helping retain minority schools. These new measures in the education are not without challenges and heavy public criticisms. The changes in the education system are causing a number of startling challenges, compelling the construction of suitable educational policies to discourse the needs of a changing society. Lack of resources both in terms of human resources and financial resources has to be handled and the curricula have to be changed but also teachers are to be trained with changing curricula.

In order for the measures of bilingualism in education taken by the states to function effectively, proper planning and research needs to be conducted and encouraged at the grassroots level taking into consideration the views and needs of all ethnic groups in each of the countries accordingly. Innovative approaches are also essential to create social awareness and change the attitudes of the minorities to appreciate the benefits and importance of bilingual education.

Notes

1. Titular language is the majority language of a nation. The titular nation is the single dominant ethnic group in the state, typically after which the state was named. The term was used for the first time by Maurice Barrès in the late 19th century.

References

Cheskin, Ammon (2015), "Identity and Integration of Russian Speakers in the Baltic states: A Framework for Analysis", *Ethnopolitics*, 14 (1): 72-93.

Cianetti, Licia (2014), "Representing minorities in the city-Education policies and minority incorporation in the capital cities of Estonia and Latvia", *Nationalities Papers*, 42 (6): 981-1001, retrieved from http://dx.doi.org/10.1080/00905992.2014.957663.

Cummins, J. (2006), "Education in a multilingual society", inK. Brown (ed.), *Encyclopedia of Language and Linguistics*, Vol. 4, 2nd edn, Amsterdam and Oxford: Elsevier, pp. 64-66.

Dooly, Melinda and Claudia, Vallejo (2009), *Educational Policies that Address Social Inequality, Thematic Report: Linguistic Minorities*, EPASI (Educational Policies that Address Social Inequality).

Dundua, Salome (2014), "The politics of language and education in Georgia (compared with the Baltic states and Ukraine)", DOI: 10.14746/pp.2014.19.3.13, pp. 171-183.

Hogan-Brun, G. and Ramoniene, M. (2004), "Changing levels of bilingualism across the Baltic", *International Journal of Bilingual Education and Bilingualism*, 7(1): 62-77

Hogan-Brun, G. et al. (2008), "Language politics and practice in the Baltic states", in Robert B. Kaplan and Richard B. Baldauf, Jr. eds., *Language Planning and Policy in Europe: The Baltic states, Ireland and Italy*, 3. *Multilingual Matters*, Clevedon, U.K.

Jarve, P. (2003), "Language Battles in the Baltic states: 1989 to 2002", in Farimah Daftary and François eds., *Nation building, Ethnicity and Language Politics in Transition Countries*, Budapest, Local Government and Public Service Reform Initiative Open Society Institute.

Hogan-Brun, Gabrielle (2007), "Language-In-Education across the Baltic: Policies, Practices and Challenges", *Comparative Education*, 43 (4): 553-570.

Kersh, N. (1998), "Current developments in education in Latvia: difficulties of renewal", *Oxford Studies in Comparative Education*, 8(2): 35-48.

Kubota, R. (2004), "Critical multiculturalism and second language education", in K. Toohey and B. Norton eds, *Critical pedagogies and language learning*, Cambridge: Cambridge University Press.

Norton, B. (2000), *Identity and language learning: Social processes and educational practice*, Edinburgh Gate: Pearson Education.

Pinnock, Helen and Gowri Vijayakumar (2009), Language and education: the missing link how the language used in schools threatens the achievement of Education for All, CfBT and Save the Children Alliance.

Simonian, Renal'd (2004), "The Russian Diaspora in the Baltic Countries", *Russian Politics and Law*, 42 (4): 67-88.

Simonian, Renal'd (2013), "The history of the formation of the Russian Diaspora in the Baltic states", *Filosofija Sociologija*, 24 (4): 161-170.

Statistical Office of Estonia, Central Statistical Bureau of Latvia and Statistics Lithuania 2011 population and housing censuses in Estonia, Latvia and Lithuania, retrieved from http://osp.stat.gov.lt/services-portlet/pub-edition-file?id=19698.

Tamim, Tayyaba (2014), "The politics of languages in education: issues of access, social participation and inequality in the multilingual context of Pakistan", *British Educational Research Journal*, 40 (2): 280-299.

Tulun, O.M. (2012), "Russification Policies Imposed on the Baltic People by the Russian Empire and the Soviet Union", *Uluslararasi Suçlar ve Tarih*, 14.

Wiley et al. (2014), "Language Policy, Politics, and Diversity in Education", *Review of Research in Education*, (38): vii-xxiii.

Zamyatin, Konstantin (2012), "The Education Reform in Russia and its Impact on Teaching of the Minority Languages: An Effect of Nation building", *Journal on Ethno politics and Minority Issues in Europe*, 11(1): 17-47.

Chapter Eight

Socio-Political Ideas of Leonidas Donskis: Nationalism, Anti-Semitism and Predicaments of Modernity in Lithuania

Chinmaya Mahanand[*]

Leonidas Donskis was a Lithuanian liberal philosopher, political theorist, historian of ideas, critic of the current ongoing Antisemitism, and a defender of human rights and civil liberties who contributed a lot in the contemporary philosophical and nationalist discourse of Lithuania. He was a strong social critic of the Lithuanian society, politics and mainstream social science discourse. His thought on nationalism is unique in the discourse of nationalism that has challenged both western and Lithuanian readers. His theorization of nationalism has a social critique with universal normative ideals that has the potential to transcend the national boundaries. His thought of nationalism is based on multiculturalism and tolerance that rejects the extreme form of 'blood and soil' nationalism. His ideas of nationalism structurally engage with the issues of intolerance and anti-Semitism that developed in Central Europe and Baltic states in general and Lithuania in particular in twentieth century. Therefore, Donskis' thought on nationalism cannot be studied in isolation of the Anti-Semitism that developed because of the radical 'blood and soil' nationalism in Lithuania. He traced the growth and development of Lithuanian nationalism theoretically from a critical perspective and also analysed the predicaments of modernity.

Donskis belong to Litvak, the Lithuanian Jewish community. Donskis was born on 13 August 1962 in Klaipėda, Lithuania. He was the son of a Holocaust survivor. According to his public statements, his father, was a Litvak who was rescued by Lithuanians during the Holocaust and raised Catholic. Donskis described himself in an interview: "I am a Jew whenever and wherever I encounter anti-Semitism,"

* I sincerely extend my gratitude to Dr. K. B. Usha for giving me opportunity to study on Lithuania. I also thank Dr. Sarunas Paunksnis and Dr. Nerijus Cepulis for their support for me to study Lithuanian philosophy and socio-political ideas of Leonidas Donskis at Kaunas Technological University under Erasmus + programme.

explaining he would never deny being Jewish out of respect for his father. Donskis was outspoken in his support of Holocaust education in Lithuania, for promoting tolerance in Lithuanian society and respecting the rights of Jews and Litvaks.

Donskis held various prestigious positions of responsibility and power. He was the deputy Chairperson of the Lithuanian Jewish Community and a notable figure in Lithuanian society and political life. In 2004, Leonidas Donskis was awarded the title of the Ambassador of Tolerance and diversity in Lithuania. Donskis acted as a Lithuanian member of the European Parliament. He represented Human Rights Coordinators of Alliance of Liberal and Democrats for Europe (ALDE) group in European Parliament from 2009 to 2014. In 2012, Donskis was appointed as EP Rapporteur for the annual report on Human Rights and Democracy in the world 2011. Until his election as a member of European Parliament, Donskis acted as a Professor of Political Science at Vytautas Magnus University in Kaunas, Lithuania. Donskis served as a Professor and Dean in the Faculty of Political Science and Diplomacy at Vytautas Magnus University from 2005 to 2009. He also served as Docent of Social and Moral philosophy at the University of Helsinki. Donskis was a visiting professor of Philosophy at Dickinson College of Pennsylvania, USA, a Swedish Institute Guest Researcher at the University of Gothenburg, a Guest Professor of East European Studies at the University of Uppasala, Sweden. Donskis has been published widely in the international refereed journals. Donksi's works originally written in Lithuanian and English have been translated into other languages as well.

Leonidas Donskis claimed that the theorists of nationalism have paid less attention towards nationalism as a social critique of society and culture. He does not confine himself in the narrow definition of nationalism of one country. He considered nationalism as a liberating force grounded with objective universal value system. According to Donskis, critical dimension constitutes the major component and symbolic organization of nationalism. The liberal nationalism should not be confused with the "blood and soil" nationalism and it cannot be located in the framework of any particular ideology and moral culture. Neither can it be represented by any particular ideology and cultural movement. He argued that nationalism has successfully accommodated itself in the ideological framework of liberalism, socialism and conservatism (Donskis 2002: 26). However nationalism underwent radical changes at the second half of the nineteenth century and first half of the twentieth century. Nationalism, having started as a phenomena of freedom and sympathetic understanding of other, became more doctrinal and exclusive in this phase. As a thought and action system, nationalism surpasses any other phenomena of consciousness, destroying the age old empires across the globe with the slogan of freedom for all (Ibid). He pointed that the explosive potential of nationalism deeply affected the downfall of the Soviet Union.

Historical Development of Nationalism and Anti-Semitism in Lithuania

Leonidas Donskis (2002) says that Lithuania cherishes the ideas of multi ethnic, multi religious and multi-cultural models of renaissance of Europe. It also cherishes the generous and noble spirited ideas of Roman Catholic liberal nationalism. In fact in 1980, Lithuania's national movement and singing revolution not only revived the springtime of the peoples for freedom, but also it became the litmus test for the soviet policies of glasnost and perestroika (Ibid). Lithuania reached its highest point in history by being the first breakaway republic from Soviet Union representing the historic triumph of nationalism over forced internationalism. However, he claimed that Lithuania departed from its noble ethics of liberal nationalism many times in past, particularly at the initial phase of its nationalism. It has also departed from its principle of its multi-ethnic, multi-religious, multi-cultural ideas. It became the country of typical homogenous actors with the slogan of "one nation, one language, one culture and one state" in the inter-war period. Before Second World War, Lithuania had more than 250000 Jewish people, however only 20000 Jews survived the holocaust (Donskis 2002: 20).

According to Donskis, Lithuanian mainstream nationalist discourse was based on the ideas of anti-Semitism. He discussed about the ideas of double genocide widespread in Lithuania[1]. In this context he writes:

> the idea of double genocide widespread in Lithuania and beyond, which is based on the assumption of the symmetry in suffering of Eastern European Jews as victims of the Holocaust, and their non-Jewish compatriots and neighbours as victims of Stalinism and Communism – as if to say that the Holocaust was only about the Jews, whereas Stalinism was exclusively hostile only to the Balts and other non-Jews, as the Jews enormously contributed to Communist causes (Bauman and Donskis, 2013: 131).

He narrated the memoirs of his colleague's ancestors to highlight how the daily life of Lithuanian Jewish was violently brought to an end. He writes: "I read the memoirs once, twice, and once again, and I was, figuratively speaking, grabbed by the throat, there was no way I could avoid digging deeper, reading more, and finding out as much as possible about what actually happened from 1941 to 1944" (Ibid). Donskis quoted Bauman:

> what do you say about a human being who, one night during the Second World War, hears a knock at the door from a Jewish child who asks for shelter in the hope of being saved? The human being has to decide on the spot, knowing very well that he is risking his own life and that of his family. Such situations cannot be wished on anyone, including oneself (Ibid: 17).

In order to understand this transition of inclusive Lithuanian nationalism into an exclusive conservative radical nationalism, Donskis, not only studied the development of Lithuanian philosophy of history and culture, but also he studied the Central/East European consciousness. He realized that Lithuanian national consciousness cannot be understood in isolation of the Central/East European consciousness.

In this context, Donskis referred Vincas Trumpa, an émigré Lithuanian historian who noted that Lithuania transformed its 'will to power' into 'will to culture' in the inter-war period i.e. from a *Naturvolk* into a *Kulturvolk* (Ibid, 27-28). However, he mentioned that though Trumpa found the contribution of philosophers like Stasys Salkauskis and Antanas Maceina in the growth of Lithuanian philosophy of culture in the interwar period, he could not reflect on their philosophy of cultures which was empirically disconnected from the reality of Lithuania (ibid).

Donskis also referred Norbert Elias's *Uber den Prozess Zivilisation* and Louis Dumont's *Essay on Individualism: Modern ideology in Anthropological perspective* to explain how Central/East European intellectuals were bewitched by the *Geschichtsphilosophie* and *Kulturphilosophie*, the German philosophy of history and culture. He discussed how German middle class intelligentsia identified the ideas of civilization with politeness, delicate manner and behaviour which was nothing but the superficiality of the court of nobility and their lifestyle and culture (*Kultur/Bildung*) with spirituality (*das rein Geistige*) (Ibid). In this way, the ideas of culture and civilization departed from the social reality among the German middle class intelligentsia and the same was followed by the others.

Donskis asserted that like Italy, which resembled Germany politically and historically in the nineteenth century, the Central/East European states were also attached to the German variant of subculture, rather than French or Anglo-American variants of modern ideology. Donskis (2002) asserted two following conclusions regarding the Lithuanian understanding of culture and history:

1. "Lithuanian social philosophy inherited, from its German counterpart/predecessor, a hypostatized model of cultural individualism, which treats national culture as a collective individual. This type of individualism leads culture to orient itself and refer to identity, rather than to multidimensional human reality. In order to demonstrate how deeply this sort of hypostatized cultural individualism is grounded in German philosophies of history and culture, it suffices to recall Herder's treatises in the philosophy of history, *Ideen zur Philosophie der Geschichte der Menschheit* and *Auch eine Philosophie der Geschichte*".
2. "The gap between culture/ideas and politics/social reality is deeply rooted in Lithuanian consciousness: it springs from the endorsement of

> "axial ideas" – a term nearly simultaneously employed by Karl Jaspers and Lewis Mumford –drawn from Germany's history of consciousness and ideas, rather than having developed from Lithuania's cultural resistance to Soviet domination, ideological and political practices, use of power, brainwashing, and so on. It must, however, be noted that the Lithuanian intelligentsia's tendency toward escapism, which developed as a reaction to Soviet ideological and political oppression, undoubtedly deepened the gap between culture and politics".

Donskis quoted one of the essay of Tomas Venclova, "*The Jews and the Lithuanians,*" written in the 1970s to show the real scope of the tragedy admitting the guilt and responsibility of those Lithuanians who collaborated with the Nazis and actively participated in the massacre of Lithuanian Jews. He mentioned that the idea of xenophobic nationalism is deeply embedded in the best intellectual traditions of Eastern and Central Europe (Donskis 2011: 125). Donskis also explained about how Lithuanian and Baltic politicians and public figure romanticize the political forces of 1941 that tried to save the independence of the Baltic states collaborating with the Nazis (ibid: 118).

Donskis stated that the history of consciousness could be considered the most appropriate research strategy for examining the questions of ethnicity and nationalism in the post-Communist societies. Many philosophers like Philippe Ariès, Michel Foucault, Louis Dumont, Vytautas Kavolis, and Hayden White developed it as an interdisciplinary and methodological approach, he claimed. He considered it as a tool not only to understand the cultural reductionism, but also to understand how European identity as a whole relates to each of its national variants.

Donskis (2002) referred J.L. Talmon' ideas of "political messianism" and characterised them as constituting a significant feature of consciousness of the post-Communist societies in Central and East Europe (Talmon, 1960). He appreciated Alfred Erich Senn, an American historian and political scientist, for pointing out a sense of vulnerability and fragility as the most characteristic features of Central/East European consciousness. He believed that the ideas of innocence and victimizations are widespread in the post-communist countries. These are nothing but an inversion of political messianism. The experience of depression and despair usually seeks symbolic compensation and most of the new Central and East Europeans counties are determined by the inadequacy of self-consciousness and collective identity, as a result they look backward in a messianic manner (Donskis 2002). In this context, he cited an example of how the Lithuanian new Romantics extol the ideas of "Third Rome of Russian Slavophiles or the Athens of the North", which are fundamentally grounded with the denial of western liberal discourse, emphasizing much on personal heritage or past (Ibid). He considered it as a continuation of the ideological clash that took place during "the time of Peter the Great between the anti-western, anti-modern Russian Slavophiles and the Hegelian Zapadniks" (Westerner). This sort of "Central/East European messianism" has a common feature of being purist and ethnic oriented which negates the liberal western discourse. This kind of ideological orientation penetrated into the Lithuanian consciousness through the works of Adam Mickiewicz, Jules Michelet's revolutionary messianism and Mazzini's vision of *Roma Terza* (Ibid).

Donskis also discussed on the existence of Eurasian thought in Lithuanian consciousness side by side with the anti-western consciousness. In the twentieth century, the self-image of Lithuania as the Athens of the north peacefully coexisted, geographically located as bridge between the East and West (Donskis 2002: 30). He found that the ideas of East and West, a synthesis of civilization were reflected in the writing of "Lithuanian philosopher, Stasys Salkauskis.[2] However this book was severely criticized by many intellectuals in Lithuania including Salkauskis's own disciple Antanas Maceina.[3] Maceina argued that the Salkauskis's vision of a bridge between East and West or the synthesis of civilizational culture was nothing but a Russian vision of Eurasia. Beside this Donskis found "Eurasianism" as a philosophical approach and as a civilizational identity in the works of Lev Karsavin, who remained in Lithuania for long time and contributed for the Lithuanian philosophy of history and culture (Ibid).

Donskis credits Salkauskis and his critic Antanas Maceina for contributing significantly in developing and shaping the Lithuanian philosophy of history and culture. He found that Maceina was deeply influenced by Nikolai Berdyaev's apocalyptic philosophy of history which believed that philosophy of history is neither a product of wonder or nor doubt, but of suffering. This apocalyptic understanding of history led by Maceina and other philosophers concluded that the acquisition of philosophy of history or historical knowledge be done through suffering only. However, Donskis argued that the people (who were considered as historical and cultural identity) and the nation (which were understood as socio-cultural phenomena) could reach to a level where the proliferation of social sciences and humanities occurred. Unlike the interwar Romanian literary and academic intellectuals who not only established humanities, but also social sciences, their Lithuanian counterparts remain closed within the framework of philosophy of history and culture to deal with the only issue of where *WE* come from (Donskis 2002: 32).

Vytautas Kavolis, a Lithuanian born American sociologist, urged the current intellectuals of Lithuania to make an analytical comparison between Maceine's ideas and Romania's 1927 Generation (Ibid). The 1927 Generation members were Nae Ionescu, Emil Cioran, Mircea Vulcănescu, Constantin Noica, Mircea Eliade, and Eugene Ionesco Nae, who could be considered as the models of Central/East European consciousness in general, who provided unending debate to locate the origin of Romanian nation historically and culturally to choose between East and West.[4] Therefore, Donskis concludes that it is possible to identify the streams of Central/East European consciousness, which is very much paradigmatic and grounded with structural isomorphism. Notwithstanding the structural isomorphism and identical structures of sentiments, Donskis claimed that the inter-war nationalist movement of Lithuania took a different form unlike its counterparts such as Romania, Poland, and other East European countries (Ibid).

In this context, Donskis discussed about Lithuanian nationalist intellectuals and philosophers who contributed in the development of Lithuanian philosophy of culture and history and nationalist discourse of Lithuania. Among them Salkauskis, Maceina, Juozas, Girnius, Vosylius Sezemanas, Bronius Stokus were prominent who contributed lot in shaping the nationalist discourse in Lithuania. Donskis (2002) discussed that the essentialist philosophy of history and culture dominated the inter-war period in Central/East Europe. Neither Anglo American nor French social and political philosophy influenced the inter-war Lithuania. He considered this as the result of weakness of social sciences that could not develop a proper methodological approach to study the social reality in that period. Hence he claims that it is not because of the influence of outside discourse, rather the absence of epistemological dimension in social science in Lithuania led to the misinterpretation and misconception of social reality. The theoretical fallacies that developed are the product of incongruity between the social reality and ineffective tools for social sciences on one hand and lack of an appropriate analytical language on the other hand (Ibid).

Donskis says, Lithuanian intellectuals were quite interested on the ideas of Oswald Spengler, Leo Frobenius, Ludwig Klages, Eduard Spranger, Anton Hilckman, and Martin Heidegger as well as the most prominent representatives of Lebensphilosophie, Geschichtsphilosophie, and Kulturphilosophie.[5] However, none of them was concerned about the thoughts of John Stuart Mill, Émile Durkheim or Max Weber. As a result, the messianic nationalism that sprang from the peripheral mode of consciousness, deeply rooted in the Central/East European linguistic and cultural politics continued to prevail in Lithuania.

Donskis claimed that the Lithuanian intellectuals of inter-war period were aware about fascism and radical nationalism in Europe. Among them, Mykolas Römeris and Valentinas Gustainis were the most prominent. In addition, Jonas Basanavicius and Jonas Šli pas, the founders of the *Aušra* (The Dawn) movement, and Vincas Kudirka, founder of the *Varpas* (The Bell) movement were also aware about the Fascism. All these intellectuals represented liberal tendency in Lithuanian nationalism. However, Donskis found quite unpleasant anti-Semitism in Kudirka's satires and pamphlets. The nature of anti-Semitism was associated with anti-urbanism during the early twentieth century Lithuania, that came from the rural peasantry. On the contrast, the *Ausra Movement* leaders held different perspective. They defined Lithuanian as one who has breathed in Lithuanian air. Through this perspective, the national identity becomes another way of conceiving freedom.

According to Donskis, Lithuanian identity and Jewish identity both existed peacefully through mutual understanding since long. Lithuania was famous for its large Jewish community before Second World War. The Lithuanian capital Vilnius was said to be the Jerusalem of north. Many internationally eminent Jews who lived in Vilnius were from Lithuania and among them were the philosophers Emmanuel Lévinas and Aron Gurwitsch, the painters Chaïm Soutine and Neemija Arbitblatas, the sculptor Jacques Lipchitz, the violinist Jascha Heifetz, and the art critic Bernard Berenson, one of the most sophisticated twentieth-century students of the Italian Renaissance (Ibid). Yet none of these intellectuals was recognized in the intellectual discourse of Lithuania, because Russian-speaking Jews were always alienated form the Lithuanian mainstream discourse. The nationalistic perspective was determined through the historical and cultural projects, rather empirically identifiable social reality. Therefore Donskis emphasised that Jews and other aliens were excluded from the Lithuanian mainstream intellectual discourse.

Donskis (2002) observed that the mainstream nationalism of Lithuania founded upon the alliance between the conservative nationalism through Roman Catholic Church and its ideological and political network that developed in inter-war period. The origin and formula for Lithuanian identity was equated with the Roman Catholic Church. The Catholic conservative nationalism became the official ideology of Lithuania during the Lithuanian President Antanas Smetona's authoritarian Regime (Ibid). Donskis considered it as the primarily factor responsible for the development of new political discourse of radical conservative nationalism in Lithuania. This led to the negation of multi-ethnic, multi-culture, multi-religious ideals of Lithuania. During this time, the ideas of one nation, one language, one religion, one state dominated the mainstream political discourse (Ibid).

The conservative nationalists started using anti-modern and anti-western rhetoric in their discourse. Especially the catholic oriented journals significantly propagated anti-western discourse. Donskis considered this anti-modern attitude of the conservative nationalists as the reflection of their fear of modernity. He found Maceina as most striking example of this fear of modernity. According to Donskis, Maceina consciously adopted the Nazi ideology and had significant influence on Lithuania's nationalistic consciousness. Maceina was the architect of the Lithuanian Activists Front (LAF), whose primary objective was to preserve the Lithuanian national racial purity during anti-Soviet agitation in 1941. Hence Maceina was not knowing English language, he could not follow much of the western discourse. As a result he misinterpreted many liberal discourses in Lithuania (Ibid). Therefore Donskis asked, how one could speak about liberalism without reading John Locke, Thomas Paine, Jeremy Bentham and John Stuart Mill?

Nonetheless, Donskis claimed about the existence of liberal tendency in the Lithuanian nationalist movement parallel to the messianic ethnocentric consciousness as an alternative discourse to the dominant mainstream. After the Second World War, this legacy was carried on by *Santara Sviesa* Movement in USA.[6] This liberal nationalism represented the most inclusive, sophisticated and human facet of nationalism in general. Donskis discussed in detail about three important émigré Lithuanian philosophers, Vytautas Kavolis, Aleksandras Shtromas and Tomas Venclova who contributed significantly in shaping Liberal nationalist discourse in Lithuania. *Santara Sviesa* Movement is not appreciated much in Lithuania and often criticized by the conservative nationalists. Conservative nationalists equate it with western conspiracy and with communism. Donskis claimed that the Liberal nationalism, which believes in critical study of society and country in terms of universal intellectual and moral criteria, is still condemned in present day Lithuania (Ibid).

Therefore, Donskis (2002) writes:

> what is surprising and embarrassing is that Maceina's ideological idioms are alive and well in present-day Lithuania. For the vast majority of Lithuanian intellectuals, nationality is merely another term for ethnicity. This confusion of political and cultural terms reaches its climax in the inability—or conscious refusal—to equate Lithuanian-ness with Lithuanian citizenship. By implication, if someone is an ethnic Pole or Russian or is Jewish, then he/she cannot be a true Lithuanian. The tendency to conceive of Lithuanian-ness in strictly ethno-cultural, rather than political, terms betrays the very narrow, rigid and exclusionary concepts of loyalty and identity that determine Lithuanian consciousness.

Donskis distinguished liberal and conservative nationalists in terms of their perspective towards Lithuanian history and cosmopolitanism. Unlike liberal nationalists, the conservative nationalists do not allow space for cosmopolitanism. According to Donskis, these anti-modern, anti-liberal, anti-cosmopolitan and anti-Semitic stances are merely different names of the same thing. In the framework of conservative nationalists, these phenomena and terms like 'capitalism', 'the bourgeoisie', 'secularization', 'liberalism', 'liberal democracy', 'cosmopolitanism', 'the Jews' and 'the West' are all combined under the same framework of 'self and civilization' (Ibid).

Donskis (2002) claimed that the Lithuanian scholars define nationalism as a phenomenon of merely a collective identity related to neither the universal system of values nor prescriptive political discourse. Therefore, he writes, "Aggressively defensive, exclusionist, victimized, and constantly searching for internal and external enemies, Lithuanian nationalism is not yet capable of theoretically reflecting upon itself. In present-day Lithuania, nationalism is either perceived as merely the cultivation of the collective self, or is described pejoratively as another term for xenophobia and the cultivation of hatred." He argued that a definition of nation, which claims to be subjective even though it recognizes territorial identity as an essential factor for self-determination must be considered objective in modern society.

Predicaments of Modernity

Donskis pointed out the crises, dilemmas and complexities in the democratic transformation in the world after Soviet disintegration. The world witnessed several crisis and predicaments such as economic crisis, environmental crisis, cultural crisis which any political ideology could correct. Therefore, he argued that the modernity is in crisis. Donskis pointed that the modernity is going through the crisis of moral blindness and insensitivity. The modernity has created a culture of sensationalism and consumerism among the people. It also creates the sense of insecurity and fear in the minds of people.

> Donskis writes; "Ours is a time of fear. We cultivate a culture of fear which is becoming increasingly powerful and global. Our self-revealing age, with its fixation on cheap sensationalism, political scandals, TV reality shows and other forms of self-exposure in exchange for public attention and fame, prizes moral panic and apocalyptic scenarios incomparably more than a balanced approach, light irony or modesty. Behind this tendency is an overwhelming fear of crumbling to the ground or merely being oneself: the fear of unimportance; the fear of vanishing in the air leaving no trace of visibility and presence; fear of being like others; fear of being beyond the TV and media world, which is tantamount to becoming a nonentity or the end of one's existence" (Donksi and Bauman: 2013: 94).

However this fear of insecurity does not go alone, it always moves with hatred, Donskis pointed. The fear wears various masks which speaks the language of existential and intimate experience. From a closer look it appears that we are in control of large segments of organized fear. He talks about horror films and horror stories that functions as an irreplaceable part of entertainment along with TV comic shows and stand-up comedians. He writes; "We don't quite fear, yet we fear. I fear, therefore, I am. Another side of that same coin, fear nurtures hatred, and hatred nurtures fear. Fear speaks the language of uncertainty, unsafety and insecurity, which our epoch provides in large quantities and even in abundance." (p. 96). Now the problems is how to live with a sense of constant uncertainty. Here he pointed on the fertile psychological conditions of the society for the emergence of dodgy politician who can promise to handle the situation and take control of everything. Thus he mentioned that fear has become a political commodity, paving the way for a wave of populism and xenophobia in Europe (Donksi and Bauman: 2013: 96).

Bauman, in the context of pointing the moral blindness of the civil society, talks about how the modernity is going through an era not only of monetary inflation, but also of the inflation or devaluation of concepts and values. Bauman writes; everything is becoming uniformly important and unimportant. My very existence places me at the centre of the world. In my experience, the pinnacle of concept inflation was reached ten years ago, when I came across articles in the American press describing the 'holocaust' of turkeys in the run-up to the Thanks giving holiday. This was probably not a simple case of a word being used unthinkingly or irresponsibly. Disrespect for concepts and language only temporarily masks disrespect for others; and this disrespect eventually bubbles to the surface (Donksi and Bauman: 2013:122).

Beside this, the martyrdom-seeking politics with total indifference has become an efficient tool of attention seeking. It is treated as a success story in our world of comparative martyrology. It always goes by denying and trivializing others suffering at the same time. Therefore the pie is expected to be shared equally among all the victimized actors of history. It means convincing martyrology or a plausible account of suffering has becomes a password through the gates of power and recognition.

In this context, Bauman talks about the concept of double genocide that is prevalent in Lithuania and in Eastern Europe. Bauman writes; Hence, the idea of double genocide widespread in Lithuania and beyond, which is based on the assumption of the symmetry in suffering of Eastern European Jews as victims of the Holocaust, and their non-Jewish compatriots and neighbours as victims of Stalinism and Communism – as if to say that the Holocaust was only about the Jews, whereas Stalinism was exclusively hostile only to the Balts and other non-Jews, as the Jews enormously contributed to Communist causes. Needless to say, the distortion of history is too obvious here to need emphasis, yet it throws more light on why and how the wave of the obfuscation and trivialization of the Holocaust became possible in Lithuania, where an attempt was made to equalize the Holocaust as a major crime against humanity and the crimes of Communism, as if to say that we have experienced not one, but two Holocausts, two parallel realities of horror and hatred, a Holocaust of the Jews and a Holocaust of Gentiles, the former orchestrated by the Nazis, and the latter by the Communists (p.123). Hence, evil is not confined to circumstances in which people are acting under extreme stress. Today it remains in the everyday insensitivity to the suffering of others, in the inability or refusal to understand them. It remains in the normality and in the triviality and banality of everyday life and not just in the exceptional conditions. In order to overcome moral blindness, one should break the vicious circle of consumerism and sensationalism to address the real problems. Here the universities and the politics, have important role to play in educating the masses to get rid of the crisis of moral blindness.

Donskis observed that the lack of rational intellectual discourse in Lithuania is responsible for this transition. Highlighting the condition of universities and intellectual discourse in Lithuania, he writes, "Like the majority of European Union countries, Lithuania is now confined to the new managerial experiments – officially labelled as a substantial structural reform – which are trying to transform the universities into semi-corporate bodies run like business companies, with a paramount mission of service and efficiency, rather than original, in-depth research and top-level teaching. These senseless experiments are far from innocent and harmless. We are at serious and real risk of bidding farewell to the university as a cornerstone of European culture and as an institution which has survived states and forms of government. Even in Italy, the new managerial class has stopped talking about the autonomy of universities. The commodification of universities and education is too obvious to need emphasis. Yet one thing is much worse – namely, a gradual disappearance of the political in the realm of the university, and also a sliding into technocracy disguised as democracy and free choice (Bauman and Donskis, 2013: 53). However he observed that the Lithuania's intellectual discourse is in transition since the last decade and acquiring criticality and self-introspection within it.

Defender of Global Human rights

Donskis remained as a strong defender of human rights and critical of de-humanization tendencies anywhere. For instance as MEP he questioned the caste based discrimination in South Asia, Africa and especially in India. He was one of the supporters of the struggle against caste oppression. He argued that caste discrimination is not a problem in just one country, India, but it is widespread global issue. He called it "one of the biggest paradoxes of 21st century" (IDSN 2013). A resolution in European Parliament against caste discrimination in India testifies his strong commitment to human rights discrimination based of caste, gender, race, religion etc.

Donskis raised the caste based discrimination and moved a resolution in this regardin EU Parliament in 2013 (The European Parliament 2013). He called for a more active EU policy to address this issue. In his speech he asserted:

> In fact caste based discrimination resolution calls for the recognition of caste based discrimination. It must be tackled together with other kind of discrimination like ethnicity, race, religion, gender or sexuality. This form of discrimination destroy the lives of hundred millions people, but the EU policies still do not reflect upon it while the EU

> has deadline on LBGTI, human rights defender, freedom for religion and belief. This be group of people suffering from caste based discrimination is not mentioned almost anywhere and this problems is not confined to India alone as President mentioned quite rightly 216 million peoples are suffering not only in south Asia but also in Yemen, Mauritania, Nigeria, Senegal and Somalia. Those suffering have no chance of development, are excluded from all public sphere and educational institutions and this obvious we fight poverty and this problems pose a serious threat to the development. Therefore the caste sensitive post to 2015 agendas has to be promoted, especially women are suffering from multiple and intercepting forms of discrimination based on caste, gender and religion. Therefore I believe that the EU must raise this question in the realm of EU-India relation, trade and investment agreement have to include clauses on caste based discrimination. Recent crackdown on Indian NGOs finance from abroad including those fighting caste based discrimination has to be on the spotlight. Finally, I have to be frank with you on every single nuances considering this story. We are aware that some countries have very strong lobbies in order to prevent this topic to reach to EU or even the EP agendas and whatever the case all the suffering people should not be left aside and forgotten (https://www.youtube.com/watch?v=Xyadld1cZkk).

On 10 October 2013, the European Parliament debated – and then adopted – a resolution on caste discrimination, calling on the EU to strengthen its policy on the issue. The resolution had been prepared by the Committee on Development (DEVE), which unanimously approved the draft resolution on 17 September (IDSN 2013).

Conclusion

Leonidas Donskis was a great philosopher of Lithuania and a social critic of Lithuanian society and politics, who continued the historical egalitarian, inclusive, multicultural legacy of Lithuania. Donskis did not consider Nazism or Holocaust as an aberration in Lithuanian or European history, but as a phenomenon of specific social condition that can grow in nay nation under similar social condition. Donskis's consistent engagement on xenophobic nationalism and holocaust is an attempt to make the civil society acknowledge the genocide it has created in past to avoid it in future. In this context, he writes, "after all, we cannot regard the history of all our civilizations as one ongoing crime and one endless genocide of some group or other. Whitewashing a concept benefits no one. Whether we like it or not, the Holocaust was the one and only bona fide genocide in human history. It was unique not only because of its scale, its praxis, and its industrial methods of annihilation but because of its determination never to call a halt to the Final Solution as long as a single Jew remained alive" (Donskis 2011, 135).

Figure 5: Leonidas Donskis (13 August 1962-21 September 2016), who became a global voice of defending human rights and resistance against discrimination based on race, caste, gender, religion and ethnicity. His works are widely acclaimed in Baltic Studies in India and use as resource for teaching Baltic political philosophy. Research scholars are attracted by his ideas on modernity and human rights. His untimely departure is a great loss to humanity. Photo courtesy: internet

Figure 6: Memorial of the main Jewish mass grave in Lithuania in Leonidas Donskis's Hometown Butrimonys

The Litvak community assembled on 23 October 2016 to say kaddish (mourner's prayer) for the Jewish community murdered there in 1941 and paid tribute to Donskis's memory in Butrimonys, where his father survived Holocaust in line with his expressed wish. Donskis said in an interview on Delfi TV on 31 August 2016, a month before his death on 21 September 2016, on the occasion of Moletai Holocaust commemoration march, "I would be happy, if while I am still alive, something similar would happen in Butrimonys... I feel a moral obligation to say kaddish there with Jews" as if it was his last wish

Source: *http://www.donskis.lt/a/en/1/1_/2538*

Photo Courtesy: Milda Jakulytė-Vasil retrieved from https://www.lzb.lt/en/2016/10/21/ethical-will-of-leonidas-donskis-kaddish-for-butrimonys/

Donskis made Lithuanian mainstream intellectual discourse responsible for the transition of Lithuania in past as he strongly realised that the philosophical discourse shapes the journey of a nation. As a social critic, Donskis identified the limitations of Lithuanian nationalist discourse and social science methodology with the objective to strengthen it further for the cause of inclusive, multicultural Lithuania and humanism. The world will remember him as the defender/champion of human rights as a global issue.

Notes

1. The concept of double genocide, one by Nazism and other by Communism, was developed by Lithuanian. It is alleged that this idea was developed to whitewash the memory of Holocaust, or the persecution of Jews by the Nazi collaborators of Lithuania.
2. Stasys Salkauskis's book '*Sur les confins de deux mondes*', written in French in Switzerland.
3. Antanas Maceina, a Lithuanian philosopher, theologist, existentialist and the architect of the Lithuanian Activists Front (LAF), whose primary objective was to preserve the Lithuanian national racial purity during anti-Soviet agitation in 1941.
4. The 1927 Generation constructed myth, theories, narratives, poetry, in terms of ideological tension between East and West.
5. Lebensphilosophie, Geschichtsphilosophie, Kulturphilosophie stand for philosophy of life, philosophy of history and philosophy of culture respectively.
6. Santara Sviesa Movement was led by young émigré Lithuanian scholars in USA against both Fascist and Soviet oppression on Lithuania. This movement promoted liberal nationalist thought in Lithuania and outside. It spoke for the independent Lithuania. It was mainly led by émigré Jews scholars in USA.

References

Bauman, Zygmunt, and Leonidas Donskis (2013), *Moral Blindness: Loss of sensitivity in Liquid Modernity*, UK: Polity Press.

Donskis, Leonidas (1999), "Between Identity and Freedom: Mapping Nationalism in Twentieth-century Lithuania", *East European Politics and Societies*, 09/01/1999.

Donskis, Leonidas (2002), *End of ideology and Utopia: Moral Imagination and Cultural Criticism in the Twentieth century*, New York: P. Lang.

Donskis, Leonidas (2003), *Forms of Hatred: The Troubled Imagination in Modern Philosophy and Literature*, New York: Rodopi.

Donskis, Leonidas (2002), *Identity and freedom: Mapping Nationalism and Social Criticism in Twentieth Century Lithuania*, Gordon & Breach Publishing Group.

Donskis, Leonidas (2005), *Loyalty, Dissent and Betrayal: Modern Lithuania and East-Central European Moral Imagination*, New York: Rodopi B.V.

Donskis, Leonidas (2008), *Power and Imagination: Studies in Politics and Literature*: New York: Peter Lang.

Donskis, Leonidas (2009), *Troubled Identity and the Modern World*, New York: St. Martin's Press.

International Dalit Solidarity Network (2013), "EP resolution on caste-based discrimination (2013)", retrieved from https://idsn.org/eu/eu-resolutions-on-caste/

Leonidas Donskis (2011), *Modernity in Crisis*, PALGRAVE MACMILLAN® in the United States—a division of St. Martin's Press LLC, 175 Fifth Avenue, New York, NY 10010.

Donskis, Leonidas (2011), *Niccolo Machiavelli: History, Power and Virtue*, New York: Rodopi.

Talmon, J.L. (1960), *Political Messianism: The Romantic Phase,* New York: Frederic A. Praeger, 1960, 242–277.

The European Parliament (2013), European Parliament resolution of 10 October 2013 on caste-based discrimination (2013/2676(RSP), retrieved from http://www.europarl.europa.eu/sides/getDoc.do?pubRef=-//EP//TEXT%20TA%20P7-TA-2013-0420%200%20DOC%20XML%20V0//EN

Voren Van, Robert (2009), *On dissidents and Madness: From the Soviet Union of Leonid Brezhnev to the Soviet Union of Vladimir Putin*, New York: Rodopi.

Chapter Nine

Historical Memory of Holocaust, "Double Genocide" Politics And Revival of Anti-Semitism in Contemporary Baltic States

K. B. Usha[**]

Introduction

Baltic states of Estonia, Latvia and Lithuania, after regaining independence from the former Soviet Union in 1991, began nation building based on the rejection of Soviet legacy, adoption of norms and values of western liberal democracy and an orientation towards "return to Europe". In this process history, identity, collective memory, the narratives of the victimhood of Soviet and Nazi crimes and "equal genocides" policy form the core elements of defining national identity, citizenship and security. The Baltic nationalist's attempts for finding historical truth and desire for renewed identity and recognition demonstrate a perceived problem of over-emphasizing the complete victimhood of the Baltic majority nationality under Soviet occupation and arguably minimizing the horrific Holocaust experience of Jewish minority under Nazi German invasion. Because, the history of Holocaust experience unravels a different story of local ethnic Baltic citizens being perpetrators of crime against humanity by voluntarily collaborating with Nazis and participating in the mass murder of Jews.[1] Overemphasising the complete victimhood of the Baltic majority nationality under Soviet occupation demonstrates the virtual underpinnings of hiding the dark spot of their own history. When looking at the nation building process of Baltic states through the prism of Holocaust, the history of Jewish experience during the Second World War reveals the complexity of revisionism, contestations and multiple dilemmas of simultaneous sympathizing with both victims and perpetrators of crimes against humanity.

Framework of Analysis

The current Holocaust revisionism in contemporary Baltic states is related to politics

---

** This chapter is a modified version of a paper by K. B. Usha published in *Country Specific Study Project:* vol. 5, 2015, Mahendra Gaur, ed, *Studies on Israel*, New Delhi: Foreign Policy Research Centre (FPRC), pp. 72-98.

of memory and identity. Memory politics is reflected in victimhood narratives, "equal genocide" policy and remembrance events. Marek Tamm refers memory politics to "a politics endeavoring to shape the society's collective memory and establish notions of what is and is not to be remembered of the past, employing to this end both legislative means (by instituting historical anniversaries, rehabilitating certain persons, condemning certain ideologies, etc.) and practical measures (organizing public rituals, erecting monuments, building museums, etc.)" (Tamm 2013: 652). Memory politics focus mainly on historical and transitional justice and also shows a normative take for transformation of meaning.

The Baltic states are determined to highlight the crimes and victimization under Soviet occupation to inform the world about their preferred past, arguing that the realities of Soviet crimes against humanity were overlooked. Therefore, they began their heated historical debates around the representation of past and pursued the agenda of promoting 'national' histories depicting themselves as "victims of 'two totalitarianisms'-the Nazi and primarily the Soviet ones" (Smirnov 2015: 65) in search of a "usable past" for legitimacy of present interests and future directions. In the Baltic context definitions of a number of concepts such as "anti-Semitism", "genocide', "Holocaust denial" and "Holocaust obfuscation" require elaboration as Baltic states are trying to re-interpret certain norms, concepts and definitions after becoming members of the European Union.

The Baltic states' approach to history and memory of Holocaust reflects recognition and revisionism. The Baltic political elites recognized the moral responsibility of Holocaust and admitted local collaboration. And regret their inability to save more Jewish lives from being victims of crimes. The "symmetry formula" of equating both Soviet and Nazi crimes as "two genocides" reflects revisionist underpinnings. The Baltic Holocaust revisionism is deeply rooted in the broader context of revival and rise of the new forms of anti-Semitism and Holocaust obfuscation taking place across Europe. After the post-war UN enforcement of international law to curtail the violation of rights of Jewish community, anti-Semitism used to be considered as a thing of past in Europe. Nazism was defeated and race-based anti-Semitism was discredited in Europe was the common belief. However, now after seventy years of the horrendous Holocaust, the revival and political manifestations of anti-Semitism/neo-anti-Semitism are a disturbing trend especially in Eastern Europe where the post-Soviet Baltic countries are located. The current trend of revival of anti-Semitism in Europe has its reflection in Baltic states. As EU members they can use the platform for interacting with nationalist groups in other parts of Europe and asserting nationalist politics in EU.

Parliamentary report of United Kingdom and the US congressional report found the growing trend of anti-Semitism worldwide. The transformation and revival of anti-Semitism in Europe has been a contemporary trend. Denis MacShane, British

Labour Party MP says that anti-Semitism which he refers as neo-anti-Semitism is back as a twenty-first century global ideology. Anti-Semitism is still persistent in Europe that needs to be prevented from any sort of escalation as happened in the past. In order to contain anti-Semitism it has to be understood in political terms and dealt with (MacShane 2008).

Steven Beller, regarding preventing anti-Semitism, suggests: "The question is how can this 'eternal' form of antisemitism be kept within minimal and 'harmless' dimensions. In those terms, the answer to antisemitism is ultimately not a Jewish state, but the establishment of a truly global system of liberal pluralism" (Bellner 2007: 119). In response to Beller's conclusion, MacShane concerns that "neo-anti-Semitism, the development of an old hate into an organized ideology with its thinkers, organizers, spokespersons, state sponsors and millions of adherents. Today anti-semitism is not about Jews. It is about us" (MacShane 2008). Alvin H. Rosenfeld supports this view that the current anti-Semitism is different from the old anti- Jewish hatred which was based on racial and religious factors. Today's anti-Semitism is transformed as a phenomenon driven by ideological biases (Rosenfeld 2013: 2). As MacShane warns, as a new global phenomenon anti-Semitism is back with a deadly vengeance. It threatens all humanity.

EU's working definition of anti-Semitism is relevant in Baltic case as they are EU members. The EU defines, "Antisemitism is a certain perception of Jews, which may be expressed as hatred toward Jews. Rhetorical and physical manifestations of antisemitism are directed toward Jewish or non-Jewish individuals and/or their property, toward Jewish community institutions and religious facilities" (European Forum on Antisemitism 2012)[2]. Anti-Semitic acts are criminal acts as defined in the provisions of legal instruments of the countries concerned. Anti-Semitic discrimination, therefore, is illegal. Anti-Semitism is expressed in various forms: the denial to Jews of opportunities or services available to others and targeted of attacks on Jewish people or property – such as buildings, schools, places of worship and cemeteries.

The legal definition of genocide according to Article 2 of the UN Convention on the Prevention and Punishment of the Crime of Genocide (1948) refers to "any of the following acts committed with intent to destroy, in whole or in part, a national, ethnical, racial or religious group, as such: killing members of the group; causing serious bodily or mental harm to members of the group; deliberately inflicting on the group conditions of life calculated to bring about its physical destruction in whole or in part; imposing measures intended to prevent births within the group; [and] forcibly transferring children of the group to another group" (Office Of The UN Special Adviser On The Prevention Of Genocide 2010: 2). This is the universally accepted definition of genocide all over the word. But the Baltic states redefined the concept of genocide diverting from the international customary law provided by the UN with the objective of qualifying Soviet crimes as genocide similar to Holocaust experience. It should be noted that the UN definition of genocide itself came as a result of Holocaust. As Siobhan Kattago points out, "... it is the memory of the Holocaust as a symbol of evil that is connected to human rights, a universal conception of human dignity and the desire to prevent future genocide" (Kattago 2015: 8). United Nations Declaration of Universal Human Rights adopted and proclaimed on 10 December 1948 as the foundation of freedom, justice and peace in the world was international community's response to Holocaust and to prevent such incidents ever happening in future.

Although evidence of Stalin's racial intention to annihilate Jews is lacking, the Soviet silence on the Holocaust is astonishing for the Jewish community. Scholars point out that except in a speech made on 6 November 1941 Stalin never made mention of Jews in his statements. He avoided mention of Jews subjected to mass murder despite Soviet army had evidence of the same. Yitzhak Arad argues, "Following the victory at Stalingrad in early 1943, the Soviet army found evidence in the liberated cities that the entire Jewish population had been murdered, but Stalin's speeches contained no mention of this fact" (Arad 2009: 536). Soviet silence on the annihilation of Jews during Second World War and after is a focus of Holocaust remembrance in Baltic states today. Despite state recognition of Holocaust, there is discrepancy between the official government policy and attitude of society towards Jews (Zizere 2005).

Holocaust is a term of Greek origin which means "sacrifice by fire". Holocaust Encyclopaedia of US Holocaust Memorial Museum defines Holocaust as "the systematic, bureaucratic, state-sponsored persecution and murder of six million Jews by the Nazi regime and its collaborators" (United States Holocaust Memorial Museum 2014). Holocaust denial and distortion are other two concepts that further expose the Baltic politics. Working definition of Ministry of Holocaust denial by Foreign Affairs of Israel refers specifically to any attempt to claim that the Holocaust/Shoah did not take place. It also includes public denial or doubt over the use of principal mechanisms of destruction (such as gas chambers, mass shooting, starvation and torture) or the intentionality of the genocide of the Jewish people. It can be found in various forms as an expression of anti-Semitism: blaming the Jews for the responsibility of Holocaust or considering it as the result of Jewish conspiracy. The Holocaust denial often aimed at the rehabilitation of an explicit anti-Semitism and the promotion of political ideologies and conditions that suit to it (Israel Ministry of Foreign Affairs 2013). The Ministry also specified that distortion of the Holocaust refers, inter alia, to:

a) Intentional efforts to excuse or minimize the impact of the Holocaust or its principal elements; including collaborators and allies of Nazi Germany;

b) Gross minimization of the number of the victims of the Holocaust in contradiction to reliable sources;

c) Attempts to blame the Jews for causing their own genocide;

d) Statements that cast the Holocaust as a positive historical event. Those statements are not Holocaust denial but are closely connected to it as a radical form of antisemitism. They may suggest that the Holocaust did not go far enough in accomplishing its goal of "the Final Solution of the Jewish Question";

e) Attempts to blur the responsibility for the establishment of concentration and death camps devised and operated by Nazi Germany by putting blame on other nations or ethnic groups (Ibid).

Dovid Katz, noted Holocaust and Yiddish historian of Lithuania, introduced the concept of Holocaust obfuscation to describe efforts currently underway. In his words:

> Holocaust Obfuscation is the systematic effort to relativize, minimize, obscure, confuse or eliminate the Holocaust, as a distinct historic entity in European history, without necessarily denying any of the documented murders. By the early twenty-first century Holocaust Obfuscation evolved as a major trend of thought in some governmental, political, press, academic and other elite circles of some new-accession states in the east of the European Union. Its ideas have been packaged in a number of declarations and proposed laws aimed at eliciting compliance from Western nations and organizations of nations. The most frequent apparatus includes: inflation of the term genocide to encompass a variety of Soviet crimes; the claim that Nazi and Soviet crimes were inherently equivalent; thereby leaving the Holocaust as a conceptual 'half' in the replacement paradigm. At the local level, variants of the model have included claims of overwhelming Jewish complicity in communism; claims that the murder of the Jewish populations in Eastern Europe was a reaction to alleged Jewish communism; claims that the miniscule percentage of Jews who survived by escaping to Soviet-supported partisan groups in the forests are a priori guilty of 'war crimes' (hence they may be investigated with neither evidence nor charges). The Holocaust Obfuscation movement frequently harbors antisemitic and racist undertones (Katz 2009: 272).

Dovid Katz, calls current scenario of Holocaust obfuscation "double genocide" which is inspired by a "movement in Europe that believes the crimes—morally, ethically—of Nazism and Communism are absolutely equal, and that those ... who 'don't think 'they're absolutely equal, are perhaps soft on Communism" (Katz Quoted in Liedy 2011). Interrelationship between current anti-Semitism and "Symmetric Approach" of Holocaust is evident in the "red-brown movement" of equalising Soviet and Nazi occupation of Baltic states (Zuroff 2005).

In the light of the above conceptual framework, the following sections try to analyse the factors – social, economic, cultural and political – that led to Baltic enmity and hostile behaviour to Jews, the reason for perpetrating violence against Jews during Second World War and the current phenomenon of new forms of anti-Semitism and Holocaust revisionism. The period of formation of sovereign Baltic states after First World War, national majority-Jewish minority relation during the interwar period, the current attempts of redefining the past, and politics of identity, culture, and nation building throw light to understand the underpinnings of revisionism in the treatment of history and memory of Holocaust and revival of anti-Semitism in Baltic states.

Politicization of Memory and History in the Nation Building Process

The creation of new national historiography by assessing selective past is a source of politics and power in Baltic nation building process. The contemporary narratives of history is represented, shaped and constructed on the premises explained by the Baltic political elites who are in the pursuit and exercise of power. They argue that the Soviet crimes were not assessed adequately by the West and perpetrators were not brought to justice as in the case of Nazi crimes in the post-War period. The Baltic states, therefore, defined them as formally occupied by Soviet Union from which they later regained their independence and democracy (Pettai 2011). The debate on the memory of Holocaust generates an irreconcilable conflict in coming to terms with this past.

Holocaust committed by Hitler's Nazi Germany aimed at complete annihilation of Jewish nation across the world is known today as the most horrific crime against humanity the Europe/world has ever experienced. On the eve of the Second World War, because of the external influence of Nazism in Germany, anti-Semitism increased in Baltic states. The hatred of Jews was because of the Baltic majority's fear of Jewish domination in the economy and culture, and their nationalist perception that Jews were loyal to Russian communists and would betray the Baltic nations. Since 18th century Baltic states, especially Lithuania, compared to other parts of Eastern Europe, had a distinctive history of modern Jewish cultural, religious, artistic, economic and intellectual life. Lithuania's capital Vilnius was known as the "Jerusalem of the North"[3] as the city hosted one of the biggest Jewish settlements in Europe (Leva 2001). The apprehensions and hatred towards Jewish minority's empowerment transformed into violence during the Second World War. A massive extermination of almost 95 percent of Jews took place in Baltic states (*Vilnews* 9 January 2011). Such a high scale of mass murder of Jews did not happen elsewhere in Europe. The Holocaust occurred in Baltic states was not possible without the voluntary active participation and collaboration of local Baltic nationality with the Nazi Germans. Since Baltic states were incorporated into the former Soviet Union after the war the Baltic Holocaust history remained unknown as the issue was silenced by the Soviet authorities to hide their own crimes during the War (Arad 2009).

Since independence in 1991, the political elites took the language, culture and territorial homeland of Baltic majority nationalities as salient features of their national belonging. State is seen not only as an aspect of national identity but also an instrument of preserving the Baltic majority ethnicity's language and culture. The old hatred of Jews who were equated with Russian communists is transformed today into nationalist sentiments against Russian speakers including Jews internally and so into an anti-Russia stance externally. In the "self/other" dichotomy of national identity construction, Russian speakers including Jews are treated as the hostile "other." The Baltic governments pursued a politics of restrictive citizenship towards minorities (Aasland 2002). Because, the Baltic national majority view Jewish minority as communists, who were closely associated with Soviet occupiers and therefore held responsible for the killings and mass deportation of the Balts to Siberia under Soviet occupation in the past (Eidintas 2000; Hanebrink 2018). Apparently, Jewish question becomes a contested issue related to the much larger political questions.

In the ethno-nationalist political agenda of Baltic states, rewriting history became an important agenda as a "truth" finding mission. The Holocaust revisionism and rewriting history, apparently, come into use as a political instrument in diluting the crime committed by local Balts against Jews. Obviously, the state supported History Commissions established in the late 1990s came up with "two Holocausts"; in other words, "double genocide" theory in effect minimising the Holocaust experience and establishing complete "victimhood" under Soviet occupation. The Baltic attempt of conciliation by asserting the principle of "equality of victimhood" under the Nazis and the Soviets is something of the denial of genocide of the entire Jewish people and getting rid of Holocaust out of history. Therefore, the Holocaust history reveals the complexity of the Baltic nation building by simultaneously following two irreconcilable political goals of sympathising with both victims and perpetrators. The paradox of the attempts to hide their own crimes for which they can use Soviet crimes as an excuse for Holocaust mystification or ultra-nationalism calls into question the Baltic democratic system.

Consequently, after nearly three decades of independence the prejudiced attitudes toward Jews has transformed into a political and ideological anti-Semitism. The process of falsifying Holocaust in the Baltic states is expressed in various forms in government policies and among the masses: rewriting history, "double genocide" theory, Holocaust education, redefining concepts related to Holocaust, legislations, desecration of monuments, commemoration events, vandalism, anti-Semitic graffiti and remarks, provocative media articles and so on (Levin 2008; Arad 2011; Pettai 2015; Katz 2017). Commemoration of Combat Support Forces of Waffen SS (*Schutzsstaffel*, Armed Protective Squadron) legions is regularly celebrating their commemoration events in all major Baltic cities despite Jewish protests. While the state is showing great enthusiasm in bringing communist crimes to justice, their reluctance to consider the complicity of local collaborators in Holocaust crimes and prosecute them, and the Baltic attempt to hide the dark spot in their own history do not match with the claim of Baltic states that they cherish the democratic values and humanistic traditions of the west. Thus, the Holocaust revisionism and new anti-Semitism have now become a part and parcel of the larger questions of identity and minorities related to the ethnocentric nation building in these countries. The paradoxical situation gives impetus to understand this under-researched aspect of the complex, rightist, ethno-nationalist political agenda in the so-called democratic nation building in Baltic states.

Jewish Community in Baltic States before the Second World War

The Jewish community in Baltic states has a history that dates back to more than 700 years. In Lithuania the first Jewish settlements appeared in the 12th century. They were merchants from southern Europe (Levin 2000). Historian Abraham Elijahu Harkavi believed that the Jews came to Lithuania in the ninth and eighth centuries from Babylonia (Greenbaum, 1995: 2). Jews were first mentioned in a document in Livland (Latvia's Vindzeme province today) in 1536. Courland (Zemgale and Kurzeme provinces of modern Latvia) also had Jewish settlements in the 15th century. In Estonia Jewish settlements appeared as early as fourteenth century. As mentioned in the written archival records (Aeltestes Denkelbuch) a man called Johannes Jode, whose name appeared in 1333, is believed to be the first Jew settled in Estonia. However, the permanent Jewish settlements of Estonia began only in the 19th century, when Russian Tsar Alexander II granted them the legal right to enter the region in 1865. In 1894 an edict of Emperor Alexander III gave the right to reside in the Baltic provinces to all Jews who had been living there permanently since 1879. Mostly they lived in the Pale of Settlements[4] since the creation of such settlements by Catherine the Great in 1791. Jews flourished through the centuries and became inseparable part of Baltic societies. Main cities like Riga, Tallinn and Vilnius became important trade and cultural centres of Jews (Gurin-Loov et al. 2001: 9). Vilnius city was named *Jerusholayim de Lite* ("Lithuanian Jerusalem") and considered to be the spiritual centre and cultural capital of Jews who call themselves as Litvaks. Jews were mostly urbanized and very few of them lived in the countryside (Weiss-Wendt 2008: 90).

However, they faced several hardships due to restrictions imposed by rulers, deportations, confiscation of their property, and difficult situations created by wars, uprisings and the like. They were accused of assassination of Russian Emperor Alexander II. In this connection pogroms were encouraged against the Jews all over Russian empire. During the Russian revolution and First World War Jews were killed in large numbers. Because of the hardships they faced throughout the centuries they participated in and supported the independent movements during 1918-1920 led by Baltic nationals, anticipating some amount of autonomy (Gurin-Loov et al. 2001). In the independent Baltic states in the interwar years (1918-1940) Jews enjoyed the rights of national minority. Jewish associations, parties, network of Jewish educational institutions, congregations and places of worships were established. However, the anti-Semitic attitudes, expressions and prejudices against Jews, prevalent in Baltic societies especially since Estonia, Latvia and Lithuania became independent states in 1918 after the First World War (interwar period) set the preconditions of Holocaust during Second World War.

Anti-Semitic feelings against Jews seem to be based on economic, religious and socio-political reasons. When the Baltic states became independent for the first time in the second decade of 20th century, Jews, despite being deprived, extended great material support in rebuilding the country after war. Baltic Jewry contributed a fair measure of aid in the rebuilding of their native countries. During the difficult transition period from 1919 to 1922 theirs was a great help. In the interwar years (1918-1940) when the new states were formed in 1919, Jews were granted minority rights in Baltic statesunlike in other countries in Europe. Lithuania (12 May 1922), Latvia (7 July 1923) and Estonia (17 September 1923) made declarations recognizing the Jewish minority rights in educational and culture spheres (Laserson 1941: 275). Jews enjoyed the rights of national minority in principle in the three Baltic states.

After the foundation of the democratic republic of Latvia, Riga, the capital city where 47 percent of Latvian Jews lived, became the political, cultural and social centre of the Latvian Jews. The Jews dominated in trade, businesses, etc. The economic condition of Jews flourished. After the foundation of the democratic republic of Latvia, the upward mobility of Jews in socio-cultural and economic spheres caused discontent among Baltic majority nationality and developed attitude of intolerance towards Jews. However, Bernhard Press says, anti-Semitism during the 1920s in Latvia was not aggressive. In Latvia prejudice against Jews existed in the form of preventing Jews from competing with Latvians on an equal basis on everyday life. Jews were excluded from government employment (Press 2000: ix).

Estonia was more liberal than Latvia in granting autonomy to Jews but there was restriction for Jews for membership in National Parliament. The Jewish community was organized and their cultural interests are served through mainly three agencies: a 27 member cultural council elected by Jewish citizens triennially, an executive committee of seven members elected by the council; and local committees (Laserson 1941).

In Lithuania Jewish community had its own National Assembly of Jewish Council with local branches and had a Ministry of Jewish Affairs until 1924. With the Christian Democratic government that assumed power in 1926 Jewish autonomy ended completely. During the period from 1919 to 1922 the Jews recognised their well-being. They showed patriotism in the newly formed state. Their loyalty to the state made them financing industrial development, fostering economic growth and participating in self-rule (Sutton, 2008).

However, Jewish autonomy remained as a crucial political issue in the later interwar years in Baltic countries when democracy changed into dictatorship in 1926 (Lithuania) and in 1934 (Estonia and Latvia). Thereafter, Baltic national majority broke the promise of autonomy. Although Jews enjoyed minority rights their entry into civil service was fully restricted. More exclusionary policies were followed by all the governments during the period of dictatorship. The perception of the Baltic majority nationality masses and leadership that Jews had monopolized the best jobs and controlled the national wealth led to further anti-Semitic policies. For instance, the Lithuanianization policies of Antanas Smetona's government carried out the exclusion of Jews (Laserson 1941).

In order to undermine Jewish socio-economic domination, leading Baltic business people and artisans formed an organization called Verslininki. On 15 January 1939, the organization's weekly journal *Verslas* published the reasons for Lithuanianization programme. It stated that Lithuania had too many Jewish manufacturers, merchants and petty shopkeepers, a situation which was intolerable. Therefore, in order to exclude Jews from economic sphere it suggested transfer of jobs to Lithuanians, immigration to other places, exclusion of Jews from state owned credit institutions, expulsion of Jews who migrated to Lithuania after 1918, elimination of Jews from restaurants, hotel and liquor industries, and elimination of Jewish university students. The extent of hatred towards Jews was further expressed by a Lithuanian Premier Jonas Cernius at a conference in 1939 organized by Verslininkithat "the Lithuanian Government will support the efforts of the Lithuanian Merchants Union to eliminate the Jews from trade" (Sutton 2008). Again on 20 January 1939 the journal published an article titled "Let Us Not Adjourn Unless the Jewish Problem Is Solved". The government also pursued policies favouring priority to Lithuanians over Jews in entry in the job market, admission to universities and so on. However, although such expressions existed, Sutton says, "Lithuanian government never instituted anti-Semitism de jure' (Ibid). In Latvia also state policies were not enacted supporting anti-Semitism. But nationalization of Jewish enterprises had been carried out. By late 1930s expression of anti-Semitism had begun to be seen in street violence and vandalism. Perkronkrust (an organization of Baltic-German Hitlerites) was the important source of spreading anti-Semitism among the masses. Unlike in Estonia and Latvia, religious confrontation between Catholicism and Judaism was a source of anti-Semitic feeling in Lithuania.

The anti-Semitism in neighbouring countries like Germany impacted such expressions in Baltic states also. Hitler's conspiracy against Jews for Soviet Bolshevism had impact on Baltic nationalists. Hitler described Bolshevik Russia as a "Slavic-Tatar body with a Jewish head". He said: "In Russian Bolshevism we ... see the attempts undertaken by the Jews ... to achieve world domination." That attitude was carried forward by Baltic Nazi collaborators during the Final Solution (Hitler quoted in Gitelman, 2013: 218). According to Laserson "There is no doubt that if Hitler had not assumed power in Germany there would have been no dictatorship in Latvia (or in Estonia where it took a moderate form)" (Laserson 1941: 282). Having said this, it could be argued that the impact of Nazi ideology and transformation happened in the inter-ethnic relation between Balts and Jews fuelled anti-Semitism. An atmosphere of anti-Semitism prevalent among the masses and nationalistic policies of governments accelerated prejudice to Jews and thereby Jewish vulnerability on the eve of Second World War.

In order to grasp the extent of Holocaust it is relevant to mention the size of Jewish community in Baltic states on the eve of Second World War. According to US Holocaust Memorial Museum "The Jewish population in the three Baltic states totalled 255,000: 95,600 in Latvia, 155,000 in Lithuania, and 4,560 in Estonia. Here, Jews comprised 4.9 percent, 7.6percent, and 0.4 percent of each country's population, respectively and 5percent of the region's total population" in 1933.29 In 1935 before the Second World War the Jewish population of Latvia was 93,479 people which comprised of 4.8 percent of the total population. In the capital city Riga 43,672 Jews lived.30 In Lithuania around 220,000 Jews were there and in Estonia the size of Jewish population was around 4,000 (United States Holocaust Memorial Museum, 2014). According certain other estimates there were around 300,000-350,000 Jews in total in Baltic states before the war (Segel 1988: 60; Levin 2008).

Influence of German Anti-Semitic and Anti-Soviet Propaganda in Baltic States

Besides the previously existed anti-Semitism and anti-Semitic Nazi propaganda, Nazi-German policy of Holocaust towards Jews in Soviet territories and wide-scale local collaboration with Nazis made the mass murder of Jews possible. According to Yitzhak Arad, Israeli Holocaust survivor and scholar, the German policy of Holocaust in Baltic states was characterized by three elements:

1. the Jews in the occupied territories of Soviet Union were the first group of Jews in German-occupied Europe to face physical and total extermination;
2. the killing was carried out by shooting, openly and in the vicinity of the localities in which the Jews lived, and was witnessed by the local population.
3. the German propaganda stressed that Soviet Jewry were the bearers of the Bolshevik ideology and the ruling elite in Soviet Union, that the target of the war was their elimination and the destruction of the communist state. For the other nations of Soviet Union German propaganda claimed that "their enemies are not the people of Soviet Union but the Judeo-Bolshevik rulers" and the German Army brings them freedom and liberation from Stalin's and Jewish yoke (Arad 2004: 175).

The Holocaust was carried out by *Einsatzgruppen* (Hitler's special action groups or death squad), Waffen SS units and the *Ordnungspolizei* (order police). In Latvia the Arajs commando and Hamman commando in Lithuania led the Holocaust in the Baltic. The vast majority of Jews were exterminated during the end of June-early July 1941 and end of July-December 1941. Ninth Fort in Kaunus, Poneriai (Ponary) near Vilnius, Rumbuli in Riga, were the main sites where the maximum number of mass killing of Jews took place. In these places and other smaller locations in the Baltic, hundreds or thousands of Jews were rounded up for execution by the Germans and their local collaborators. The number of Jews killed during 1941-42 in Baltic states were reported to be 80,311 in Lithuania, 30,025 in Latvia and 474 in Estonia (Yahil, 1990: 256). Estonia was the first country declared as *Judenfrei* (free/ clean of Jews). In Latvia around 90 percent of Jews were slaughtered. In Lithuania 95 percent were murdered (Yad Vashem 2016). A total of approximately 300,000 Jews were killed. The specificity of Baltic Holocaust is its highest level of mass killing that has happened in Europe. The question of how such a terrific pattern happened points towards the fact that without local Baltic ethnic majority's participation such a massive extermination would not have happened.

Shoah, the Baltic Jewish Tragedy: Local Collaboration, Complicity and Cruelty

The role of local nationals of Baltic states in collaborating with Nazis in the mass murder of Jews is a controversial question. Historical documents, Holocaust literature and survivor's testimonies and diaries available in public domain testify the participation of local Balts, i.e., ethnic Estonians, Latvians and Lithuanians, in Holocaust and their collaboration with Nazi legions. The Baltic states exterminated Jews to such an extent that elsewhere in Europe did not happen. Richard Rushke who reviews the scope and brutality of Baltic collaboration with Nazis confirms:

1) Estonian and Latvian Militia and Police collaborated with Nazis in the execution of their Jewish and Gypsy populations; 2) without their assistance, making those countries *Judenfrei* would not have been possible; 3) the motives for this indigenous collaboration were varied; and 4) Estonia and Latvia are still struggling to understand and accept responsibility for their part in the genocide (Rushke 2013).

Because of the problems of limited manpower and communication barriers Germans recruited local population from Baltic, Belarus, Ukraine, etc. to kill Jews. A lot of testimonies are provided by witnesses and officials regarding the brutal nature of Baltic collaborators in the Holocaust pogroms. As one German officer puts it, "we are actually frightened at the blood thirstiness of these people". Rushke says that the details of Lithuanian Nazi collaborators' degree of complicity with Nazi orders are available in Nazi war crimes testimony and *Einsatzgruppen* field reports found by US Army and Red Army in files in Berlin. He cites an example:

> EinsatzgruppenA received orders in October 1941 to liquidate all the Jews in the Belorussian town of Sluzk. The group commander divided his battalion into four companies, two of which were made up entirely of Lithuanian volunteers. After the operation was completed, the commander reported to Berlin, "with deepest regrets" that the action bordered on sadism ... with indescribable brutality on the part of both German police and particularly the Lithuanian partisans (Ibid).

G. Reitlinger, the author of The Final Solution: Hitler's Attempt to Exterminate Jews of Europe, 1939-1945, himself wrote about the Baltic involvement in the holocaust and brutality:

> The savagery of Lithuanian and Latvian gangs who carried out the pogroms, coupled with the indifference of nearly the entire population towards the more scientific extermination practiced by Germans, must have given an unusual degree of satisfaction to Hitler and his circle. But to those who in pre-war days had attributed to an almost Scandinavian respectability to the Baltic republics, the news of the massacres that leaked to was very credible (Press 2000: xi).

Historian Bernhard Press who is a survivor of Riga ghetto evacuation explains the brutal extermination incident begun in the chilled morning on 30 November 1941:

> First the policemen, rolling drunk, forced their way into the old age home and the neighbouring houses. In the old age home they machine gunned old people, sick people and invalids in their beds. They drove out of apartments ... people who were still in the midst of their preparations for the supposed evacuation, with truncheon blows, and shots, curses and threats. Anyone who did not obey fast enough was shot on the spot. Small children were hurled out of windows onto the street. In the dark of night, Latvian

policemen on foot and on horseback ... drove people down the street like a panicky herd of animals. According to an eyewitness report Herbert Cukurs (the butcher of Riga) tore an infant from its mother's arms and smashed the baby's head against the curbstone. As the mother threw herself with a wild scream on the lifeless, bleeding body, he riddled her head with bullets from his revolver. Anyone who couldn't keep up was killed with a shot in the neck. Some of the old people were pushed into buses and driven off; these unfortunate ones had no idea where they were going (Ibid: 103).

About a pogrom which took place in Kaunas on 25 June 1941 it has been described that "Women with children on their arms pushed their way to the front rows while laughter and shouts of 'bravo' echoed to the sound of the iron rods and wooden clubs used to beat the Jews to death. At intervals one of the killers struck up the national anthem on his accordion, adding to the festive mood of the day" (Weiss-Wendt 2010). Sexual atrocities were also being perpetrated against women. The above testimonies establish that local collaborators were mostly brutal and actively participated.

However, there were also incidents that local people saved Jews. The dominant view is local collaboration was through conscription and voluntary participation. In most cases the local people were indifferent and even the intelligentsia kept their silence probably out of fear. As Karen Sutton observes, local collaboration with Germany in the Holocaust "was not a spontaneous response to something that had happened in a short time earlier. It had a history of its own, the result of deeply rooted sentiments that stemmed from the teachings of the Church, modern nationalism, and political and socio-economic conditions" (Sutton 2008).

After the war Baltic Nazi collaborators were granted permission to immigration to America because Nuremburg Tribunal and the US High Commission in Germany defined the members of Baltic Legion as freedom fighters protecting their homeland from Soviet communist invasion and was not members of criminal Waffen SS. Baltic Nazi collaborators from Estonia, Lithuania and Latvia managed to flee to America after the war as they received a special treatment from the US Displaced Persons Commission (DPC). The Baltic legions were given permission to be immigrants in US and considered that they hadn't done anything harmful to US interests. The Jewish protests that the US ruling in favour of Baltic legions was anti-Semitic remained unheard although DPC Commissioner Harry N. Rosenfield opposed through dissenting vote (Rushke 2013). The Holocaust was largely ignored when the Baltic states were incorporated into Soviet Union after the Second World War. The Holocaust history remained unknown and unaddressed during Soviet period. However, many years of Holocaust research established today in detail that the DPC's ruling about Baltic legions was wrong. After the Baltic states regained independence they started dealing with the Holocaust issue. Consequent upon such reductive approach and policies of respective governments towards Jewish minority, expressions of anti-Semitism is reviving in Baltic states.

Holocaust Memory Politics and Rise of Anti-Semitism in Contemporary Baltic States

Policies and practices of state reflect minimizing of Holocaust in the attempt of highlighting severity of Soviet crime experienced by Baltic nationalities. Baltic states in the late 1990s appointed History Commissions to rewrite history in accordance with its nationalist political agenda and geopolitical imperative. They came up with new interpretations and new narratives of equality of victimhood under Germans and Soviets. The new narrative on Holocaust known as "double genocide" has now replaced the Holocaust denial (Katz 2009).

Figure 7: Holocaust memorial at Ninth Fort, Lithuania.

Ninth Fort that was built by Russian empire in the 19th century was used as prison. It is located in the northern part of Silainiai elderate, Kaunas, Lithuania. The Fort was used as a field of killing Jews from Kaunas Ghetto and German, Austrian and Czech Jews brought to Kaunas during Holocaust the Second World War. Detainees were kept in the underground cell under inhuman conditions. Around 45000-50000 Jews were slaughtered in the Fort. Today it stands as a Monument of Nazi Holocaust. The road from Kaunas Ghetto was known as the "Way to Heaven" in the past. Today it is called the "The Way of Death". The Fort has a museum depicting both Nazi Genocide and Soviet crimes as "equal genocides".

Source: *https://www.jewishvirtuallibrary.org/ninth-fort.*

Photo by: *K. B. Usha*

The transformation and redefining of justice system reflect the nationalistic genocide politics. Baltic states updated their criminal codes with new provisions interpreting crimes against humanity and punishment for such crimes. However, the criminal codes of all the three Baltic states simply define genocide as "broadly directed against a group of people defined by nationality, ethnic origin, race, religion, social or political beliefs" (Pettai and Pettai 2015: 79). The Baltic approach of genocide and the legal framework for prosecuting perpetrators of crimes during the Soviet era is centred on its "applicability of repressive acts committed during Soviet occupation" (Ibid: 80). They tried to get legal recognition of the crimes and atrocities committed under the Stalinist Soviet regime as genocide so as to escape Holocaust revisionism. They insisted the European parliament to recognise their demand to include a clause to make illegal the "condoning, denial or trivialization of crimes against humanity" committed under the Stalinist Soviet regime but was rejected by other members (Archdeacon 2007). The attempt is in effect to cover both Nazi and Soviet crimes as equal genocide and Holocaust denial in the Criminal Code.

Likewise, a bill which provides to impose up to two years' imprisonment for anyone who might deny or underestimate Nazi or Soviet genocide was passed by the Lithuanian parliament in June 2010. Dovid Katz explains, if a historian will say "Soviet crimes in Lithuania were horrific but they do not rise to genocide; there was only one genocide here, that perpetrated by the Nazis and their partners," he or she is potentially liable to prosecution (Katz 2010). This is a dangerous and undemocratic situation restricting freedom of expression and speech of a person who refuses to signify the Soviet crimes as genocide and expresses a different opinion.

Removal and renovation of monuments by changing original inscriptions is another tactic. The controversy over removal of Bronze soldier victory memorial in Tallinn in 2007 was a provocative incident. Another provocative event is the opening of Bauska monument honouring the Waffen SS legion by Latvian government in September 2012. The monument dedicated to "Bauska's Defenders Against the Second Soviet Occupation" has another inscription "Latvia is for Latvian" (*Pravda* 18 September 2012) which invited criticism of rehabilitation of Nazis. Holocaust education is initiated to teach the Holocaust in a local point of view and minimize it as minor evil.

Figure 8: The Bronze Soldier Monument in Tallinn

This monument of a bronze statue of a common soldier unveiled in Tallinn on 22 September 1947 by Soviet Union in the honour of Red Army soldiers who fought and sacrificed their lives in the Second World War. It was originally named as "Monument to the Liberators of Tallinn". After the restoration of independence this monument became a controversial one when Estonian authorities decided to remove it as per the War Graves Protection Act of 10 January 2007 that led to riots by Russians. Estonians and Russians have two different views on the monument. The controversy whether it represents occupation or liberation remains.

Photo by: K. B. Usha

Prague declaration of 3 June 2008 is another important instrument to defend double genocide and falsify history. The main demands in the declaration include: "recognize Communism and Nazism as a common legacy"; "recognition that many crimes committed in the name of Communism should be assessed as crimes against humanity serving as a warning for future generations, in the same way Nazi crimes were assessed by the Nuremberg Tribunal"; "ensuring the principle of equal treatment and non-discrimination of victims of all the totalitarian regimes"; "a day of remembrance of the victims of both Nazi and Communist totalitarian regimes"; and "adjustment and overhaul of European history textbooks so that children could learn and be warned about Communism and its crimes in the same way as they have been taught to assess the Nazi crimes" (Senate of the Parliament of the Czech Republic 2008). Dovid Katz points out the five occurrences of the word "same" in the declaration indicative of "double genocide" narrative. Association of Lithuanian

Jews in Israel in its protest statement condemned the declaration as it is a symptom of new and dangerous of strain of anti-Semitism (Katz 2010).

Commemoration events organized by the governments reflect "double genocide". For instance, Lithuanian President Dalia Grybauskaite when she visited the Holocaust memorial at Paneriai, near Vilnius on 9 May 2015 said, "Having divided Europe for half a century, Second World War took dozens of millions lives. It was the great pain of the XX century, giving rise to the Holocaust and Siberia forced labour camps." *(Delfi* (Vilnius) 8 May 2015). She equates the two painful events. But she paid silent tribute and did not say that it was liberated by Soviet Union. Holocaust minimization is the effect of such silence. During Russia's commemoration of victory day on 9 May 2015 glorification of Nazism occurred in many places in Europe like Ukraine, Baltic states of Estonia, Latvia and Lithuania, which is a noticeable fact in terms of nationalist political agenda coupled with rise of anti-Semitism.

Several questionable incidents are happening in the Baltic which reveals the glorification of Nazism and revival of hatred towards the Jews. A Latvian nationalist political activist, Janis Iesalneiks, argued for the inclusion of "intelligent anti-Semitism" in public discourse in 2010 (Auers 2015: 152). Honouring of the Waffen SS in Estonia and Latvia and reburial of the pro-Nazi Prime Minister Juozas Ambrazevicius in Lithuania with full state honours in 2012 are ultranationalist neo-Nazi efforts to rehabilitate Nazism. The ultranationalists want "*Lietuva lietuvams*" (Lithuania for Lithuanians) despite the pluralism in society. Refusal of Lithuania and EU, US, Ukraine and Canada to support the UN resolution moved by Russia on 21 November 2014 for "Combating Glorification of Nazism, neo-Nazism and other practices that contribute to fuelling contemporary forms of racism, racial discrimination, xenophobia and related intolerance" (New Cold War.org Nov 21, 2015) denotes the western support for glorification of neo-Nazism and Nazi perpetrators and collaborators in some of the new EU members like Ukraine, Baltic states and Poland.

Anti-Semitic contents appeared in the press. The main topics of these articles were the collaboration of Jews with the Communists in the Soviet period, Jews tarnishing Latvia's good name in the West, and Jewish businessmen striving to control the Latvian economy (Alster 2015). In 2004 a Lithuanian daily newspaper Respulika published anti-Semitic caricature in the front page depicting a globe and two individuals – one gay and the other a stereotypical crooked nosed Jewish individual –and posing the question: "who controls the world?" (Auers 2015: 152). A stage musical in October 2014 celebrating the life of Latvian Nazi mass murderer Herbert Cukurs, infamously known as 'Butcher of Riga,' for his crimes against Jews in Riga ghetto is an anti-Semitic expression which Israel Foreign Ministry "strongly condemned" (Yashar 2014). An Estonian museum exhibition mocking the Holocaust, using phrases such as genocide is even entertainment, and there was humour in the gas chamber experience, was highly provocative event which created a huge controversy (Alster 2015).

Desecration of museums and vandalism are incidents occurring in the Baltic states frequently. Every year on 16 March, the Remembrance day of the Latvian legionnaires, Waffen SS organises march in central Riga. On 16 February on Independence Day neo-Nazis organize march in Lithuania. Street names are there in the capital city for honouring the Nazi collaborators of Holocaust (Auers 2015). The governments commemorate the Nazi collaborators. Baltic governments are eager to punish Soviet war criminals but as of now they failed to punish Baltic perpetrators of Holocaust. Such double standards demonstrate the moral bankruptcy of Baltic democracies. As Yiddish scholar Dovid Katz points out, "We have to say that the support of Hitler and rewriting history to turn Hitler into a liberator of this area is not a western value..." "If you're repatriating Nazi war criminals to be re-buried and honored as part of national history, that is not behaviour compatible with western ethics and values." (Alster 2015).

In the Baltic states 22,800 Jews were there in 2001. Among those 12,300 were in Latvia, 7,500 in Lithuania and 3,000 in Estonia. At that time around thirty five Jewish organizations were functioning in Baltic states. Those organizations aimed at Jewish education, preservation of Jewish culture and traditions, commemoration of Holocaust, combating anti-Semitism and helping the poor (*Defending History* 6 March 2013). But now how Jewish citizens feel about their safety in the newly independent Baltic states is important. Jewish community expressed fears about their security and safety in these countries. Across the Baltic states of Latvia, Lithuania and Estonia, Jewish leaders say their communities are feeling increasingly uncomfortable as anti-Semitism once again appears to be increasing. In its report about Latvia, The European Commission against Racism and Intolerance (ECRI) observed increasing anti-Semitic discourse, "particularly on the Internet, for instance in the context of commemorations of the Second World War events and the debate around the issue of the draft law on compensations for confiscated properties" (Alster 2015).

Zvi Gitelman identifies several tactics being used to downplay historical anti-Semitism and Holocaust such as denial or ignoring Holocaust, denial of participation, reinterpretation of collaboration with the Nazis as a national liberation struggle against Soviet communism and diluting the genocide of Jews as just a large scale loss of life (Porat and Stauber, 2002). Daunis Auers (2015: 152) points out that the incidents of anti-Semitism exist in all three Baltic states; although not severe but at times certain disturbing incidents such as occasional attacks on holocaust memorials and Jewish monuments, anti-Semitic media editorials, etc. occur (European Commission against Racism and Intolerance 2012). The US State Department report of 2005 observed manifestations of intolerance, xenophobia, racism and anti-Semitism in three Baltic states of Estonia, Latvia and Lithuania in the form of expressions of incitement of hatred, events of commemorations, incidents of desecration of cemeteries, vandalism, and anti-Semitic graffiti and remarks, sending anonymous anti-Semitic proclamations to state institutions, and so on. Such expressions are basically of the sort of ideologically and politically motivated anti-Semitism favouring historical revisionism rather than the old racial and homophobic kind. But it creates a climate of hate towards and distrust on Jews (Gitelman 2013: 225).

Jewish communities responded and criticised government policies for the failure of governments to confront the bloody Holocaust history. Prague declaration invited worldwide criticism and even members of European parliaments criticised it. Jewish organizations in Baltic states and Israel sent protest notes. A Seventy Years Declaration "that recognises the unique dimensions of Nazism and the Holocaust" is proposed (http://www.seventyyearsdeclaration.org). A conference on Holocaust debates held in Vilnius University in April 2015 organized by Rūta Vanagaitė calls for an honest debate on all sides of the history.

Conclusion

In the modern Jewish history Holocaust remains as the most significant event and one of the most brutal genocides humanity has ever known. Baltic states experienced the crimes against humanity under Nazi German and Soviet occupations during Second World War. Although approximately six million Jews in Europe were murdered by the Nazis, Baltic countries were the only place in Europe where 90-95 percent of the Jews were exterminated. Mass murder in such a large scale happened due to the active local collaboration with the Nazis. Today, nation building politics in Baltic states gives the impression that they predominantly intend to depict the three nations as complete "victims" of Soviet occupation by adopting "two genocide theory" in order to whitewash the dark spot in their own history. The minimizing of Holocaust remains at the centre of politics as a contested issue related to the larger issues of identity and minorities with internal and external dimensions.

The narrative of blaming Russia and her President Vladimir Putin as responsible for the Baltic vulnerability due to which they are forced to depend on NATO, US and EU for security guarantee is part of the "return to Europe/west" identity politics. The current anti-Russian stance seems to have its roots in Hitler's conspiracy against the Jews for Bolshevism, i.e., the "Judeo-Bolshevism" propaganda. The on-going government sponsored projects of minimization of Holocaust and glorification of Nazi collaborators reflects revisionism. Far-right nationalism and commemoration practices led to the rise of anti-Semitism in contemporary Baltic states. Nation building by simultaneously following two irreconcilable political goals of sympathising with both victims and perpetrators for historical reasons contradict with their claim of orientation to principles and norms of western liberal democracy. The paradoxical attempts to hide their own crimes by using Soviet crimes as an excuse for Holocaust falsification or ultra-nationalism calls into question the evolving democratic system in Baltic states in the 21st century. As Lithuanian Philosopher Leonidas Donskis expressed, the question of "who is suffering the most?" and the sense of fragility and vulnerability looms large in the Baltic consciousness in "coming to terms with the past."

Notes

1. It is also undeniable that a few humanistic ethnic Lithuanians by risking their lives helped Jews to escape.
2. This definition has been removed from the EU website later on.
3. It was Napoleon Bonaparte who named Vilnius the *Jerusalem of the North*. Vilnius was probably the first and only "Jewish city" Napoleon would ever see where a rich Jewish culture and traditions flourished. Therefore, "Napoleon named Vilnius 'Jerusalem of the North'" (*Vilnews: The Voice of International Lithuania*, 9 January 2011). The existence of mythical Yddishland emerged under the influence of Jewish language, Yiddish. There was a proverb about Yiddishland, "To earn a living, go to Lodz, Warsaw, or Odessa, but to gain wisdom, go to Vilnius" (Leva 2011).
4. The Pale of Settlement was the Western region of Imperial Russia to which Jews were restricted by the Tsarist Ukase of 1792. It consisted of the territories of former Polish-Lithuanian Commonwealth, annexed with the existing numerous Jewish population, and the Crimea (which was later cut out from the Pale).

References

Alster, Paul. (12 March 2015), "Jews in Baltics fear creep of anti-Semitism", *Fox News*, retrieved from http://www.foxnews.com/world/2015/03/12/jews-in-baltics-fear-creep-anti-semitism/

Arad, Yitzhak. (2004), "The Murder of the Jews in German-Occupied Lithuania (1941–1944)", in Alvydas Nikzentaitis, Stefan Schreiner and Darius Staliunas eds., *The Vanished World of Lithuanian Jews*, Amsterdam: Radopi B. V., pp. 175-204

Arad, Yitzhak. (2009), *The Holocaust in the Soviet Union*, Lincoln: University Nebraska Press and Jerusalem: Yad Vashem.

Arad, Yitzhak. (2011), "Popular Collaboration in Baltic States: Between Evasion and Facing a Burdensome Past", in Roni Stauter ed. (2011), *Collaboration with the Nazis: Public Discourse after the Holocaust*, London: Routledge, pp. 53-68.

Archdeacon, Talis Saule. (25 April 2007). "European Parliament passes genocide law, rejects Baltic demands", *The Baltic Times*, retrieved from http://www.baltictimes.com/news/articles/17737/

Aasland, Aadne (2002) "Citizenship status and social exclusion in Estonia and Latvia," *Journal of Baltic Studies*, 33(1): 57-77.

Auers, Daunis. (2015), *Comparative Politics and Government of the Baltic States: Estonia, Latvia and Lithuania in the 21st Century*, London: Palgrave Macmillan.

Beller, Steven. (2007), *A Short Introduction to Anti-Semitism* (Oxford: Oxford University Press.

Eidintas, Alfonsas (2000), "A Jew-Communist Stereotype in Lithuania, 1940-1991," retrieved from www.tspmi.vu.lt/wp-content/uploads/2017/11/2000.pdf, pp. 1-36.

European Forum on Antisemitism, (2012), "Working Definition of Antisemitism", retrieved from http://www.european-forum-on-antisemitism.org/working-definition-of-antisemitism/english/.

European Commission against Racism and Intolerance, (21 February 2012), *ECRI Report on Latvia*, retrieved from https://www.coe.int/t/dghl/monitoring/ecri/Country-by-country/Latvia/LVA-CbC-IV-2012-003-ENG.pdf.

Gitelman, Zvi. (2013), "Comparative and Competitive Victimization in the Post-Communist Sphere", in Alvin H. Rosenfeld, ed., *Resurgent Antisemitism: Global Perspectives*, Bloomington: Indiana University Press, 215-235.

Greenbaum, Masha (1995), *The Jews of Lithuania: A History of a Remarkable Community, 1316-1945*, Jerusalem: Gefen publishing House Ltd.

Gurin-Loov, Eugenia, Gennadi Garmberg, and Eesti Juudi Kogukond. (2001), *Jewish Community of Estonia,* Tallinn: 2001, retrieved from http://eja.pri.ee/Community/Community_eng.pdf.

Hanebrink, Paul (2018), *A Specter Haunting Europe: The Myth of Judeo-Bolshevism*, Cambridge: The Belknap Press of Harvard University Press.

Israel Ministry of Foreign Affairs, (23 October 2013), "A Working Definition of Holocaust Denial and Distortion", retrieved from http://mfa.gov.il/MFA/ForeignPolicy/AntiSemitism/Pages/Working-Definition-of-Holocaust-Denial-and-Distortion.aspx

Kattago, Siobhan (2015), "Introduction: Memory Studies and its Companions", in Siobhan Kattago ed. (2015), *Ashgate Research Companion to Memory Studies*, Farnham: Ashgate Publishing Ltd., pp. 1-22.

Katz, Dovid. (2009), "On Three Definitions: Genocide; Holocaust Denial; Holocaust Obfuscation", in Leonid Donskis, ed., *The Litmus Test Case of Modernity: Examining Modern Sensibilities and the Public Domain in Baltic States at the Turn of the Century*, Bern: Peter Lang AG, 259-278.

Katz, Dovid. (30 September 2010), "Why Red is not Brown in the Baltics", *The Guardian*, retrieved from http://www.theguardian.com/commentisfree/cifamerica/2010/sep/30/baltic-nazi-soviet-snyder.

Katz, Dovid. (2017). "The Extraordinary Recent History of Holocaust Studies in Lithuania", *Dapim: Studies on the Holocaust*, December, 31(3): 285-295.

Laserson, Max M. (1941) "The Jewish Minorities in the Baltic Countries", *Jewish Social Studies*, July, 3(3): 273-284.

"Latvia unveils monument to Nazi butchers", *Pravda*, 18 September 2012, retrieved from http://english.pravda.ru/news/world/18-09-2012/122194-latvia_waffen_ss_monument-0/

Leva, "Vilnius: Jerusalem of the North – The Center of Litvak Culture, Religion and Art", *Litvakes*, 4 April 2011, retrieved from http://litvaks-lithuanian-jewish.com/vilnius-jerusalem-of-the-north/.

Levin, Dov. (2000), *The Litvaks: A Short History of Jews in Lithuania*, Oxford: Berghahn Books.

——— (28 May 2008), "Disinformation and Antisemitism: Holocaust Denial in the Baltic States, 1945-1999", retrieved from http://www.hagalil.com/archiv/2008/05/denial.htm

Liedy, Amy Shannon. (7 March 2011), "Holocaust Revisionism, Ultranationalism, and the Nazi/Soviet "Double Genocide" Debate in Eastern Europe", retrieved from http://www.wilsoncenter.org/event/holocaust-revisionism-ultranationalism-and-the-nazisoviet-double-genocide-debate-eastern.

"Lithuanian president pays tribute to WWII victims" (8 May 2015), *Delfi* (Vilnius), retrieved from http://en.delfi.lt/lithuania/society/lithuanian-president-pays-tribute-to-wwii-victims.d?id=67920764

MacShane, Denis. (2008), *Globalizing Hatred: The New Antisemitism*, London: Weidenfeld & Nicolson.

New Cold War.org (21 November 2015), "Canada, U.S. and Ukraine vote no, Europe abstains, on UN resolution condemning racism and neo-Nazism" retrieved from https://www.newcoldwar.org/canada-us-and-ukraine-vote-no-europe-abstains-on-un-resolution-condemning-racism-and-neo-nazism/

Office Of The UN Special Adviser On The Prevention Of Genocide (OSAPG), (2010), "OSAPG Analysis of Framework of Legal Definition of Genocide", retrieved from http://www.un.org/en/preventgenocide/adviser/pdf/osapg_analysis_framework.pdf

Pettai, Eva-Clarita. (2015), "Interaction Between History and Memory: Historical Truth Commissions and Reconciliation", in Siobhan Kattago ed. (2015), *Ashgate Research Companion to Memory Studies*, Farnham: Ashgate Publishing Ltd., pp. 237-250.

Pettai, Eva-Clarita and Vello Pettai. (2015), *Transitional and Retrospective Justice in Baltic States*, Cambridge: Cambridge University Press.

Porat, Dina and Roni Stauber eds., (2002), *Antisemitism Worldwide, 2000/1*, Lincoln: University of Nebraska Press.

Press, Bernhard. (2000), *The Murder of the Jews in Latvia, 1941-1945* (translated from German by Laimdota Mazzarins), Illinois: North Western University Press.

Rosenfeld, Alvin H. (2013), "Introduction", in Alvin H. Rosenfeld, ed (2013), *Resurgent Antisemitism: Global Perspectives,* Bloomington: Indiana University Press, 1-7.

Rushke, Richard. (2013), *Useful Enemies: John Demjanjuk and America's Open Door Policy for Nazi War Criminals,* New York: Delphium Books.

Segel, Zvi. (1988), "Jewish Minorities in the Baltic Republics in the Interwar years", *Journal of Baltic Studies*, 19 (1): 60-66.

Senate of the Parliament of the Czech Republic, (3 June 2008), "Prague Declaration on European Conscience and Communism", Prague, retrieved from http://www.praguedeclaration.eu/

Smirnov, V. (2015), "The Role of Political Elites in the Development of the Politics of Memory in the Baltic States" *Baltic region*", 2 (24): 58—72. Retrieved from https://journals.kantiana.ru/upload/iblock/752/Smirnov_58-72.pdf

Sutton, Karen. (2008), *The Massacre of Jews of Lithuania*, Jerusalem: Gefen Publishing House.

Tamm, Marek (2013), "In search of lost time: memory politics in Estonia, 1991–2011", *Nationalities Papers*, 41 (4): 651-674.

"The Seventy Years Declaration: Defending Truth in History", retrieved from http://www.seventyyearsdeclaration.org/

United States Holocaust Memorial Museum, (20 June 2014), "Introduction to Holocaust", *The Holocaust Encyclopaedia*, retrieved from http://www.ushmm.org/wlc/en/article.php?ModuleId=10005143

US State Department. (5 January 2005), *Report on Global Anti-Semitism*, retrieved from http://www.state.gov/j/drl/rls/40258.htm

Vilnews: The Voice of International Lithuania, 9 January 2011, retrieved from http://vilnews.com/2011-01-napoleon-named-vilnius-%E2%80%98jerusalem-of-the-north%E2%80%99.

"Vilnius Street Name Proposed for Rescuer Out in Boondocks; But Please Remove Nazi Collaborators from City Center!", *Defending History*, 6 March 2013, retrieved from http://defendinghistory.com/vilnius-street-name-proposed-for-rescuer-please-remove collaborators-street-names/50532

Weiss-Wendt, Anton. (2008), "Thanks to the Germans! Jewish cultural autonomy in interwar Estonia", *East European Jewish Affairs*, April, 38 (1): 89-104.

Weiss-Went, Anton. (2010), "Why the Holocaust Does not Matter to Estonians", in Marko Lehti and JorgHackmann eds., *Contested and Shared Places of Memory: History and Politics in the Northern Europe*, Oxon: Routledge.

Yad Vashem (5 August 2016), "The Kovno Garage Massacre - Lithuanian nationalists clubbing Jewish Lithuanians to death, 1941", retrieved from https://rarehistoricalphotos.com/kovno-garage-massacre-lithuania-1941/

Yahil, Leni. (1990), *The Holocaust: The Fate European Jewry, 1932-1945*, Oxford: Oxford University Press.

Yashar, Ari. (23 October 2014), *Israel Condemns Latvia's 'Butcher of Riga' Musical*, retrieved from http://www.israelnationalnews.com/News/News.aspx/186521

Zisere, Bella. (2005), "Jewish Community in Post-Communist Latvia," *European Judaism: A Journal for the New Europe*, Autumn, 38(2): 82-98.

Zuroff, Efraim. (2005), "Eastern Europe: Antisemitism in the Wake of Holocaust-Related Issues", *Jewish Political Studies Review*, Spring, 17(1-2): 63-79.

Chapter Ten

Ethnicity, Exclusion and Minority Rights in Baltic States: The Case of Jewish Community in Lithuania

Anju Devi

Introduction

After regaining independence from the former Soviet Union in 1991, Baltic states of Estonia, Latvia, and Lithuania began their nation building process according to the values and norms of western liberal democracy. The nations are defined in these countries on the basis of history, memory, ethnicity and language. Historical legacy and collective memory have become the core elements of national identity formation. Baltic states experienced both Soviet occupation and Nazi German Holocaust during the Second World War, The Baltic political leadership equates the Holocaust with Soviet occupation and brought the narrative that they had experienced two "equal genocides". This narrative in effect leads to trivialization of memory of Holocaust experienced by the Jewish population, as a national minority. In Baltic states the "victims of genocide" is dominantly applied to Stalinist terror, and the local collaboration in Holocaust is not addressed adequately. The Jews were treated as Bolshevik communist supporters and thereby, facilitators of Soviet invasion and occupation. Therefore, this chapter tries to explore the politics centred on Holocaust memory in nation building process in Baltic states by taking the Jewish community in Lithuania as a case in point.

National Identity Formation: Ethnicity, Exclusion and Minority Rights

After 1991, politics of memory, historical justice and preservation of culture of titular ethnic identity became important nation building instruments in the Baltic states, there exist difference in interpretation of Soviet history between Russo phone Jewish minority and Baltic titular ethnic majority. While Russian speakers view Soviet occupation as a positive thing in terms of jobs, social welfare and industrialization, the ethnic Balts view Soviet past as occupation and show themselves as victims of Soviet occupation and oppression. They defined the nationhood on ethnic lines. This led to exclusionary policies of citizenship and language laws depriving the Russian speakers of political, economic and social rights, especially in Estonia and Latvia, in Lithuania citizenship policies are not exclusionary. Foreign policies are also based on historical narrative of occupation, collective memory and ethno-national identity in order to distance from Russia and be closer to Europe (Usha 2015: 74).

The Different identity and memory narratives were perceived as hostile and antagonistic acts. Russian immigrants are viewed as instruments of Soviet oppression and a potential fifth column to be used by revanchist Russia, in the "self other dichotomy of national identity construction, Russian speakers which also include Jews are treated as the aggressive other" (Usha 2015: 73). In this definition, "language, culture and territorial homeland have become important features of belonging to the nation; state is seen as an aspect of national identity and as an instrument of preserving the Baltic ethnic majority nationality's language and culture. The discrimination experienced under Soviet occupation based on Molotov-Ribbentrop Treaty of 1939 has been emphasized as the core of defining national identity, citizenship and security return to Europe west narrative of political elites highlighting the small size and vulnerability of these nations as they are situated on the periphery of the former Soviet empire and sharing direct boundary with mighty Russia, their potential enemy and therefore NATO and the EU should come for their security against threat from Russia" (Usha 2015: 73).

The Baltic majority nationality's perception about Jewish minorities is that they were equal to communists or closely associated with Soviet occupiers. It is dominantly perceived that Jews were partially responsible for the killings and mass deportation of Lithuanians to Siberia during Soviet occupation. Therefore, a few may view that the Jews deserve punishment. This is the basis of putting pressure by many groups for equating Holocaust with Soviet terror. "The groups pushing for the equation of the two are often the direct heirs of the very nationalist groups, for example, Latvians, Lithuanians, and Estonians, who cooperated with the Nazis in the annihilation of the Jews, by equating the two and asserting that the core of the Communist party was comprised of Jews, they are suggesting that what happened to the Jews was, in some fashion, a deserved punishment" (Usha 2015: 75). Lithuanian government pursues a politics of restrictive citizenship towards minorities. Thus, prejudiced attitude towards Jews is transformed into a political and ideological anti-Semitism; such attitude can lead to their social exclusion and deprivation of their rights as a minority community. (Usha 2015: 75).

Jewish Community in Lithuania: Historical Background

Jews have a history of more than 700 years as an inseparable part of Baltic society.

Jewish settlements were said to have found in Lithuania as early as eighth century. Historian Abraham Elijahu Harkavi believed that "the Jews came to Lithuania in the ninth and eighth centuries from Babylonia" (Masha 1995: 75). The first Jewish settlements in Lithuania appeared in the 12th century. They came from southern Europe as merchants (Levin 2001: 6). The Jewish population played a prominent role in social and political sphere of the Baltic states. In the 14th century, they were invited by Gediminas, Grand Duke (ruler) of the Lithuania to settle in that area (Voren 2011: 23). Vytautas, Gediminas's grandson granted Jews many privileges such as religious freedom and protection of individuals and property to Jews in the 15th century. During his reign the size of Jewish community increased considerably. By the 16th century Poland-Lithuania became a new cultural centre of Jews in Europe. Litvak, the Lithuanian Jews, established their communities throughout the western part of Grand Dutchy and Jewish life flourished in Lithuania (O'Connor 2015: 32).

Figure 9: Monument of Vytautas the Great in Kaunas

Grand Duke Vytautas/Vytautas the Great (1350-1430) was one of the most distinguished rulers in the history of Lithuania. He was the ruler of Grand Dutchy of Lithuania from 1392-1340. Under his rule Lithuania became the largest kingdom in Europe in the 15th century, stretching from Baltic to Black Sea. In today's modern Lithuania Vytautas the Great stands as the symbol of national pride, people's unity, freedom and prosperity.

Photo by: K. B. Usha

However, permanent settlements appeared only in the 18th century when Lithuania was under the Russian Empire. The Jewish community of Lithuania was known as Litvaks. They developed in all spheres over the centuries and became an integral part of Lithuanian society. Vilnius in those days was known as the "Jerusalem of the North" (Leva 2014: 3). Jewish community contributed to the national intellectual and cultural tradition of Lithuania and enriched the country's economy, culture, science, and education.

Until 1940, this area was safe and secure for them from the brutality and discrimination. In 1940 the emergence of ethnic violence as a reaction against perceived Jewish involvement in Soviet state. These incidents made an unsolvable split between Baltic nationalities and Jewish population, it happened again in the 1980s. In this decade, the rise of Baltic nationalism filled a disappointment within the Jewish population. The decades of 1980s and 1940s, have been challenging for Baltic national movements which were trying to create 'a guiltless national consciousness'. Lieven (1993) nicely summed up one of such incident; the construction of Jewish monuments in Vilnius would remind people of a different truth and could have implications for the whole Lithuanian view of its national past. Baltic area has a total of 8 million people out of which 5 millions belongs to 'titular' nationalities. These three nationalities have played a pivotal role in bringing down the Soviet, as a consequence to this, they have engrossed substantial amount of attention from politicians, journalists, scholars and diplomats (Voren 2011: 23).

Even though there is a common tendency among outsiders to see these three groups as the same, in fact they have different cultures and histories. The Estonians speak the language of Ugro Finnic origin. Latvians and the Lithuanians speak what they call as Baltic languages. The Lithuanians share much of the history with Russians and Poles. Latvians and Estonians share the history of the German and Swedish. World Wars brought them together into the category of Baltic states. They were the 'Baltic Republics' under the Soviet authority. The Soviet authorities tried hard to keep them from forming an alliance. In the events of the last six years they tried to cooperate closely. However in the words of historian Andrejs Plakans, "several years later, with independence in hand, the countries are not stressing the Baltic theme as much as they used to" (Voren 2011: 27).

Holocaust and Local Collaboration in Lithuania

Lithuania was a country which did not pursue any anti-Semitic state policies before the Second World War. But, historical prejudices against Jews among the masses were already prevalent in Lithuania in the 1920s and 1930s. Stereotyped and prejudiced imagination prevalent in the consciousness of Lithuanians was that Jews use the blood of Christian babies for their rituals. Such acts of Jews that ended up in political trials or manifestations explicitly describe Jewry as a clandestine and treacherous force (Donskis 2009: 10).

In Lithuania two differently parallel cultures, Jewish and Lithuania existed and it was a multiethnic national society. In Lithuania anti-Semitism should be stressed that exclusion and alienation became the fate of Jewish throughout Central and

Eastern Europe Including Lithuania (Donskis 2009: 11). During the 17th and 18th centuries the relation between the Jews and non-Jews as well as between the Jews community and influential Catholic Church in the Lithuanian-polish Republic developed in the sector of economy and intertwined with growing religious intolerance (Vareikis 1941: 2).

Jews community and Lithuanians lived in isolated and distant social and cultural world, as a result, developed negative stereotypes sentiments to each other. Presumably this gap between Jews and Lithuanians was one of the major factors that facilitated the rise of mutual suspicion and anti-Semitism that violently exploded in the mid-twentieth century (Balkelis 2010: 49). Lithuanian society was strictly Catholic, and it was the Catholic Church that was the main driving force behind the popular belief that the Jews had not only killed Jesus Christ and needed to be punished for that (Vareikis 1941: 2). Moreover the myth also that the Jews maintained the ritual of using fresh blood of Christian children in preparing matzos, often intensified anti-Semitism (Jones 2011: 236).

Public Discourse on Holocaust in Post-Soviet Lithuania

Almost 95 percent of Jews were exterminated in the Holocaust that took place with the active local Lithuanian participation and collaboration with German Nazis (Voren 2011: 19). Such a scale of mass murder did not happen anywhere else in Europe. It is also true that Lithuanians had undergone repression under Soviet rule. However, despite accepting the gravity of Soviet terror, the experience of Holocaust and Soviet occupation cannot be equated. The Holocaust is considered as the biggest crime against humanity the Europe or the world had ever witnessed. But, the Lithuanian political elites' narrative of "two parallel genocides" equating both Holocaust and Soviet occupation has become a political ideology in Lithuania in the attempt of earning international prestige. The state sponsored strategies are criticised as often involved in the politics of "fixing Holocaust" through a "double genocide" politics (Voren 2011: 19). The politics of "double genocide", i.e. establishing the symmetry between Nazi and Communist crimes was strong in Lithuania (Zuroff 2010: 1) and could be seen as an attempt of distortion and falsification of history of holocaust experience of the Baltic Jewish community by minimizing or hiding the role played by the Lithuanian Nazi collaborators in the execution of Jews.

Anti-Semitism refers to injustice against Jews as individuals and as a group. This discrimination has a long and dark history in mainly the Christian lands of Europe, marked by expulsions forced conversion to Christianity, and massacres. Anti-Semitism based on many stereotypes that target Jews as a member of the group, their religious faiths, and beliefs (Brustein and King 2004: 35-53). It is a social phenomenon against Jews and represents a special phase of the group conflict

(Reich 1945: 294-302).A European Union working definition of anti-Semitism is given in the Fundamental Rights Research (FRA) wing that is applicable to Lithuania as one of the EU members. EU defines, "Anti-Semitism is a certain perception of Jews, which may be expressed as hatred toward Jews. Rhetorical and physical manifestations of Anti-Semitism are directed toward Jewish or non-Jewish individuals and/or their property, toward Jewish community institutions and religious facilities" (Reich 1945: 294-302).

Baltic peoples felt what, in the words of Alfred Kaarmann, one resistor in Estonia, who expressed his views about the Nazis and Soviets to the BBC: "The difference between them was that the Germans enslaved us and took our land. But the Russians destroyed the Estonian nation. They opposed and still oppose Estonian independence." The toll on the Baltic states was substantial. Timothy Snyder (2009) included the Baltic states in the region he dubbed the "Blood lands", not just for the toll of the war and three waves of foreign occupation, but also for the devastation wrought by the Holocaust, other mass killing policies undertaken by the Soviets and Nazis, and massive displacement.

Estonia, the only country to be declared "free of Jews" after its 4,000 Jews were deported by the Soviets during the initial occupation, killed in the Holocaust, or escaped with Soviet troops during their retreat, was deeply affected, but it was by no means the worst. It was reported that between 1940 and 1945, the Estonian population seems to have declined by large numbers. This was terrible, the "demographic consequences of Stalinism in peacetime proved even more devastating to the population of Estonia than the upheavals of Second World War," By comparison, half of the people in Belarus were killed or displaced during the war (Stevick 2012: 89).

Legal Protection for Minorities in the Baltic States

Linguistic minorities faces serious problem in all Baltic states. There has been much controversy over the law passed in post-Soviet period, which declared national language as the official language. The Baltic states have been at the forefront of this controversy because they have faced the issue of linguistic minorities and enacted some strong laws to promote the national languages. In the USSR, linguistic origins were usually an important part of ethnic identity. In the Baltic states also, language was always closely linked to ethnicity. However, in all states, customs and traditions played a larger role in ethnic identification than language. Soviet linguist groups never recognized this reality and insisted that even in these states, language was always a key factor in ethnic identification. In keeping with Marxist theory, the leaders of the Soviet Union from Stalin to Gorbachev maintained that "linguistic identity" paves the way for changes in "ethnic identity." As Kozlov notes, "The importance of the community of language for general economic, political and other spheres of human activity is very great. Groups of individuals, who change languages usually, in the long-term, also change their ethnic identity," (Sonia Bychkov Green 1997: 57).

The laws in the Baltic states also do not violate international law. International law extends its protections to various kinds of minorities, including ethnic, racial, and, in some cases, linguistic minorities. Article 1(3) of the UN Charter states that it is the aim of the United Nations to "encourage respect for human rights and for fundamental freedoms for all without distinctions as to race, sex, language, or religion" Both the Universal Declaration of Human Rights and the International Covenant on Economic, Social and Cultural Rights provide freedom from discrimination on the basis of language. The UN General Assembly also passed a resolution aimed at protecting the rights of ethnic, religious, and linguistic minorities (Wright 1999: 605-629). However, it is a widely accepted norm in international law that states are free to establish their own laws on citizenship.

The strongest arguments against the laws of the Baltic states have been arguments stressing potential human rights violations. One immediate response to this criticism is that the citizenship and language laws of the Baltic states have been reviewed by the UN, the Council of Europe, the European Commission, and CSCE delegations. The reviewers have consistently found that the legislation does not violate human rights standards. For example, a European human rights study found that Lithuanian rules on citizenship did not violate any international standards. In fact, even after Lithuania's independence, over forty thousand Russians immigrated to Lithuania. Moreover, the Baltic states, unlike the Soviet Union, have tried to protect linguistic minorities as much as they could. All three states have enacted legislation to protect linguistic minorities. The Latvian language law was even found to grant a sufficient allowance for Russian as a second language and to give extensive facilities to Russian-speakers. During the time of Soviet occupation, the international community argued that the Baltic groups and their culture and languages deserved protection (Green 1997: 220-271).

In 1991, Estonian and Latvian adopted citizenship act according to which all the residents who had been citizens since 16 June 1940 and their family had their citizenship rights restored. This restoration meant that all post-war settlers and their descendants, about 740,000 inhabitants of Latvia and 500,000 of Estonia, overnight became outsiders or aliens in Estonia's terminology (Muiznieks, et. al, 2013: 288-308). Accordingly, these non-citizens could not participate in the first post-independence parliamentary elections took place in 1992, and 1993 in Estonia and Latvia respectively. Thus, legal means were used to weaken the political influence of post-war settlers and their descendants, who were left with three options: taking the citizenship of another country mostly Russia, naturalizing or remaining non-citizens or aliens. The Estonian authorities initially required all aliens to acquire temporary residence permits, implying the possibility that they could be revoked and that aliens would then lose their right to residency in Estonia. This generated significant fears among aliens about their status, and many acquired citizenship of the Russian Federation. In Latvia, a 1995 law granted non-citizens permanent residence rights automatically. However, on 1 May 2013, 122,746 persons in Estonia had citizenship of another country, of which 93,795 or 76.4 per cent were citizens of the Russian Federation. At the beginning of 2013, Latvia, by contrast, had only 66,188 foreign citizens, of which 43,586 (65.9 per cent) were citizens of the Russian Federation (Ibid).

In Estonia, naturalization began in 1992, while in Latvia not until 1995. Naturalization initially took place in Estonia according to the rather liberal provisions of the 1938 law on citizenship. More than half of all naturalizations (87,712 of 154,874) from 1992 to 2012 took place in the period 1992 through 1996. In a 1995 law, citizenship requirements were made stricter and all candidates had to pass a language examination, leading to a significant drop in naturalization rates. In 1994 Latvia adopted a citizenship law that implemented rather strict linguistic and other requirements; it also created a system of age brackets whereby a timetable was created in which different categories of non-citizens were allowed to submit applications depending on where and when they were born and arrived in Latvia. As a result of concerted arm-twisting by the EU, the Organization for Security and Cooperation in Europe (OSCE) and some member states, Latvian legislators proposed amendments to remove the system of age brackets that had limited the scope of those eligible to apply for citizenship, and to allow the possibility of registering stateless children born in Latvia without any examinations. The amendments were sufficiently controversial that they were put to a referendum in October 1998 in which the majority of citizens approved them. In December 1998, the Estonian parliament also amended its citizenship ac t to grant citizenship on easy terms to stateless children.

Despite the fact that some form of citizenship became accessible to almost all post-war settlers in Estonia and Latvia, many have not taken any steps to naturalize. Survey data of non-citizens suggest that the lack of inspiration to naturalize is the result of a combination of psychological barriers, like finding the process humiliating or considering that citizenship for them should be automatic, and linguistic concerns including being unable to pass the language examinations. Thus, at the start of 2013, Latvia had 297,883 non-citizens and Estonia had 90,533 aliens. While the latter have the right to vote in municipal elections, non-citizens in Latvia do not. However, both sets of non-citizens have internationally recognized travel documents and benefit from facilitated travel to Russia and the CIS countries. They also had social and economic rights as citizens, though Latvia has barred non-citizens from working in most civil service jobs in accordance with the Latvian State Civil Service Law. (Ibid)

"After the Soviet Union signed the Helsinki Final Act of 1975, committees began to develop all over the empire; the human rights provisions of the Helsinki agreement provided a legal status for struggle against the Soviet regime. The Lithuanian Helsinki Group (LHG) was established in 1976 (Miniotaite 2013: 19) Initially the committee comprised of experienced resistance activist Viktoras Petkus, priest Karolis Garuckas, the poet and former political prisoner Ona Lukauskiene-Poskiene, the poet Tomas Venclova, and the scientist Eitan Finkelstein, the group emphasized the legal and peaceful character of its activity we will neither support violent struggle, nor participate in it" (Miniotaite 2013: 17).

During this time so many people from Baltic states approached the group for help, "it seemed to be an almost official establishment for the protection of their rights, the LHG closely cooperated with the Moscow Helsinki Group, though it differed from being as much concerned with national rights as with individual rights. In its first manifesto, the LHG stressed that it sought the restoration of the independent Lithuanian state, as it existed before its illegal occupation by the Soviet army on 15 June 1940" (Miniotaite 2013: 17).

"However, strongly nationalist, the group was also concerned with violations of the rights of national minorities in Lithuania: Byelorussians, Germans, Jews, Tatars, and Karaites, in the first half year of its activity, the group issued some 20 documents, then persecution began Venclova was deprived of citizenship, Petkus and Balys Gajauskas were imprisoned, The average period of a member's activity before being arrested by the KGB was half a year, the Lithuanian Helsinki Group was destroyed with the arrests of leaders Vytautas Vaiciunasand Mecislovas Jurevicius, however, even after the functional end of the LHG, human rights activities (and arrests) continued. Letter writing and petition campaigns for political prisoners were launched in 1982 and 1984" (Miniotaite 2013: 17).

Anti-Semitism

Anti-Semitism emerged in the Baltic states as a result of hatred and prejudice against Jews prevalent among the Baltic masses. Anti-Semitism emerged in Europe since the 19th century and it had an impact in Baltic states. These countries were greatly influenced by the political developments that took place in Europe, especially in Germany. As far as the rise of anti-Semitism in modern Europe is concerned, the year 1899 to 1939 is commonly accepted as a highpoint (Brustein and King 2004: 36).

"This phenomenon can be analysed by examining the reactions in various countries to specific Holocaust-related issues that have emerged as central questions in Eastern Europe since the fall of Communism and the dismantlement of the Soviet Union. Lithuania, a democratic country, and a member of European Union and NATO, still closely following the policies of the government on Holocaust-related issues over the years, could not have failed to discern a deep-seated reluctance to honestly confront its Holocaust past and especially the extensive collaboration of local Nazi collaborators in the mass murder of Jews." Primarily inside Lithuania and its borders similar to other East European countries, Lithuania also followed almost the same path (Zuroff 2010: 8).

Zuroff wrote in *The Guardian* that "Lithuania has been the leader of an insidious campaign to try to distort the history of the Holocaust by seeking recognition that Communist crimes were just as terrible as those of the Nazis, This false equivalence would unjustly rob the Shoah of its universally-accepted uniqueness and historical significance, turning the worst case of genocide in human history into merely one of many tragedies" (*The Guardian* 29 November 2010). Lithuanian authorities very rhetorically had tried to equate the killing of Jews by Nazi Germany with crimes done by the communist regime.

However, there have certain efforts against the holocaust denial to punish the revisionists for the false premises of the issue. For instance, in 2010, the new right-wing government in Hungary passed a law that effectively criminalized the opinion that there was only one genocide in the region during Second World War, maximum jail-time for offenders: three years (Katz 2009: 8). He pointed out that this was rapidly followed by a similar law passed by the Lithuanian Parliament and signed by its president (with two years of maximum jail term). Momentum for this trend picked up in 2014 when a similar law was passed by the Latvian parliament (up to five years of imprisonment). Lithuanian young anti-fascists from Antifa Lietuva staged a march in Kaunas, protesting the glorification of the Lithuanian Activist Front, which unleashed murder upon Jewish citizens in 1941 in dozens of locations; the banner tells, "Real heroes rescued people instead of killing them. Remember the victims of the Holocaust" (*Katz 2009: 8).*

Response of State for the Protection of Jewish Minority

Minority rights have been having the strong protection by law and regulation. But, in these three countries, they were suffering from so many problems such as continuous exclusion and discrimination. Jewish Community was also excluded by the local Baltic people, and they faced the Holocaust during Second World War. When the Nazis broke off the alliance and invaded territories held by the Soviet Union, they had good reason to mislead the Baltic peoples about their ultimate intentions.

Entrance of the Memorial Site

A Memorial Monument

Jewish Memorial

Polish Memorial

Russian Memorial

Soviet Memorial

Figure 10: Poneriai Holocaust Memorial Complex

The Paneriai or Ponary was the site of mass murder of up to 100,000 people by German SD and SS and their Lithuanian collaborators during Second World War. Around 70,000 Jews, 20,000 Poles, and 8,000 Soviet Prisoners of War were murdered at Paneriai. The murders took place between July 1941 and August 1944 near the railway station at Paneriai, a suburb of today's Vilnius, Lithuania. Source: http://military.wikia.com/wiki/Ponary_massacre

Photos by: K. B. Usha

If people in the Baltic states believed that supporting the German forces offered the best opportunity to regain independence from the Soviets, they were more likely to enlist and perhaps more likely to act in consonance with the Nazis' racial ideology. Indeed, one of the most difficult issues for the Baltic states has been the degree of complicity of the Baltic nationals in the persecution of their Jewish minorities.

The Nazis' ultimate ambitions, however, encompassed more than the Jewish residents of the region. According to *Generalplan Ost* (GPO), the Nazis anticipated and intended the elimination of 50 million people in the western Soviet Union, a toll that would have included most of the Baltic peoples (Snyder 2009). These ambitions are not well-known in the Baltic states. Those Baltic nationals who enlisted in German units are often depicted today as freedom fighters and national heroes (Stevick 2012: 89).

Estonia and Latvia have two types of minority participation. First, active political participation of minorities considered indicator of stable democracy. Second, low level of participation is belonging to disaffection with the political process and the political system. Disaffection and disengagement from the political process have been explained because of non-responsive political institutions; that persistently do not reflect minority preferences. Where political systems are not open and responsive, people of the country do not feel that the system reflects their needs and demands (Regemann 2014: 1-18).

In Latvia, some tensions emerged in 2012, when in a referendum the use of the Russian language was granted as second state language. While Latvian people interpreted this referendum as a challenge to their ethnic identity, Russian people rallied for political representation and inclusion about political and social issues at the national level. Russian people collected signatures for the referendum to be prepared by the state. Support for the referendum was seen by the Latvian political institutions as a clear sign of disloyalty to the state and this further reinforced ethnic cleavage. This allowed for the Latvian part of those who were eligible to cast their votes in the referendum to represent their issues. This referendum was later used by opportunistic majority political elites to justify the Latvian Constitution as the sole bearer not only of the statehood but also of democracy in the country (Agarin 2016: 81-99).

Conclusion

The history of Jewish community owes certain linkages with Baltic states as these countries have been home for the Jews since centuries. In the entire Eastern Europe, Lithuania became the most important country as far as the Jewish community is concerned. With the passage of time the Jewish community became an integral part of the Lithuanian society. Jews in Lithuania has tremendously contributed to the development of the country's economy, culture and education. However, the intensity of the problems faced by the Jews remains a significant issue even till today. The question of amalgamation and the coexistence of the Jewish community with the indigenous Lithuanians paved the way for the emergence of a new issue linked with the identity. The devastating impact of holocaust on the Jewish community in Lithuania made their life miserable and they are still struggling for their life and justice and making efforts to establish their own identity in the Lithuanian society. The approach of Lithuanians toward the Jews and the growing anti-Semitist feelings pose a serious challenge to the entire Jewish community in the contemporary Lithuanian society. The reaction of the state to these problems is another most challenging factor that needs to be studied.

The life has been difficult for the Jews both in past and present times. The adversary policies against the Jews continued even today. Even before the disintegration of the Soviet Union and the Independence of Lithuania, the Jewish community faced various discriminatory policies at different depths. Ever since Lithuania freed itself from Soviet occupation, the official position of Lithuania towards the Nazi war criminals and Soviet oppressors remained somewhat neutral which was later on supported by the majority of the Lithuanians. Even though the political culture of Lithuania since 1990 has been demonstrating a fresh political willingness to accommodate the diverse culture, things are however far more intricate as far the Jewish community is concerned.

The rise of anti-Semitism poses a serious threat to the existence of Jewish community in Baltic states in general and Lithuania in particular. Anti-Semites justify the holocaust of the Jews on basis of the collaboration of Jews with the Soviet authorities in 1940-1941. This approach culminated in justifying the assassination of Jews by the local population when the Nazi invasion occurred. The history of anti-Semitism in Lithuania has been inextricably linked with their historical existence in the country. Over the centuries, Lithuania had developed one of the most distinguished Jewish communities in Eastern Europe.

In the Lithuanian state, the issue of the Jewish identity, crucial for the discourse on heritage, is quite complex when it comes to definition. Starting in the fall of 2007, and even more so during 2008, the Lithuanian government began to intensify its efforts to challenge the accepted historical narrative of the Holocaust and to more actively deflect international criticism in response to its failings in addressing specific Holocaust- related issues. The primary problems in this regard were the government's abysmal failure to punish a single Lithuanian Holocaust perpetrator despite an abundance of potential suspects, and the continuing efforts of government leaders and officials to promote the canard of historical equivalency of Communist and Nazi crimes.

After the disintegration of Soviet Union, Lithuania emerged a democratic independent country. Even after the independence, the Jewish community has been discriminated and the growing anti-Semitism has remained unchecked. The Lithuanian state failed to manage the social harmony within the country despite the process of the state building based on democratic values and humanitarian traditions. There is a reluctance to bring those who committed Holocaust crimes to justice and less attention is shown towards the rise of anti-Semitism from the part of the state.

References

Agarin, Timofey (2016), "Extending the Concept of Ethnocracy: Exploring the Debate in the Baltic Context", *Cosmopolitan Civil Societies: An Interdisciplinary Journal*, 8 (3): 81-99.

Arad, Yitzhak (2009), *The Holocaust in the Soviet Union*, Jerusalem: Nebraska Press.

Brustein, William I., and Ryan D. King (2004), "Anti-Semitism in Europe before the Holocaust" *International Political Science Review*, 25 (1): 35-53.

Corney, Frederick (2012), "Dealing with the Past in the Baltic states", Russia's Periphery, Student Authored Website, January 2012. retrieved from http://russiasperiphery.blogs.wm.edu/baltic-states/

Donskis, Leonidas (2009), *Troubled Identity and the Modern World,* New York: Palgrave Macmillan Press.

Green, Sonia Bychkov (1997), "Language of Lullabies: the Russification and De-Russification of the Baltic states", *Michigan Journal of International Law* 219, 19 (1): 220-271.

Greenbaum, Masha (1995), *The Jews of Lithuania: A History of a Remarkable Community, 1316-1945*, Jerusalem: Gefen publishing House Ltd.

Katz, Dovid (2009), "*7 Kingdoms of the Litvaks*" International Cultural Program Center, Lithuania.

Leva (2014), "Vilnius: Jerusalem of the North – The Center of Litvak Culture, Religion and Art," *Litvakes*, 4 April 2011, retrieved from http://litvaks-lithuanian-jewish.com/vilnius-jerusalem-of-the-north/.

Levin, Dov (1990) "On the relations between the Baltic peoples and their Jewish neighbors before, during and after World War II", *Holocaust Genocide Studies*, 5 (1): 53-66.

Levin, Dov (2001), *The Litvaks: A Short History of Jews in Lithuania*, Jerusalem: Yad Vashem.

Lieven, Anatol (1993), Baltic Revolution: *Estonia*, Latvia, *Lithuania*and the Path to Independence, New Haven and London: *Yale* University Press.

Miniotaite, Grazina (2013), *Nonviolent Resistance in Lithuania: A Story of Peaceful Liberation*, the Albert Einstein Institution.

Muiznieks, Nils, Juris Rozenvalds, and Ieva Birka (July 2013), "Ethnicity and Social Cohesion in the post-Soviet Baltic states," *Patterns of Prejudice*, Taylor & Francis Online, 47 (3): 288-308.

O' Connor, Kevin (2015), *The History of the Baltic States,* Santa Barbara: ABC-CLIO, LLC

Regemann, Ada-Charlotte (2014), "Introduction – Minority Participation in Estonia and Latvia," *Journal on Ethnopolitics and Minority Issues in Europe*, 13 (1):1-18, retrieved from http://www.ecmi.de/fileadmin/downloads/publications/JEMIE/2014/Regelmann.pdf.

Reich, Nathan (1945), "Anti-Semitism", *Journal of Educational Sociology*, 18 (5): 294-302.

Senn, Alfred Erich (1994), "Race and Violence in Germany and Europe", *Contemporary European History* (Cambridge University Press), (3) 3: 315-330.

Snyder, Timothy (2009), *The Red Prince: the Fall of a Dynasty and the Rise of Modern Europe*, London: Random House.

Stevick, Doyle (2012), "The Holocaust in the Contemporary Baltic states: International Relations, Politics, and Education". retrieved from http://www.ceeol.com.

Truska, Liudas, and Vareikis, Vygantas (1941), "the Preconditions for the Holocaust; Anti-Semitism in Lithuania", 113-116.

Usha, K.B. (2015) Holocaust Revisionism and Revival of Anti-Semitism in Contemporary Baltic states, CSS Israel: FPRC New Delhi 72.

Voren, Robert van (2011), *Undigested past: the holocaust in Lithuania*, Amsterdam, New York: Rodopi Press.

Wright, Jane (1999), "Minority Groups, Autonomy, and Self-Determination", *Oxford Journal of Legal Studies* (Oxford University Press), 19 (4): 605-629.

Zuroff, Efraim (2010), *The Guardian*, 29 November 2010, retrieved from https://www.theguardian.com/commentisfree/cifamerica/2010/nov/.../holocaust- Lithuania.

Zuroff, Efraim (2012), "Lithuania 2012: Holocaust Distortion as Background for Increased Anti-Semitism" retrieved from: www.wiesenthal.

Chapter Eleven

Political Participation of Women in Post-Soviet Lithuania

Karamala Areesh Kumar

Introduction

Women are in position of minority in governing and public institutions compared to men throughout the world. Political power is considered as one of the most influenced factor for women's empowerment in the global level. Lithuanian women also do not have equal share in power structure. According to the population statistics of 2015, Lithuania's women population is estimated as 1,526,678 out of total population of 2,850,400. Women are not able to enjoy equal rights even though they dominate men being 53.2 percent of total population (Lithuanian Population Report: 2016). Lack of trust on the state institutions, trade unions and political parties is also one of the primary reasons for less representation of women. With an exception of the presidency, the other political representative institutions failed to gain the public trust. In Lithuania, less than one third of the population trusted in the parliament, courts, local governments and political parties. As Grybauskaite in her speech stated, "Lithuanian institutions and political parties became small Lithuanian duchies. Nearly 80 percent of the people in Lithuania no longer trust the political parties, politicians and public institutions (Grybauskaite: 2010).

Women's representation in Lithuanian politics is fluctuating since its initial independence. Several women representatives were elected for the parliament after the Russian revolution. Lithuanian women lost their political rights under the Soviet Union regime. Gorbachev's political reforms (*Glasnost*[1] *and Perestroika*[2]) allowed Lithuanian women to fight for their rights. Disintegration of Soviet Union, end of cold war, globalization, liberal market policies and women's movement throughout the world has shown major impact on Lithuania. Lithuania also adopted education and health policies for women's empowerment.

Lithuania regained its independence from the former Soviet Union in 1991. After independence, Lithuania began its political transition from authoritarianism to parliamentary democracy and from planned economy to liberal market economy. Lithuania has introduced political institutions required for a democracy such as constitution, parliament, regular competitive elections, party system and an organised legal system. On 25 October 1992, Lithuania adopted its present constitution. Article 29 of the constitution grants equal status to men and women. Further, it states, "all persons shall be equal before the law, the court and other state institutions and officials. The rights of the human being may not be restricted, nor may be granted any privileges on the ground of gender, race, nationality, language, origin, social status, belief, convictions or views" (Constitution of Republic of Lithuania: 1992). In addition to this equal treatment provision, Lithuanian parliament (*Seimas*) adopted the "Law on Equal Opportunities for Men and Women" in 1998 to protect women's rights. This law prohibits discrimination against men and women in public and private institutions, which are bound to implement gender equality (Republic of Lithuanian Law on Equal Opportunities for Women and Men: 1998).

Lithuania witnessed progress in women's empowerment in political structure by electing Dalia Grybauskaite as its first woman president in 2009. Lithuania's integration into European Union (EU) and North Atlantic Treaty Organization (NATO) also influenced the government in favour of women's empowerment. Lithuania is one of the countries in Central and Eastern Europe with the highest women representatives in the parliament. However, Lithuania has to achieve more regarding women representatives compared with Sweden, Denmark and Finland (Purvanneckiene 1999: 115). This chapter focuses on the Lithuanian women's access to power and political rights. It discusses on how women used political power for their empowerment. It also examines the obstacles for women to participate in Lithuanian politics.

Women's Movement in Lithuania

Women's movement in Lithuania has historical background since Russian revolution. In 1908, Lithuanian Women's Union was formed during Tsarist rule. It was the main organization of the Lithuanian women's movement with democratic and social democratic trends. It was operated illegally since Tsarist Russia refused to register it officially (Birmontiene and Virginija 2012: 85). This organization advocated social, economic and political rights of Lithuanian women during the initial independence of Lithuania between the two world wars. All women's organizations and movements were abolished during the soviet rule. All political parties including women's organizations were declared illegal. Communist Party of the Soviet Union (CPSU) emerged as the only political organization in the Union. In 1985, when

Gorbachev became president of Soviet Union and introduced political reforms, Lithuania could help reorganise its political organizations.

As a result of collective efforts of political groups emerged during the late 1980s, independence was granted to all the three Baltic Republics in September 1991. A newly elected Lithuanian government reclaimed its independent status, which it had lost during the red army occupation in 1940. The Lithuanian transformation was peaceful and the intelligentsia played a specific role in the process of transformation (*Janusauskiene* 2001: 25).

Various political organizations emerged in Lithuania during the transition period. Thirty-three women's organizations have been set up or re-established during the country's transition (Dalia 1998: 107). Among them is the Society of Mothers of Lithuanian Soldiers, the Widows Association, the Women's Home, the Association of Lithuanian Business Women, the Lithuanian Society of Catholic Women, the Women's League, the Lithuanian Society of Polish Women, the Lithuanian Society of Christian Democratic Women and others. Each in its own way fought against certain legal, social and moral issues (Ibid).

In 1990, women of Lithuania formed a Lithuanian Women's Organization, which started as a non-governmental and non-political group with a secular idea of uniting women of different nationalities, faith and views, interested in equal rights, education and ecological issues. To ensure women's involvement in decision-making in political economic and social spheres, to help women become active members of society through education and development of skills, etc. are the main objectives of the organization. The symbol of the organization is a woman with a child in her hands. The organisation is a member of International Alliance of Women (since 1992), and International Council of Women (since 2002) (Kilukaite 2016; Birmontiene and Jreniene 2012: 92).

In Lithuania, there has been a significant increase in the number of women's organizations. They have been actively participating as well as been vocal in the policymaking. At present more than 63 women's organizations are active in Lithuania (Taljunaite 2004: 1). According to Taljunaite (2004), two different types of organizations are working for women's empowerment in Lithuania. These are women's groups within political parties and the public women's organizations as well. Five of the largest parties in Lithuania have women's groups. They are women section of Lithuanian Centre Union, Lithuanian democratic women's group, Lithuanian social democratic women's union, Union of women's conservative, and the women's section of the Lithuanian Christian Democratic Party (Ibid).

All political party women's wings developed their strategy to tackle the women oriented issues. According to the statue of the LSDP Women's Union, the main objectives of the union are: spreading the social-democratic ideas and values, change the SDP and all members of the society towards women's political participation and decision-making of public interest, achieve equal rights for men and women, economic and legal guarantee for children and family building and achieving equal opportunities in the labour market and business (Labour Party Program: 2012). Public women's organizations are very diverse in Lithuania. At the national level, many organizations are active, while a few others work at the regional or city level. Many of these organizations have set goals of equal rights and equal opportunities. Cooperation among women's organizations is strong and more than ten international organizations are working in Lithuania (Taljunaite 2004: 5).

After regaining independence, Lithuania adopted new constitution in 1992. To attain the status of a democratic state, Lithuania introduced the rule of law, universal suffrage, a free press and business organizations. It enjoys a democratic system of government, presence of political stability, and respect for the rule of law along with the successful implementation of political rights and civil liberties (Goehring 2007: 416). In order to ensure political, economic and national stability in the country, Lithuania joined several international organizations like the United Nations (UN), the European Union (EU) and North Atlantic Treaty Organization (NATO). Major political forces and a strong public opinion of Lithuania supported this integration process. Aspiration for European Union membership drove the country's sweeping political economic and administrative reforms (Ibid). To join the European Union, states had to fulfil the economic, political and administrative conditions known as the Copenhagen criteria (Svensson 2010: 59). According to Svensson, Lithuania adopted the democratic institutions, rule of law, protection of human rights and minorities and market economy in order to fulfil the criteria required to join the EU (Ibid: 2). These developments helped Lithuanian women claim their political, economic, social and cultural rights.

Women's Representation in Seimas

Women played a significant role in the Lithuanian politics. After regaining independence, Lithuania adopted new constitution in 1992 and Parliamentary form of government has been introduced. A unicameral legislature (*Seimas*) consisting of 141 members of which seventy one are elected from constituencies by majority votes and seventy by proportional representation has been introduced. The president is directly elected by people for a period of five years and the prime minister and other ministers are appointed by president for a four-year term subject to the approval of the parliament (*Seimas*). These new democratic institutions encouraged Lithuanian women to participate in political activities of the country.

Lithuanian women participated in every election under the banner of different parties and received significant positions in the *Seimas*. More than 35 percent of all deputies in the Lithuanian Soviet Socialist Republic were women, while their representation dropped in the first post-communist multi-party elections. During the transition period, the representation of women was considerably very low (Taljunaite 2004: 1). The tradition of women's participation in national politics was revived with the *Sajudis* national revival movement, and Kazimiera Prunskienė, the first prime minister of independent Lithuania symbolized it.

Table 4: Women Representatives in the Seimas

Year of election	Men	Women	% of women seats
1990	127	14	9.90
1992	131	10	7.10
1996	113	24	18.10
2000	126	15	10. 64
2004	110	31	21.99
2008	116	25	17.73
2012	107	34	24.11
2016	111	30	21.28

Source: Election Commission of Lithuania (2016).

In 1992, female representation in the *Seimas* dropped to its lowest at 7.1 percent although with left wing majority, which appointed only three female deputy ministers. During the 1996 elections wooed by conservative HU, the share of women in the *Seimas* increased to 18.3 percent and seven women joined the government. Legislative representation dropped to 10.6 percent in 2000; however, women maintained a relatively strong position within the cabinet, with three ministers (including finance) and eight deputy ministers during the term (Forest 2011: 75). Women's access to executive positions remained quite unchanged even after their representation at the *Seimas* hit a record high of 22 percent in 2004.

Since the 2008 elections, only 18 percent of women were participating in the parliament with only one female minister. Women's position has been reinforced by the growing credibility of female presidential candidate. In 2009, Dalia Grybauskaite was brilliantly elected in the first round of the presidential elections (Ibid). In 2012 general elections, 34 women representatives were elected with 24.11 percent share in the parliament. The 2016 elections also witnessed growth in women's representation with slight decline compared to previous elections. The women candidates who contested in the 2016 general elections were 442, among 1,415 candidates in total. However, only 30 women representatives were elected to the parliament (Central Election Commission of Lithuania: 2016).

Women's Representation in European Parliament (EP)

Lithuania joined European Union in 2004 with the public support. Lithuania elects 12 members to the European Parliament. The electoral system is based on proportional representation. The representation of Lithuanian women in the European Parliament (EP) now has drastically declined since its integration to European Union (EU). In 2004 EP elections, women members elected to the 2004-2009 legislature were 38 percent. The women representation of Lithuania in EP sharply dropped from the next election onwards. It was dropped to 25 percent in the 2009-2014 legislature elections. The 2014-2019 legislature elections witnessed high decline in women representation with only 9 percent (European Commission: 2006).

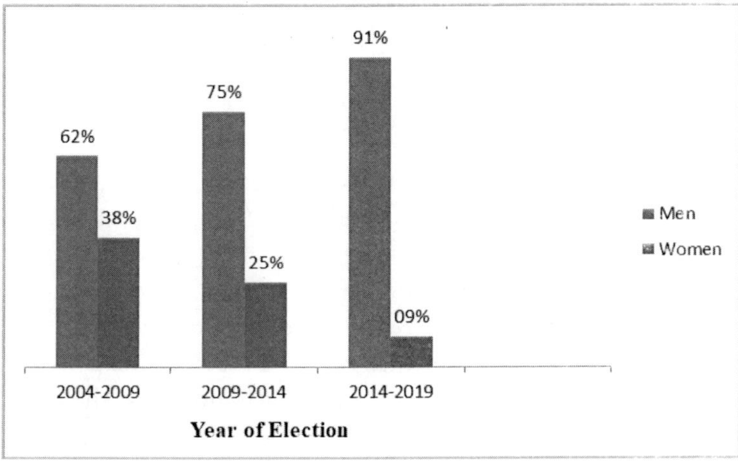

Figure 11: Women Representation in European Parliament (EP)
Source: Election Commission of Lithuania (2016).

Lithuanian women were found highly successful in guaranteeing representation in the first elections in June 2004 to the EP. Five of them were women among the 13 individuals elected to the body. Except the Labour Party, which nominated three women candidates, some parties including the Liberal and Centre Union did not include any women among their five candidates (Taljunaite 2004: 3). Slowly the percentage of women representatives of Lithuania in EP declined due to several reasons. Political parties' unwillingness is the main reason for the decline of women representation in EP.

Major Political Parties of Women

The Lithuanian Party of Women (LPW) is an independent volunteer political organization, which unites members to take part in political activities and solve problems. The party works on the principle of equality of all its members. LPW is a lawful body, which has a seal and a current bank account. The party follows the constitution and laws of the Republic of Lithuania (Dalia 1998: 96-97). After gaining 101 out of the 141 seats in the Lithuanian Supreme Council, *Sajudis*[3] nominated Kazimiera Prunskiene as a first female prime minister. Later she resigned from office in 1991 and joined the Farmers Party (Forest 2011: 75). In 1995, Prunskiene co-founded the Lithuanian Women's Party as a way of capturing public attention (Bugajski 2002: 143). Her initiative influenced the major parties to nominate more female candidates (Forest 2011: 75).

Following are the main objectives of the Lithuanian Women's Party:

- To establish a new non-patriarchal environment in Lithuania.
- To train women in self-expression, formalities and responsibility concerning the working of the state.
- To develop an environment that encourages the participation of women in political and government activities (Dalia 1998: 97).

The New Democracy-Women's Party (ND-WP) was also founded by the former Prime Minister Kazimiera Prunskiene on 20thApril 1995. The party was an outcome of the Lithuanian Women's Association formed in 1922. Having a membership of 1000 supporters, it sought to represent women and their difficulties in the national legislature. Generally, the party was centrist and felt the necessity to incorporate diverse views of women in the Lithuanian society. In spite of Kazimiera Prunskiene winning a seat in the *Seimas*, the party missed its entry into the parliament by slightest number of votes (Bugajski 2002: 143).

The party proposed to unite its members to participate and to solve the problems related to the women community. It gave significant importance to the development of women's self-expression, patriotism and responsibility towards the state affairs. The party endeavoured to create conditions encouraging women's participation in politics and in state governance. The ND-WP worked with Lithuanian Centre Union (LCU), the Lithuanian Social Democratic Party (LSDP), and the Lithuanian Peasants Party (LPP) in order to improve the position of Prunskiene as a *Seimas* representative (Ibid).

Conclusion

There is a lack of political participation among the Lithuanian women community due to the lack of legal, economic and political support. The emerging women's movement, NGOs and educational opportunities are offering alternative solutions for the problems faced by the women's communities. It is very much essential to improve women's political and social participation in Lithuania to create gender equality. Higher participation of women is important to bring new, positive enthusiasm to the political life of Lithuania, and thus improving the strength of the political party system.

Notes

1. Glasnost (openness) was the Soviet policy permitting open discussion of political and social issues. Under Glasnost, people could criticize the government system and policies without being punished.
2. Perestroika was a policy of restructuring or reforming the economic and political system, practiced in the Soviet Union under the leadership of Gorbhachev. Its foremost objective was to restructure the soviet economy and bureaucracy. But it eventually led to the end of central planning in the economy.
3. Sajudis was a new mass organization called the Lithuanian movement for restructuring, later known simply as Sajudis (1988). At the beginning, Sajudis was a movement that united various strata of Lithuanian society, including nationalists, liberal intellectual and communist reformers. After the declaration of independence Sajudis movement gave birth to several political parties. In fact, multi party system was started with the disintegration of Sajudis.

References

Birmontiene, Toma and Virginija Jureniene (2012), "The development of women rights in Lithuania: striving for political identity", in Blanca Rodriguez-Ruiz and Ruth Rubio-Marin (eds.), *The Struggle for Female Suffrage in Europe: Voting to Become Citizens*, Boston: Brill.

Bugajski, Janusz (2002), *Political Parties of Eastern Europe: A Guide to Politics in the Post-Communist Era*, New York: The Centre for Strategic and Institutional Studies.

Central Election Commission (2016), Election of the President and Election of the Seimas of the republic of Lithuania retrieved from http://www.vrk.lt/en/home.

Constitution of Lithuania (1992), Article 2 in the Constitution of the Republic of Lithuania retrieved from http://www.litlex.lt/Litlex/Eng/Frames/Laws/Documents/CONSTITU.HTM.

Dalia, Teiserskyte (1998), "Why and How the Party of Women was formed in Lithuania", in Suzanne Lafont (eds.) *Women in transition: voices from Lithuania*, Albany: State University of New York Press.

European Commission (2006), The EU mutual learning programme in gender equality, women in political decision-making, Lithuania, retrieved from http://ec.europa.eu/justice/gender-equality/files/exchange_of_good_practice_si/lt_comments_paper_si_2016_en.pdf.

Forest, Maxine (2011), "Central and Eastern Europe", in Bauer Gretech and Tremblay Manon (eds.), *Women in Executive Power: A Global Overview*, New York: Routledge.

Goehring, Jeanntee (2007), *Nations in transit 2007: democratization from Central Europe to Eurasia*, New York: Freedom House.

Grybauskaite (2010), Speech of The President: the overriding principle – the Individual – the State – the Future, *Lithuanian Tribune and Baltic reports* retrieved from http://www.lithuaniatribune.com/2010/06/08/the-president-the-overriding-principle-%E2%80%93-the-individual-%E2%80%93-the-state-%E2%80%93-the-future/.

Janušauskienė, Diana (2001), *Post-Communist Democratization in Lithuania: Elites, Parties and Youth Political Organizations*: 1998-2001.

Kilukaite Jovita (2016), Lithuanian Women's Organization, retrieved from http://www.womenngos.eu/2013/11/lt-lietuvos-moteru-draugija-lithuanian.html.

Labour Party Program (2012), "Labour Party Program" [Online: web] retrieved 19 April 2012, URL: http//www.darbopartija.lt//.

Lithuanian Population (2016), Population of Republic of Lithuania, Country Meters retrieved from http://countrymeters.info/en/Lithuania.

Purvanneckiene, Giedre (1999), Women in Lithuanian Society, *Lithuanian Human Development Report*, pp.115-125.

Republic of Lithuania (1998), Law on Equal Opportunities for Women and Men, 1 December 1998, No VIII-947, Vilnius.

Svensson, Jenny (2010), "Governance through Mediation: EU Twinning in Lithuania", in Bengt Jacobsson (ed.), *The European Union and the Baltic states*, London: Routledge.

Taljunaite, Meilute (2004), "*The Women's movement in Lithuania: Discourses and lobbying strategies*", A paper presented at the Gender issues conference, the implementation of quotas: European experience, Budapest, *IDEA/CEE*: 22-23 October 2004.

Chapter Twelve

The Baltic States' Policy towards Russia: The Problems of Politics of Identity and Securitisation

Anoop Kumar

This chapter examines the problems of identity politics and securitization in Baltic states' policy towards Russia in view of their perspectives and new discourses on identity, national interest and security in the post-Soviet period. Baltic nation building process has the underpinnings of a strong ant-Soviet/Russian approach. National identity is constructed based on Russian otherness and European sameness which bring both domestic and international repercussions. The Baltic security perception includes the dimensions of integration and identity, and a security discourse centred on "danger" from Russia and "protection" from EU, NATO and the US. In the post-Soviet era, the Baltic issue was framed as a test for measuring the direction of development of Russia as either a true democratic state or a threat to international community, and for the West it is capability to handling the Baltic issue in connection with NATO enlargement (Usha 2015). Given this situation, the desire of Baltic states to return to European security politics generated multiple dilemmas, as the consolidation of their independence was assessed in terms of the balance of power between the West and Russia. The Baltic independence was viewed by the West as their victory and by Russia as loss and decline of great power status. The West treats Russia's conduct towards these states as a measure of Russia's commitment to international norms and laws. Baltic states' policy towards Russia is determined by factors such as geopolitical vulnerability, politics of history, memory and identity, threat perception and security policies, energy dependency and Russophobia.

Geopolitical Vulnerability of Baltic States

The Baltic states had a history of foreign domination in the past. They were dominated by Sweden, Denmark, Germany and Russia. The foreign domination was not because of their fault but because of their location at a geopolitically vulnerable area. Their situation is such that the big neighbours' politics affect their sovereignty. They lost independence during Second Word War and became part of Soviet Union. That memory frightens them as they think if the past repeats. Such a perception encourages their securitization measures against Russia. The memory of trauma of the past shapes their securitization policies.

During the recent crisis, the Baltic support for the Ukraine to come under the ambit of the European Union shows their reliability on the security structure of which they are part. Russia in the Baltic states' conception represents the security threat against which they have to create their security structure; and the US and NATO take them as their 'litmus test'. K.B. Usha argues that since these states are considered a 'litmus test' between the west and east, it has created a security dilemma for the Baltic states (Usha 2015). The Baltic states are suspicious about the intention of Russia especially after the Georgia war and Ukraine crisis. They are also skeptical about the cultural association of the Russian minority present in the Baltic states. Although the Baltic states have categorically supported their integration in the European Union they could not assimilate themselves completely with the EU because the cultural association is not there. The Baltic states are culturally different from the other states in the EU and therefore could not fully integrate themselves in the EU culture.

Baltic States' Policy towards Russia: Politics of Identity and Securitization

The three interlinking concepts are vividly evident in the political existence and integration of the Baltic states. The identity politics, informed and constructed by memory, is shaping the national interest, security and foreign policy to a great extent in case of the Baltic states. The reflection of memory politics is visible in the choices of the Baltic states to secure their national interest of "return to Europe" and erase Soviet legacy. Identity determines the national interest and determines the directions of policy and state action. Baltic national interest is reflected in their support to the enlargement policies of the NATO and the US which they consider as their primary security providers. Their participation in the EU Atlantic security structure and economic integration under the EU evidently secures their national interest.

Notwithstanding the fact that the Baltic states are relying on the US and EU for the fulfilment of their national interest, energy security could be a problematic area as this seems a weak point. The Baltic states had to take extraordinary work in order to create and justify identity formation which is based upon memory and history. Rein Taagepera does explain the anxiety and difficulty of the Baltic states to create the historical narrative in their favour. He stated that the painful history of the Baltic states was not even known and Russia could create history on their behalf, but certainly the narrative which suits them. For instance, till 1990 the perception of the west towards the Baltic states was grimly informed which was "steadily affected by how they perceived Baltic history: whether it even existed and if so, what did its most recent phase represent – occupation or voluntary union?" (Taagepera 2009). So, the transformation of memory into history was much conscious effort taken up by the Baltic states which reflected evidently in the identity politics of the Baltic states especially in relation to the securitisation.

The identity politics consoles itself with the presence of commonality of history, culture and socio-political goals. The Baltic states which have transformed themselves with the complete structural overhaul of their system and goals after the independence. In the process of forging commonality the narration had to be naturally created around the discourse of identity and memory. Although to a great extent the Baltic states in a span of two decades could create narrative around their identity and history but the challenge they face from the Russian speaking minority is a difficult one. The Russian speaking people or group is certainly not dependent on Russia for their economic goals and there is no association so to speak based upon the economic aspirations of the Russian speaking people. Ammon Cheskin analyses the problem of integration of the Russian speaking people into the identity of the Baltic states in which the two identities differ by culture, tradition, language and occupation (Cheskin 2015). So, the incorporation of Russian speaking people was great challenge and it still is so in the Baltic states. Russian speaking people are viewed with suspicion. The identity politics of the Baltic states, which are to some extent enveloped by Russia, and the historical relation between the two is hampering in the creation of the identity of the country and therefore hazardous for the securitisation which is constantly built around the discourse of identity.

The politics of identity has greatly influenced the discourse of national interest in the Baltic states as the national interest is a highly volatile and fragile motivation in the current political scenario. The national interest of the Baltic states which is laden with the identity and security of the states which they have tried to ensure by accepting the western political and economic norms and their assimilation into the structure of the western security model is a tale of securing their national interest defined in terms of their distinct identity which is in constant dialogue with the fear of Russia. Russia in the perception of the Baltic states is a constant threat which in the opinion of the Baltic states is evident in few of the recent incidents. Russia's intention of relations with the Baltic states is highly suspicious in their security discourse, which led them to view the history of world war in new light and they hold opinion that they have supported Hitler in order to keep Stalin at check (Onken 2007). In the light of the present political scenario in the international arena, one does not support this view that the Baltic states should view Russia as an enemy. In the world politics, Russia is gaining importance and status and the difference between Russia and its western counterpart is not much visible. The America-Russia relations are improving and the west considers this view that the negation of Russia as a political force would not be a viable solution to resolve issues the world is grappled with.

The perception of the security in the Baltic states suggest integral interdependence between their security and identity which encourages structuring of the foreign policy priorities keeping in view the relation between identity and security. The significance of national identity, in terms of collective self, envisages in case of the Baltic states that the security concerns are leading these relatively new independent states to bring out foreign and even commercial policies in relation to their identity and security. Andrei P. Tsygankov in an analysis of the policies of Latvia has identified the quintessential interconnecting relation between security and policies (Tsygankov 2000). The dialectical interdependence between identity and foreign policy is intriguing in the case of the Baltic states (Estonia, Latvia and Lithuania). The process of identity formation reflects conspicuously the relation between forging of the Baltic states' foreign policy and identity construction. The history of the Independence of the three states is the history of war, occupation, suffering, peaceful resistance and discovery of their collective self. The Baltic states and their people are still haunted by the imagery of war and occupation. The consequence of this imagery is evident in their very psyche which is explicitly evident in their foreign policy choices, security concerns and identity formation. Is this imagery real or they are haunted by the echo of their voices, is to be investigated in the light of the modern security concerns.

The very process of the independence of the Baltic states reflects the complete transformation socially, politically and economically. The Baltic states have preferred to move towards liberal democratic principles, democratic form of government and liberalism in the arena of economy. It could not just be categorized as a complete overhaul; instead it was a restructuring of the system from the very scratch. The causation to follow a particular structure was highly compulsive in nature because of the political and security dilemma and therefore it could not be smooth. Yaroslav Bilinsky stated that the transition of the three Baltic states was not smooth because they had to go through a complete restructuring and they were not ready to receive such kind of changes so suddenly (Bilinsky 2006). The defining factor in the restructuring of their political and economic system was the fear of Russia, as the independence of the Baltic states was taken as a blow by Russia and their assimilation into the western security structure fuelled this feeling. Stephen Blank stated through analysis of facts that Russia could not digest the assimilation of the

Baltic states in the western security structure and their becoming members of the NATO. It was evident that Russia was extremely opposed to the idea of the Baltic states joining NATO because it would threaten its security (Blank 1998). On the one hand the historical experience of the Baltic states had increased their propensity to tilt towards the west, and on the other they were left with not many choices to use their free judgment.

At the core of their struggle to gain independence from the Soviet Union lies the issue of identity. The Baltic states, skeptical about the intention of Russia, were seeking new identity. Resurgence of Russian military presence in the area enhanced their suspicion about the further intentions of Russia, as "the Baltic is more important than ever as a defense zone for the Russians; in particular, the airspace over the Baltic has taken on an increased significance in Russian air defence" (Bitzinger 1992). The discourse around the security and the sour experience of the freedom struggle, occupation and the natural fear they had from Russia, shaped the future course of the formation of their Identity. The Baltic securitization of Russia fuelling the eternal fear they have vis-à-vis Russia, has become a reality. Russian invasion of Czechoslovakia in 1968 and Georgia war in 2008 had posed great psychological threat because the latter was "the largest Russian military incursion into a foreign state since the collapse of Soviet power, [which] have also prompted fundamental questions about the motivations and objectives of the Russian leadership" (Allison 2008).

The Ukraine crisis of 2014 is another historical occurrence that strengthens skepticism in the Russian intention towards the Baltic states. The Baltic states tried intensely to assimilate themselves with the western world through institutions whose presence in that geopolitical space is questionable, such as North Atlantic Treaty Organisation (NATO). Their compulsive security choice pushed them to take few unlikely steps such as participation in the Afghanistan war. The Baltic states are living in a paradoxical situation, where their freedom and volition is in constant jeopardy. After little more than two decades, the Baltic states are still grappling with those problems in their political analysis and therefore their politics and policies reflect an opposition to the Baltic's securitisation of Russia.

Problems of Politics of Identity and Securitization of Russia

The intrinsic elements of the identity formation reflect the historical and foreign policy choices which might be the outcome of compulsion but serve them to draw back their existence from almost a century's crisis. In response to the situation of the Baltic states the west was also baffled as the situation was putting them in dilemma after the disintegration of the Soviet Union. The Baltic is dilemma defined "as a choice between support for the moral precept of Baltic self-determination or the more pragmatic policy of quietly endorsing Mikhail Gorbachev as he endeavors to open Soviet society without dismembering his nation" (Mantenieks 1990: 167-169).

The foreign policy therefore, unlike in other nation states, consists in case of the Baltic states their political, social and cultural anxiety. The euphemism for the process of the formation their identity after independence is their foreign policy concerns. The Baltic states' experience as an independent unit seems ephemeral in the psyche of the political leadership and the people. The politics of fear which seems significant and relevant in case of the Baltic states, as it is posed by one of the most powerful nation states in the world, can cause serious damage to the political establishment. The riddle to solve for the Baltic states is whether the constant fear or threat from Russia is a potential reality or just an illusion to be pricked as Russia's influence is diminishing with time. Until recently, Moscow comfortably thought of the Baltic Sea as its rightful sphere of influence. But Russia has only two remaining bases for its once huge Baltic fleet (Blank 1998).

There is not much space to build up a discourse contradictory to the historical situation and experience, as the presence of fear has basis in the same but the necessity is to dig the reasons for the enlargement of fear which still affects the whole policy choices of the Baltic states. The most evident political choices are their membership of the NATO and their assimilation in the European Union (EU). At the expense of their political and economic rights as independent nations they have preferred rather to be part of the EU and NATO. In case of the Baltic states they had to go through the process of establishing military and domestic security institutions in order to comply with the requirements of the EU. The worthiness of such investment which is not even directly defending their borders vis-à-vis Russia can be questioned unless the historical and political reasons behind this are not understood. Russia is evidently skeptical about the NATO enlargement as it would be a challenge to its security. "If NATO military structures were to approach Russian borders and its troops were to appear on the territories of new member-states, Russia would be forced to adjust to these challenges to its security" (Pushkov 1997). This essential security conflict between Russia and the Baltic states would further sore the already stressful relations. The Baltic states' assimilation in the western security structure could not enable them to survive with maintaining any relations with Russia. The Baltic states are dependent upon Russia for their energy needs and have considerable economic and trade relations.

The security concerns of the Baltic states vis-à-vis Russia are not solely based on the illusory presumption, but are embedded in the history of Russian occupation of the Baltic states. These concerns are also based upon some of the facts which are continuously causing anxiety in the three countries. The Baltic states since their Independence are unconsciously or consciously spurred by the security dilemma produced due to the powerful states. The making of the Baltic states as Independent states and their continued effort to maintain independent existence is always paradoxical. The strategic security measures and association with the European Union (EU) entail discussion especially in the changed world order and new relations which emerged after the economic and technological development. As Karen A. Cerulo states, the shift in identity studies is due to three reasons and one of them is social and nationalist movements (Cerulo 1997). In case of the Baltic states the significance of political movements in the formation of identity is highly important. Its long history of attack and occupation has shaped almost all the later developments especially in the arenas of security and foreign policy.

The freedom struggle by the Baltic states is the epitome of nonviolent struggle. It is popularly known as Singing Revolution in which more than two million people participated and formed a human chain. This movement was characterized by songs and music and therefore known as singing revolution. This nonviolent resistance inspired by Gandhi and Maritin Luthur King's philosophy of political nonviolence contributed not only to their freedom but also to the disintegration of the Soviet Union. The singing revolution exhibited their will to freedom through nonviolent means and challenged power through peaceful resistance (Smidchens 2007). The Baltic states suffered economic sluggishness, political volatility, and social uncertainty during the Soviet occupation. Their identity remained fragile under constant threat from the cultural and political attack from the Soviet Union. Singing revolution was a remarkable movement for independence securing its political, historical and cultural identity. The Soviet Union occupied the Baltic states for nearly five decades; "the Soviet empire stretched its geopolitical power deep into Central Europe and the Balkans, posing a potential threat to the West at many points" (Bildt 1994: 72-85). The Baltic states after the restoration of independence relied on the western economic and political model. As a result they not only came up to the terms of the liberalization and democracy but also prospered. They chose to become members of the EU in all the spheres, economically, politically and culturally. Their geopolitical importance attracted their western partners to assimilate them in the western security structure.

The political movement for the independence of the Baltic states was extremely important in the formation of their identity as it shaped them as they are today. Although it remains essential in making an understanding of the forging of their identity, there are other factors which are constantly contributing to the same. The present geopolitical location, presence of Russia militarily and culturally in the region, enhancement of the power of Russia which is evident in Russia's actions in Ukraine and Georgia are some of the factors which are contributing to the identity formation. The strategic and natural choice, which emerged out of their security concern, made the Baltic states associate with the European Union and eventually become the member of the North Atlantic Treaty Organisation (NATO). The defining element in their choice to assimilate themselves with the EU was the security concerns. Cultural disassociation with Russia was another element in their choice to desire the EU's membership. The Baltic states politically and culturally do not want to be associated with Russia. The Baltic states do not represent culturally one coherent unit. The three Baltic states are not a coherent unit culturally (Boiko 2002) but what unite them are their common history of struggle and the process of their identity formation. The Baltic states were forced into constant fear of attack or occupation. Georgia war and Ukraine crisis contributed further to the securitization of the Baltic states in the recent times as contributed in the identity formation.

The Baltic states gained independence in the last decade of the twentieth century in 1991. The three states have a long history of struggle to gain and secure their independent existence from the Russian occupation. In the year 1918 after the end of First World War, the Baltic states gained independence. The former Soviet Union again threatened them to attack, if they would not provide military bases in order to attack Poland as a result of Molotov-Ribbentrop Pact between the Soviet Union and Germany. The Baltic states could not sustain their independence in such an environment for a long time. They fell under the Soviet Union's occupation in 1941 and later on attacked by Germans which continued till 1945. After the German occupation they again became prey to the Soviet Union till they finally gained independence in 1991. Although the EU and the US readily came forward to provide security to the Baltic states, their intention to do so had favourable reasons for them. The United States of America (USA) has built its security structure in the form of NATO utilising the fear of the small nation states around the world. So, to save them from Russia, the Baltic states exercised its volition in favour of the US. George J. Viksnins has argued otherwise in 2003 that the Baltic states and other three countries, which were then joining the NATO, have received funding or military aid from the United States (US) and the reason being that they were not signing the immunity which the US was seeking and later on the EU presidency also declared that the countries which are joining the EU are supposed to follow the convictions of the EU, which clearly in his opinion shows the problem these countries are facing in associating themselves as an allies of America and the EU (Viksnins 2003). It was understood that in the post-Cold War era the former Soviet Union would lose its credential as a superpower and would not be able to present substantial resistance to the US. Contrary to the belief, Russia emerged as a powerful state, and after the Georgian war, it has established its authority as a militarily strong nation.

The strategy of the US on the other hand is to counter Russia and present a formidable control which could be ensured by its presence around the borders of Russia. In a security expansion over the EU and to counter the hegemonic role which

Russia could play especially in Baltic Sea area incited the Baltic states hurriedly to join NATO which was certainly fuelled by the US. Despite the view held by many that the Baltic states' assimilation into NATO security would seriously jeopardize America's relation with Russia, the US was enticed by the prospect of Baltic states becoming part of NATO (Larrabee 2003). Because, it would give leverage to America to pose serious challenge to Russia, though it would always remain burdensome to the Baltic states as they have to comply with the policy priorities of the EU as well as NATO. So the modern imagery of Russia has intensified the already established notion regarding the securitization of the Baltic states affecting them in each and every action including all the policy decisions. The politics which revolves around the Baltic securitization has its significant role in the making of the foreign policy perspectives. The evident relation between the two seemingly independent elements of the nation states, i.e., security and foreign policy, is blurred in case of the Baltic states.

The Independence of the Baltic states in 1991 coincided with a great historical upheaval in world politics. The structure of the world politics was at the brink of crumbling down. The world was witnessing unprecedented changes in the international arena. The Soviet Union got disintegrated and with it the bipolar world order was no more defining factor in international relations. Identity which is solely political or ideological couldn't exist and the nation states had to resort to new methods of identity formation. The new identity which was emerging after the cold war was not laden with political as well as cultural overtones, and this was not the case with the Baltic states exactly. The Baltic states underwent the same process but couldn't eradicate the impressions of the cold war political identity. When regional integration became rampant due to the disintegration of Russia, the Baltic states, though still under the influence of Russia, moved forward in this direction in which not only these three states came together but also endeavoured to assimilate into the European Union. Hafeez R. Khan and others have argued that the future of the world order is difficult to speculate but it will be characterized by the presence of significant elements as dependence on other nation states, non-violence and pursuit of the goals defined by UN charter or international community (Khan et al. 1992). The Eastern and Western security dilemma which was not very sharp in the later years in the world political scene affected the process of identity and politics of the Baltic states. In the liberal democratic political structure with the presence of international institutions to safeguard peace, constant threat to any nation states is unlikely to happen. In the case of the Baltic states, the narrative is full with fear, cultural intervention and political threat from Russia.

The Ukraine crisis for instance questions the integrity of Russia as a responsible liberal democratic country which respects the charter of the United Nations.

Intervention in Ukraine was totally uncalled for as K.B. Usha argued that it was the biggest crisis after the Cuban missile crisis (Usha 2015). It not only surprised Ukraine and its people, but also created reverberations in the present political scenario putting the global security in crisis. It again marginalized the Baltic states by intensifying the fear and showing the potential and possibility of Russia. Russia's ambition as a nation state came into conflict with the proposition which they had at the end of cold war, and became more evident with two major incidents, the Georgian war and the Ukraine Crisis. There are some other issues which do not come in the traditional categorization of security threats, as they are greatly dependent on the factors other than military. Cultural issues are increasingly inciting the fear in the psyche of the masses in the Baltic states. In the modern world which has abundant ways of spreading information beyond the national boundaries without any hindrance, the political fear can be realized and rationalized through the use the modern technology. The presence of the Russian population in the three Baltic states provides the opportunity to spread such information not through people but using technology. This political tool is used not for the first time in any conflict; there are many occurrences which provide evidence for the same sort of strategy. Although similar to some extent but not clearly analogous, the Israel-Palestine conflict carries the use of similar strategy by Israel in Palestine. The situation in the Baltic states is not that grim but it certainly increases the constant fear which they carry always.

The political scenario of the Baltic states, from the very beginning, is questioning the very existence and their constant existential paradox reflects in the policy decisions. The quintessential objective or motivation behind the policy priorities of the Baltic states is to safeguard their hard earned independence. They are psychologically appalled at different levels from time to time. So, the dialectical relation between the foreign policy priorities and its identity is extremely important and significant. Whether it is about locating them politically and economically with the EU or becoming part of the NATO reflects the essential standpoint with Russia. NATO, the Baltic states and Russia underwent much heated debate in the academic circles as Mark Kramer, Stephen Blank and others had written about the dichotomy of security between the Baltic states and Russia keeping in mind the NATO's enlargement (Kramer 2002; Blank 1998). Their association with the western security structure pushed them to move ahead peacefully to some extent towards the process of the realization of their identities and develop economically and flourish socially. Despite the safeguard which they have received as a consequence of their assimilation could not reduce the degree of difficulty they had and having to forge new identity. In the European Union there are different nation states which function together economically and politically but the distribution of the power and benefits is sometimes unequal. This unequal distribution of resources and power pushes them to be in consonance with the requirements of the groupings they are part of. The formidable question remains that they might be a part of the Union for almost three decades; their acceptance in the groupings is not a part of natural political strategy of the EU. In reality their association still needs tremendous effort on the part of the Baltic states. Despite their continuous endeavour and adventure to be part of the European society they could not assimilate themselves combining all the features of one society.

The inherent internal contradictions of the east and west Europe are also causing anxiety in the life of the Baltic states. Contradictions in the domain of culture seem less relevant as they are not that evident in normative political and economic life. Though these cultural and psychological contradictions are subtle, they are blatantly visible in the social behaviour, which ultimately find space and reflection in the other fields of action. The incessant struggle of the Baltic states don't end here, but it penetrates vividly other vital fields such as economic, political and above all security. One of the instances of the contradictions in the field of politics and security is the support of the Baltic states to the NATO forces in Afghanistan. The Baltic states also became part in the international interventionism in Afghanistan where big powers were using their military might to invade Afghanistan (Morini 2010), despite their historicity is not in consonance with the present actions. The history of Afghanistan is also characterized by pain, suffering and occupation and still going through the extremely painful process of war. The Baltic states have started establishing army from the scratch primarily not to defend themselves but to follow the standards of the NATO forces. The volition of the Baltic states seems not very significant in choosing the most pertinent issues such as war. The countries which have similar experience are unlikely to support such war with whom they are directly associated even. The presence of the Baltic states in Afghanistan is not very supportive of their historical narrative because the support in the war could provide justification also for their being occupied, and their struggle for independence could be in vain.

Conclusion

The process of the Baltic securitisation and formation of the identity is an on-going process in the Baltic states, as the context which was relevant in the decade of 1990s is still relevant after passing of the three decades. This whole process of identity formation is compulsive and doesn't seem natural as it was in the lack of other choices. The Baltic states are grappled by the irreverent situation which could not be very helpful in the formation of their identity in terms of collective self because collective self is the natural outcome of the combination of the history, culture, traditions, problems, and struggles. The very discourse of the identity in the Baltic states proposes altogether different sort of hypothesis which mainly suggests that the identity formation is directly associated with safeguarding the independent existence which is highly questionable. Lithuania has incorporated in their academic studies not only o their history but also the Lithuanian language to trace its origin and they are working on mythology and digging deep to know the historicity of the construction of collective self. In the realm of the formation of their foreign policy, it would not be the best choice to shape their choices solely based upon their historical experience. The world is changing rapidly and negation of Russia as a powerful neighbouring country is no discernible choice. The Baltic states' dependence on Russia shows a different picture altogether. The policy priorities which could take into consideration Russia and manage to maintain working relations could serve the purpose of the Baltic states better.

References

Allison, Roy (2008), "Russia Resurgent? Moscow's Campaign to 'Coerce Georgia to Peace'", *International Affairs* (Royal Institute of International Affairs 1944-), 84 (6): 1145-117.

Bildt, Carl (1994), "The Baltic Litmus Test", *Foreign Affairs*, 73 (5): 72-85.

Bilinsky, Yaroslav (2006), "Toward the West: Baltic Realignment and Russia's Reply", Harvard International Review, 28 (1): 60-63.

Bitzinger, Richar A. (1992), "The Baltic: A Changing Security Situation", Scandinavian Studies, 64 (4): 606-613.

Blank, Stephen (1998), "Russia, NATO Enlargement, and the Baltic States", *World Affairs*, 160 (3): 115-125.

Boiko, Martin (2002), "Baltic and Balts: On the History of Notions and the Question of Baltic Regionalism", *The World of Music*, 44 (3): 7-19.

Cerulo, Karen A. (1997), "Identity Construction: New Issues, New Directions", *Annual Review of Sociology*, 23:385-409.

Janušauskas, Ramūnas (1994), "Russia's Interests in and Policies Towards the Baltics: Socio-economic and Military Aspects", *Perspectives*, 3: 97-116.

Cheskin, Ammon (2015), "Identity and Integration of the Russian Speakers in the Baltic States: a framework of analysis", *Ethnopolitics*, 14 (1): 72-93.

Khan Hafeez R., Mushahid Hussain, Sultan Ahmad and Fakhruddin G. Ebrahim (1992), "The Future World Order", *Pakistan Horizon*, 1: 29-52.

Larrabee, F. Stephen (2003), *NATO's Eastern Agenda in a New Strategic Era*, RAND Corporation.

Maley, William (1995), "Does Russia Speak for Baltic Russians?" The World Today, 51 (1): 4-6.

Mantenieks, Maris (1990), "The Baltic Dilemma", *Foreign Affairs,* 69 (3): 167-169.

Mark, Kramer (2002), "NATO, the Baltic States and Russia: A Framework for Sustainable Enlargement", *International Affairs* (Royal Institute of International Affairs 1944-), 78 (4): 731-756.

Morini, Daryl (2010), "A Diplomatic Surge in Afghanistan, 2011-14", *Strategic Studies Quarterly*, 4 (4): 68-100.

Onken, Eva-Clarita (2007), "The Baltic states and Moscow's 9 May commemoration: Analysing memory politics in Europe", *Europe-Asia Studies*, 59 (1): 23-46.

Pushkov, Alexei K. (1997), "Don't Isolate Us: A Russian View of NATO Expansion", *The National Interest*, 47: 58-63.

Smidchens, Guntis (2007), "National Heroic Narratives in the Baltics as a Source for Non-Violent Political Action", *Slavic Review*, 66 (3): 484-508.

Taagepera, Rein (2009), "The Struggle for Baltic History", *Journal of Baltic States*, 40 (4): 451-464.

Tsygankov, Andrei P. (2000), "Defining State Interests after Empire: National Identity, Domestic Structures and Foreign Trade Policies of Latvia and Belarus", Review of International Political Economy, 7 (1): 101-137.

Usha, K.B. (2015), "The Ukraine Conflict, Fear of Russian Aggression and Security Dilemma of Baltic States", South Asian Journal of Diplomacy, 6: 39-56.

Viksnins, George J. (2003), "New Europe, New Problems: The Case of the Baltic States", The National Interest, 73: 85-91.

Chapter Thirteen

Role of European Union in the Discourse of Minority Rights in the Baltic States

Akanksha

Introduction

This chapter traces the historical evolution of the concept of the minority protection in Europe. The focus of the chapter is on the standard setting of membership criteria to enter the European Union (EU) and the changes in the region regarding minority rights before and after membership of the EU. It examines the need for the Baltic states to deal with the issues of the minorities inhabiting in the states. It discusses the main features of accession negotiations, their likely effects on the ratification deal, and possible further developments after the EU enlargement.

Estonia, Latvia and Lithuania known as the Baltic states have experienced many political and social changes since their secession from the Union of Soviet Socialist Republics (USSR) in 1991. These states were dominated by the Soviet policy as the member states of the USSR. With the disintegration of USSR, Baltic states got the opportunity to return to their former independent status. This transition was long awaited and hoped for but it did not occur without any challenge. There were several challenges such as economic integration, social integration, etc. ahead of the Baltic states to have the transition from dependent states to independent states. With the economic integration to the rest of the world, the Baltic states felt the dire need of establishing themselves in the political regime. In order to facilitate this process, each of the three states hoped to become a member of the European Union (EU), and they became full members in 2004, though their applications were officially submitted in 1995.

Mechanisms to Deal with Minorities

All the member states of "European Union" have national or ethnic minorities in which there is a symbiotic relation among the "majorities" and "minorities" with both pros and cons. The borders of the states are mostly marked by history; however, there is not any specific demarcation between the dominated areas of the people and "ethnic groups" in Europe in fact it is often coincide. Presence of ethnic minorities in these regions remains challenge and there is strong need to protect and recognize the basic "rights" of these minorities. Since beginning, Europe was considered as "cradle of the ideology of the nation state". Now, the idea is contradicting itself due to presence of several ethnic and national minorities, which insist on "internal self-determination" as a group and claim for their fundamental rights. From this standpoint, frequently ethnic or national minorities are facing a sort of accusation of making the "fifth column of their respective kin-state" (Benedikter 2008: 108). To undertake the minority issue, which is common in most of the European countries, common rules are formulated with internationally agreed frameworks.

The Organization for Security and Cooperation in Europe (OSCE), the Council of Europe, the Framework Convention for the Protection of National Minorities (FCNM), the European Union, and various mechanisms were adopted to deal with this issue of minorities.

The OSCE Framework

After the disintegration of USSR in 1990, the need to develop a new relationship between different states and several "ethnic groups" existing on its region increased with more prominence. This was initially encouraged by the "Conference on Security and Cooperation in Europe (CSCE)", especially the "Copenhagen document". Its directory of "principles on protection of ethnic, cultural, linguistic or religious minorities" is most important because it was the first time that almost all European Member States (28) arrived at "an agreement on minority rights" (www.eurac.edu).

The CSCE procedure was initiated in 1975 with the concluding act of the "Helsinki Conference" and ended with the "Copenhagen Document of 1995". In 1991, the politics to give acknowledgement to the "minorities" started with a very simple proclamation by CSCE authorities that "Issues of national minorities and the implementation of international agreements on the rights of minorities are a rightful international question and do not symbolize just an internal affair of a certain state". Further, this new principle was confirmed in Moscow Conference on Security and Cooperation concerning the human dimension in 1992. However, constancy and harmony cannot be established without a suitable resolution on minority questions. Hence, the French Prime Minister Balladur in 1993 commenced the Stability Pact for Europe, which was aimed to offer security and stability for Central and Eastern Europe, by Promoting "good neighbourliness including border and minority questions, Regional cooperation, and Strengthening of democratic institutions"(Bendikter 2008: 109). The "Stability Pact for Europe" was signed and approved by 52 state parties and it became necessary for all candidates to give their consent to the European Union such as Lithuania, Latvia, and Estonia with other central and eastern European countries.

Framework of the Council of Europe

The Council of Europe (CoE) was established in 1949 as an inclusive organization of all European states. Later, it followed the principles of the European Convention on Human Rights (ECHR), which was effective since 1953. The CoE organised two international gatherings whose objectives were to oblige the minority questions. These are "the European Charter for Regional and Minority Languages (ECRML)" implemented in 1992, and "the Framework Convention for the Protection of National Minorities (FCNM)" implemented in 1994 (Zabielska 2008: 110). Both these plans were implemented in 1998, which were agreed by the most of the national parliaments.

The Framework Convention for the Protection of National Minorities

The basic objectives of the FCNM have been examined in the "Recommendation of 1134 of the Assembly of the Council of Europe" in 1990. The parliamentary body of the Council of Europe (CoE) has identified the principles which must be applicable to protect and recognize the national minorities of the member states of the Union. This has also been further stated in the "Vienna Declaration of the OSCE summit" where in it was expressed that the "CoE must compressively change the OSCE's political commitment to minority protection in legal provisions". This was followed by the convention on 5 February 1995, where the convention was approved by the committee of Ministers and implemented in 1998 after being ratified by 12 member states. (Benedikter 2008: 110)

The FCNM is the "first multilateral and legally binding instrument" which is solely dedicated to the "protection of the European Minorities". The main objective of the FCNM was to "protect the existence of national minorities within the respective territories of the state parties". The convention sought to promote the equality of the national minorities and requiring the states to create the necessary conditions which would facilitate the people belonging to national minorities to protect and develop their culture and also to retain their identity (Packer 2004: 43-51). Its sets out "principles to persons belonging to national minorities in the sphere of public life, such as freedom of peaceful assembly, expression and thought, association, conscience and religion and right to use media as well as in the sphere of freedoms relating to education, language and cross-border cooperation" (www.eurac.edu).

The European Charter for Regional and Minority Languages

This agreement was assumed as a Convention by the Committee of Ministers in June 1992 and proposed to regard it as a recommendation. The key conceptual basis of the ECRML is the postulation that the protection of the regional, historical or minority languages of Europe, which are in threat of eventual extinction, may contribute to the preservation and development of Europe's cultural prosperity and traditions (Lantschner 2008: 116).

The principle objective of the ECRML is to protect and preserve the regional language and language of minorities. It also intends to promote these languages as a means to preserve Europe's cultural heritage. This has been evident by the various steps taken by the ECRML which has tried to ensure that these languages play a vital role in the public and private sphere such as education, mass media and also in spheres of legal, economic and governmental fields. However, The Charter does not establish "individual or collective rights for the speakers of regional or minority languages" but rather obligates the member states for their "legal system and political undertaking" (Benedikter 2008: 117).

The Framework of the European Union

The Copenhagen Criteria was adopted by the European Council which is the supreme decision-making body of the European Union in 1993. This step was taken as a fundamental basis to acquire the membership to the European Union with regard to its Eastern enlargement. Precedence was given to the full respect of institutional stability which would guarantee not only democracy and rule of law, but also a high respect for human rights and protection of the minorities. The main criterion for the admission of the new candidates for the membership to the European Union is to meet the obligations set by the Union. These criteria were considered to be very important in order to gain accession for membership to the future candidates in South-eastern Europe.

The key objective of the integration process of European Union is to promote peaceful co-existence of states and it does certainly include "harmonization of cultures". This has been repeated in the Lisbon Treaty of European Union in 2007, where in it has been expressed that EU is "bound to be mosaic and not a melting pot". Therefore all citizens of European Union are expected to create awareness among themselves a key element to being a part of the Union is to respect the diversity that comes with embracing multiculturalism. Hence, the EU leadership is committed to the same.

Role of the European Union in Estonia

The most regular monitoring of minority rights during the first half of the 1990s was conducted by the OSCE and its High Commissioner on National Minorities, Max van der Stoel who first visited Estonia in January 1993 and issued a preliminary set of recommendations in the· month of April urging the Estonian government to increase awareness about its laws and employ the use of the Russian language in this exercise. He also suggested that government of Estonia should create a National Commissioner on Ethnic and Language Questions (Van der Stoel 1993). He tried to set to rest all apprehensions that he was trying to alter Estonia's fundamental policies. He stated that he was simply trying to blunt the edges of laws that might instigate open conflict among the different ethnic groups of Estonia.

Some of his recommendations were instantly followed up by the Estonian government but it did not pay much heed to the seven letters that he wrote to the Estonian Minister of Foreign Affairs until 1997. Van der Stoel played a very crucial role during the 1993 Aliens Act crisis during which he went to the northeast of Estonia and talked to all the sides (Zaagman 1999). The OSCE had also set up a long-term mission for Estonia, which kept an eye on the developments in the country on a day-to-day basis. The mission had an office in Tallinn as well as in the northeast towns of Johvi and Narva and its mandate was continually extended till January 2002 when the mission was closed.

It was only because of the pressure exerted by the European Union that compelled Estonia to take heed of the OSCE's policy suggestions. The OSCE mission played the role of providing a continuous flow of information from Estonia and it was in "tandem with the political muscle of the EU" that desirable changes were made as seen in the case of the granting of automatic citizenship by the Estonian government to children who would have otherwise remained stateless after the European Commission mentioned the issue in 1997 in its Opinion on Estonia's application to join the European Union (European Commission 1997: 19).

However, the European Commission made it amply clear by including Estonia in its initial "first wave" of EU accession countries that it would not make "Estonia's citizenship and minority policy an issue of fundamental conditionality or demand a major liberalization of Estonia's policies". The European Union preferred to make use of its pre-accession financial instruments as the weapon to influence policy in Estonia. The European Union invested a total of EUR 6.8 million in support of Estonian language and training programme for non-Estonians and in exchange the EU was able to secure a seat on one of the programme's steering committees and it was thus able to continually monitor the "spirit and practice" of the policy.

The European Union had started targeting particularly controversial aspects of Estonia's minority legislation. It criticized the Estonian language requirement for electoral candidates in 1999 as a violation of the UN's International Covenant on Civil and Political Rights, which ultimately led to the requirements being done away with in November 2001. The EU also opposed a series of amendments to Estonia's language law, which were intended to make the use of Estonian compulsory in private business. The European Union opposed this on the ground that such requirements militated against the EU principles of open labour market and was thus illegal (European Commission 1999: 2000).

There are varied opinions regarding the impact of international conditionality on Estonia. There are some scholars who claim that European organizations have been rather lax while others have claimed that Estonia has been subjected to a level of scrutiny, which has not been applied to many Western countries (Ozolins 2003). Judith Kelly has therefore remarked that:

> "... while the OSCE and the Council of Europe often helped facilitate the actual modalities of reaching a compromise on certain minority rights issues, either by dispatching a team of experts or providing behind-the-scenes diplomacy, the political muscle in each case was exerted by the EU and its conditionality in terms of future accession" (Kelley 2003: 36).

The European Union was undoubtedly able to pressurize Estonia to roll back measures that were in clear violation of either the international or EU law. For instance, the European Union had sent a clear signal that "accession was in play" when it stated that Estonia's language policy restrictions could engender "non-compliance by Estonia of the political criteria for membership" (European Commission 1999: 15).

Hughes and Sasse have looked upon the role of the European Union in promoting minority rights as "groping for international benchmarks that do not exist" and have described the alliance of the EU with that of international organizations as an attempt "to shift responsibility from its own monitoring process by internationalizing the benchmarking of the candidate countries with respect to minority protection" (Hughes and Sasse 2003: 17, 19). Pettai and Kallas, however, state that the EU had albeit limited but clearly defined goals. (Pettai and Kallas 2009: 106). They are of the opinion that the Accession Partnership guidelines issued by the European Council have proved to be a much more valid indicator of the EU's political content rather than the monitoring reports which tend to represent a rather late assessment of the prevailing situation.

The Accession Partnership agreements were a set of prescriptive goals to be achieved during a period in the future. Thus, the Council stated in its first guidelines from March 1998 that "Estonia should take measures to facilitate the naturalization process and to better integrate non-citizens including stateless children and to enhance Estonian language training for non-Estonian speakers" (European Council 1998: 28).

These were the only goals that the Council had set concerning Estonia's compliance with the political part of the Copenhagen Criteria. The Council issued a revised set of guidelines in December 1999 as Estonia had adopted new Estonian language requirements for the public and private sector, which were unpalatable to the European Union. Thus, the Council added these concerns to its demands for Estonia as part of the next stage of accession. When the Council issued its final partnership document, Estonia had begun implementing its large-scale integration programme and the language issue had almost totally dissipated.

The Council called on Estonia to "continue the integration of non-citizens by implementing concrete measures, including language training for non-Estonian speakers; to provide necessary financial support for the implementation of these measures and to ensure that the implementation of language legislation is in line with both international standards and the Europe Agreement and that it respects the principles of justified public interest and proportionality" (European Council 2002: 31).

The European Union was thus extremely "astute in picking up an endogenous process" that was already taking place in Estonia and the EU clearly expressed its intent of supporting the consummation of the process. The EU assisted vitally in making this process irreversible by making "Estonia's own catchphrase of integration" a part of its first binding political documents.

The European Union created "a kind of undergirding for the policy", which ensured that it became politica1ly sustainable. In addition to this, huge amount of money pledged by the EU explains as to how the European Union's conditionality played a role in moderating Estonia's ethno-political situation. Thus, Estonia did not become a binational or a multicultural state but the degree of "ethnic control" and "ethnic imbalance" was considerably reduced.

The future of relations between the majority and the minorities seem to be promising, even three years after Estonia became a member-state of the European Union in 2007. The government was on the verge of completing the initial 2000-07 time span of its integration policy and was busy preparing for a new phase for 2008-2013. There was a dearth of international financing for a range of integration projects but Estonia set aside a part of the EU structural funds to carry on work in this field. Among ethnic Russians, the number of people who claimed to have a "good" knowledge of Estonian had reached 42 per cent and only 8 per cent among Russians in the 15-29 age group reported of not knowing any Estonian. Thus, socio-economic disparities between Estonians and non-Estonians registered a decline and Estonia's economy continued to boom.

In this backdrop, the riots that erupted in Tallinn on 26-27 April 2007 proved to be a major setback in view of the recent positive developments towards integration. Prime Minister Andrus Ansip's determination to relocate a "Soviet-era memorial known as the Bronze Soldier" from a location in downtown Tallinn to a faraway cemetery led to the resurfacing of an old issue'. While the Estonians saw the monument as a "painful reminder of the Soviet occupation of their country", the Russians viewed it as a symbol of the "Soviet Union's victory in the Second World War". Russia also interfered in the crisis in early May 2007 by allowing the pro-Putin Nashi movement to protest before the Estonian embassy in Moscow. However, polls among Russian-speakers showed almost 80 per cent believed that the decision to move the Bronze Soldier was wrong, 70 per cent stated that they still considered themselves to be a part of Estonian society (Rechel 2009: 114-115).

The crisis prompted intervention by the European Union and the German Chancellor Angela Merkel, serving as the EU President, asked Prime Minister Ansip and President Putin to exercise restraint. When the blockade of Estonia's Moscow embassy began to suffer, the European Union stated that the Russian government should take steps to stop all kinds of disruption so as the Russian government had an international obligation to safeguard diplomatic outposts. However, the European Union undoubtedly found itself caught in a very difficult situation because it had the unenviable task of defending a member-state, which was responsible for the crisis. The disturbances showed that minority relations in Estonia continue to be a salient issue and that European Union largely has nothing more than soft persuasion to offer for resolving such issues unlike the earlier days when it wielded the power of conditionality.

Role of the European Union in Latvia

The international community proved to be "an active participant" in influencing Latvian minority policy throughout the 1990s and the early 2000s focusing largely "on legislation and policy pertaining to citizenship and language". This involvement took the form of official visits, monitoring reports, evaluations of draft legislation and recommendations by officials from the United Nations, the OSCE, the Council of Europe, the Council of the Baltic Sea States and the European Union.

The international interest and involvement began soon after the restoration of independence in 1991 and continued up to Latvia's accession to the European Union and the North Atlantic Treaty Organisation in 2004, after which there was a rapid decline in its intensity and impact. The OSCE and the Council of Europe played a prominent role in the early to mid-1990s while the EU took the mantle from them in the latter part of the 1990s until accession. The Council of Europe was considered to be a necessary intermediate station on the road to membership of the EU while the OSCE High Commissioner on National Minorities (HCNM) served as the "gate keeper" to membership in the case of Latvia and many other accession countries (Kemp 2001: 7). The European Union more often than not "frequently echoed and publicly supported" the recommendations of the HCNM. The representatives of the three organizations worked in coordination as part of joint expert groups and issued joint public statements (Kubicek 2003).

Conditionality became the most "critical part" of this international involvement and operated through the threat of non-membership in the Council of Europe and subsequently in the European Union. International involvement was also seen in the form of providing language training and social integration programmes as provided by the United Nations Development Programme (UNDP) (Simane and Muizieks 2005: 64-72). The representatives of international and regional organizations frequently engaged in direct lobbying, provided advice on draft legislation and attempted to persuade Latvian officials to liberalise minority policy. The threat of non-membership proved to be instrumental in convincing the Latvian president to veto the initial version of a Law on Citizenship in 1994, which did not take into account the opinion of the OSCE and the Council of Europe experts. Thereafter, the desire to join the Council of Europe proved to be critical in convincing the Latvian lawmakers to adopt a revised law (Kubicek 2003: 35-36).

However, the lawmakers were also known to have ignored a number of recommendations made by the OSCE HCNM by opting for a more drawn-out naturalization schedule than suggested and by not granting citizenship automatically to all children born in Latvia. The outcome however, represented a "normative compromise" (Dorodnova 2003: 34). International organizations renewed pressure on Latvia to liberalise the Law on Citizenship. The publication of the European Commission's Opinion on Latvia in July 1997 included a number of recommendations to facilitate naturalization. While the Opinion did not state in specific terms that the law should be amended, the EU officials, the representatives of influential member-states and the OSCE exerted intense pressure to amend the law and threatened Latvia both directly and indirectly with non-admission to the EU. (Kubicek 2003: 39-42). The electorate approved of the liberalizing changes by a vote of 53 per cent in favour and 45 per cent against the changes.

The international community made use of conditionality yet again when Latvian parliamentarians sought to adopt a new law, which provided for the extensive regulation of Latvian language use in both the public and private sector in 1999. The representatives of the OSCE, the Council of Europe and the European Commission coordinated their efforts for persuading Latvia to pay heed to human rights norms as well as EU standards and lift the restrictions on the use of minority languages. This persuasion was followed up with the use of the threat of non-membership in the EU, which was supported by many foreign dignitaries and by the president of Latvia (Kubicek 2003: 46). It was only after continued pressures and threats that the parliament adopted an amended law in December 1999, which was deemed by the HCNM to be "essentially in conformity with Latvia's international obligations and commitments" (Zaagman 1999).

Dorodnova has rightly concluded that "political arguments linked to EU accession negotiations proved more effective than the reference to international human rights norms" (Dorodonova 2003: 127). There is indeed a widespread agreement among scholars that the role of conditionality has been quite significant in influencing Latvian minority policy. Morris has stated that "Latvia's desire to join the EU has been crucial in the reform of citizenship legislation". Elsuwege has similarly stated that:

> "...the EU pre-accession conditionality has together with the efforts of other international organizations such as the UN, the Council of Europe, NATO and the OSCE resulted in a number of amendments to laws on education, language and the status of non-citizens, efforts which can be praised as largely eliminating the possibility of ethnic violence" (Elsuwege 2004: 54-55).

Muiznieks and Brands Kehris (2003: 50) agree that conditionality related to EU membership was clearly essential in convincing Latvian politicians that concessions had to be made. However, Hughes seems to have another point of view that "it is difficult to reconcile claims of successful international intervention with an outcome which has left some 700,000 persons stateless and without fundamental political and economic rights" (Hughes 2005: 752).

Although Dorodnova considers the impact of the HCNM on Latvian minority policy very significant in terms of operational, normative and substantive effectiveness, she considers the situation of Russian-speakers to be "rather unsatisfactory" (Dorodnova 2003: 149-150). Muiznieks and Brand Kehris pointed out that "sensitive legislation was liberalized in conformity with European standards", which was by no means an ordinary trend (Kubicek 2003: 50).

It is largely felt that the status of the minorities in Latvia has remained almost unchanged since the country became an EU member in May 2004. The relationship between the state and the minorities has not undergone any major overhauling but there has not been any unrest of the kind witnessed in Estonia in April 2007. Latvia has been a witness to largely peaceful social protests over the education reforms described earlier that came into force in September 2004. Although, Latvia undoubtedly faces "considerable challenges" with respect to its large Russian-speaking community, social integration in Latvia is a long-term objective, which has been strengthened by EU membership. Most people who are part of the minority population in Latvia are "relative newcomers" who have arrived in the early Soviet period in pursuance of the policy of colonization and industrialization.

Thus, the situation in Latvia can be better compared with that of France, Germany and the United Kingdom that have "recent immigrant populations" rather than with its "counterparts" in Central and Eastern Europe. This "different situation of Latvia" has had a large impact on minority policy. Successive governments have encouraged social integration, which can be referred to as a "half-way point between policies of assimilation and policies of autonomy". This approach was applied in different issues (Rechel 2009: 141).

Latvia permitted all those who were willing to appear for the naturalization exams in conformity with the mandate of the referendum held in 1998. The Latvian government simultaneously established "a social integration project", which encouraged the "acquisition of Latvian as a second language among minorities" and naturalization among those who arrived after the Second World War. The Naturalization Board had received naturalization applications concerning 138,074 persons out of which 127,786 individuals including 13,572 under aged children have been granted Latvian citizenship until December 2007, which was twelve years after the Latvian state began accepting citizenship applications. (Naturalization Board of the Republic of Latvia Report 2008)

The number of new citizens per year has increased drastically after changes were made in the citizenship law in 1998, which coincided with the moment when Latvia was named a forthcoming EU member-state. The rate of naturalization sharply increased in 2000 as part of the drive by non-citizens to acquire EU citizenship. Naturalisation numbers were lower between 2001 and 2004 and it rose again after Latvia became part of the EU and it declined sharply in 2007.

It is thus apparent that EU membership proved to be an incentive to apply for citizenship. The enlargement provided the Latvian citizens with the opportunity to work abroad in states such as "Ireland, Sweden and the United Kingdom" that had unlocked their employment markets to the new member-states of the European Union. The non-citizens were denied the automatic right to work abroad. The constraints on the mobility of non-citizens suited the Latvian state and it was amenable to the logic of the social integration project. The attraction of labour mobility influenced the non-citizens to opt for naturalization and they were required to learn the Latvian language sufficiently in order to pass the language part of the naturalization examination (Ibid).

There were only 6,826 naturalizations in 2007 because the people who were interested in the process did so either shortly before or after the enlargement. Moreover, the labour markets of many EU member-states have been opened to Latvia's non-citizens, which have led to the elimination of a powerful incentive for undergoing the process of naturalization. This has led to a large number of non-citizens who may never wish to naturalize. One of the most prominent disincentives for many young non-citizen males to naturalise was the requirement to do obligatory military service. However, Latvia opted for a professional military in 2006, which could lead many such non-citizens to reconsider their decision. Non-citizens have largely remained passive and alienated which requires the need for caution in the predictions about future behaviour. About 362,902 ethnic Russians were citizens of Latvia, 278,213 were non-citizens and 22,115 were citizens of Russia (Naturalization Board of the Republic of Latvia Report 2008).

The Latvian parliament passed a new education law in 1998, which called for a shift to a primarily Latvian language curriculum in all state-funded schools. The stage was set in Latvia's schools for the battle of social and linguistic integration in the case of the next generation Russian speakers. This was the most crucial phase during which the state thought that it would be able to achieve maximum social integration. The response of the minority community was rather slow. Organised opposition to the law occurred only after the October 2002 parliamentary elections although the education law was adopted in 1998. The result of the protests was that the now defunct People's Harmony Party, Equal Rights and the Latvian Socialist Party, which were the three left-wing minority parties succeeded in securing the second highest share of votes (Ibid).

Opposition to the law became intense in 2003 and 2004 and it was marked by weekend protests in parks in the city centre of Riga as well as outside the Ministry of Education and Science with banners saying "SOS: Save our Schools" and "Latvian-Russian and not Russian-Latvian". The protesters however, did not demand that the teaching of Latvian in minority schools should be stopped. The protesters organized a number of rallies, sit-ins, walkouts and other protest methods when the reforms were implemented at the beginning of the new school year. However, the opposition lost its tenacity and intensity as the school year progressed and then disappeared completely.

It has been alleged by many Russian activists in Latvia, the government of the Russian Federation and some Western observers that the Latvian government has discriminated against minorities. The verdict of the sociological surveys conducted throughout the 1990s was that the Russian-speakers expected to be treated in the same manner as ethnic Latvians by the employers, service providers and the police and in the spheres of health, housing and social security (Rose 1995: 39-40). A survey commissioned by the National Human Rights Office (NHRO) in 2006 found out that 13 per cent of non-Latvians answered in the affirmative as compared to 9 per cent of Latvians when asked as to whether they had experienced human rights violations or discriminations over the previous three years. This was regarded as a considerable improvement from a previous survey in 2000 when the corresponding figures were 31 per cent for non-Latvians and 18 per cent for Latvians (Baltic Institute for Social Science 2006).

Very few persons have approached the court or filed discrimination complaints in the National Human Rights Office (NHRO). The NHRO received five written complaints on racial or ethnic discrimination, one on linguistic discrimination and gave 16 oral consultations (NHRO Report 2006: 62). The court awarded compensation to a Roma woman who was denied employment because of her ethnicity in the first case of ethnic discrimination in 2006 (European Commission 2007: 28). The most common victims of harassment have been the Roma and the racially different minorities such as Blacks and Asians (Lukumiete 2005: 13).

The differences between citizens and non-citizens have not evoked much criticism when compared to the restrictions in private sector employment. Only citizens have been able to practise as attorneys, notaries, notary assistants, heads of detective agencies and security guard managers (Mitrofanovs et al. 2006: 79-83). The government has justified the restrictions on the ground that attorneys and notaries are "inextricably" tied to the judiciary while managing detectives and security guards might endanger public safety. However, the "United Nations Human Rights Committee" and the "Parliamentary Assembly of the Council of Europe" have expressed their concern and have asked Latvia to undertake a review of these requirements (Human Rights Committee Report 2003).

The language policy of Latvia has also come under the scanner. When Ingrida Podkolzina, a plaintiff from Latvia questioned the language requirement for standing for public office before the European Court of Human Rights in 2002, the Court stated that "requirements of that kind pursued a legitimate aim despite the fact that the procedural rights of the plaintiff had been violated" (European Court of Human Rights Report 2002). The Latvian authorities however, did away with the language requirements because of the compulsions linked to Latvia's bid to join the EU and NATO. This was followed by the ruling of Latvia's Constitutional Court that certain language restrictions were discriminatory. The first case that came up for hearing before the Court in this context was in 2003 and it was concerned with a law, which restricted the use of languages other than Latvian in private radio and TV broadcasting. The second case took place in 2005 and it was concerned with a law that allowed the state to subsidize only those private schools that employed Latvian as the medium of instruction. (EU Monitoring and Advocacy Program Monitoring Report 2005)

Thus Latvian language policy shall continue to be questioned in the private and public sector. However, the immediate legal difficulties are connected with the European Commission infringement procedures against Latvia for incomplete transposition of the "Race Equality Directive". The "European Union Agency for Fundamental Rights" thus noted, "Malta and Latvia have been very slow in adopting the necessary legislation in compliance with the directive" (European Commission 2007: 20).

Impact of the Framework Convention

Latvia finally ratified the Council of Europe's Framework Convention for the Protection of National Minorities (FCNM) mainly due to a different domestic constellation and the realization that the convention leaves the states a large measure of discretion. Latvia "defined national minorities as Citizens of Latvia who differ from Latvians in terms of their culture, religion or language, who have lived in Latvia for generations and consider themselves to belong to the State and society of Latvia, who wish to preserve and develop their culture, religion or language. Persons who are not citizens of Latvia or another State but who permanently and legally reside in the Republic of Latvia, who do not belong to a national minority within the meaning of the Framework Convention for the Protection of National Minorities as defined in this declaration, but who identify themselves with a national minority that meets the definition contained in this declaration, shall enjoy the rights prescribed in the Framework Convention, unless specific exceptions are prescribed by law" (Council of Europe 2007).

This definition denies the non-citizens the symbolic gratification of recognition as minorities but it does extend the protection of the FCNM to them. No laws or regulations have been modified to implement the FCNM. However, several subtle changes have taken place because of ratification. For instance, there has been a considerable increase in the allocation of additional government funds for the national minority NGOs. However, several obstacles need to be overcome. Minority policy remains controversial and there happens to be no consensus among the political elite on significant minority issues. There have been frequent changes in the governing coalition, which has led to inconsistency of policy and implementation. A secretariat is the same as a Ministry and Special Assignments Ministers are "full cabinet ministers". The secretariats are "ostensibly set up to address specific issues within a limited period" and therefore the long-term fate of the office remains uncertain. (Council of Europe 2007)

The impact of external influence on Latvian minority policy after accession to the European Union has waned considerably and political mechanisms have given way to legal battles over minority rights. The issues that remain unresolved are the "needs of a large non-citizen population, the transposition of the EU Race Equality Directive and the legal challenges to various restrictions on minority languages". The European Court of Human Rights and the Latvian Constitutional Court have given unfavourable rulings in the cases that impinge on minority rights primarily on issues dealing with language use. Despite the existence of numerous challenges, minority policy in Latvia has become increasingly "institutionalized" and funding for the preservation and development of minorities and their language and culture has increased. (Muiznieks 2006: 122)

Role of the European Union in Lithuania

There have been enough questions on the EU influence on Baltic states for setting up their rules and regulations to deal the minority rights both before the membership to the European Union and after it. Merje Kuus has therefore explained the "ritual of listening to the foreigners" at the time of Estonia's accession to the European Union. She has stated that "the importance of local actors especially their power to interpret or ignore norms should never be underestimated". She has suggested through her case studies that "national actors played critical role in influencing the reinforcement of minority rights in Central Eastern Europe" (Kuus 2004). It was not international actors affecting more minority rights policies in these countries. Grabbe (1999) has however acknowledged and emphasised on EU's actions influencing minority issues and stated:

> "...The vast literature on "Europeanisation" has identified diverse activities of EU influencing minority rights during the accession process, including "legislative and institutional templates", rule of law, financial assistance, observations and consultation on how to incorporate norms and laws."(Grabbe 1999: 36)

The local elites of Lithuania however, do not seem to mention the influence of international actors in the course of analysing the development of the framework of minority rights in their country. Their post-colonial thinking which has come from the historical roots make it difficult to promote the harmony between different ethnic and racial groups of the country. After conducting a study in 2007 many scholars like Adomenas have argued that Lithuania has failed to inculcate civic understanding of "nation" which has ultimately made difficult to build a culture of tolerance. It could have positively impacted the anti-discrimination mechanisms of European Union.

> "...Attempts at keeping an "archaic" ethnic identity, which is still recognised as being threatened, created a "passive political culture" and disrupt the improvement of a tolerant and progressive political community". (Adomenas et al. 2007: 51)

These observations put a question mark on the capability of a post-Soviet society to be able to create a culture, which would endorse progressive legislation for ensuring the protection of minority rights.

Lithuania's Legal Framework

Lithuania has given a positive projection of majority and minority peaceful co-existence in its society by having a liberal policy for citizenship after the independence. Since then it has been trying to show itself as ideal democracy at international platform. Lithuanian politicians as well as the elites have been successful projecting it as peaceful co-existence society by putting minority rights supporting legislation in place, as it was one of the conditions to get membership of European Union and NATO.

One of the important parts of legislation reads that: "the 1989 Law on Ethnic Minorities that recognized the rights of minorities to cherish and foster their cultural traditions, history and language; the 1989 Law on Citizenship that extended the citizenship of Lithuania to those residing in Lithuania in 1990; and the 1991 Law on Education that granted access to minority language education and schools for Russian and Polish minority groups. The constitution of Lithuania, adopted in 1992, guarantees cultural minority rights and prohibits discrimination based on ethnicity. It allows Lithuania's ethnic minorities to foster their language, culture and customs and grants minorities the right to administer independently from the state of affairs of their ethnic culture, education, organization and charities" (Rechel 2009).

The "legal framework" of Lithuania ensures that it supports the rights of minorities and that these minorities residing in the state are faithful to their host state. Lithuania's legal provision to protect the rights of the vulnerable people has got a positive feedback from international organization such as the "European Commission" in the late 1990s, the "UN Human Rights Committee" for managing the effective application of the "International Covenant on Civil and Political Rights", and "the Council of Europe Advisory Committee on the Framework Convention for the Protection of National Minorities".

In 1997, despite the fact that Lithuania was not asked to start the membership negotiations with the European Union unlike other two Baltic countries Estonia and Latvia, the "Commission Opinion on Lithuania's Application for Membership" stated that the condition of minorities living in Lithuania was good enough to start the negotiations for membership in EU by emphasizing the positive role of the 1991 Law on Citizenship. Because, based on 1991 citizenship law, Lithuania granted "citizenship to all the persons resident" in the state. It tried to accommodate all under one national umbrella, which was praised by the European Commission. The Commission further stated that the Lithuania's minorities had the freedom to manage their cultural and educational affairs and freedom to use their language for official communication in the area where they are in majority in the state (European Commission 1997). Thus, it was observed that the Commission approved of the minority rights model implemented by the government of Lithuania. The monitoring reports of Lithuania, before state acquired membership of the EU in 2004, also confirmed that Lithuania's ethnic and racial communities were given the well-established rights which were supported by the legal framework of the state.

Two trends have been shaping Lithuania's minority rights regime since the early 1990s. On one side, the state government put in place "minority friendly" laws and programmes, which included the transposing of EU anti-discrimination directives in order to gain approval of the international community while on the other side, the government passed various laws to strengthen the "ethnic core" of the country for example the language law and the dual citizenship law of Lithuania. This point was illustrated with the deep analytical study of the widespread debate which surrounded the revised Citizenship Law of 2002 and the ambiguous future of the 1989 Law on Ethnic Minorities.

However, the revised Law on Citizenship promoted the difference between the Ethnic population and non-ethnic population of Lithuania. This is one of the major reason why the revised law attracted debate and it was closely analysed with undecided future of 1989 law on citizenship. This new law came to be debated intensely because of its discriminatory character. This law did not allow dual citizenship, which was allowed before such as ethnic Jews, Poles, Russians, Belarusians and other minorities were allowed to keep both Lithuanian and other state citizenship.

This new law got criticisms from the International actors as well. The "European Commission against Racism and Intolerance recommended that the Lithuanian policymakers should make sure that the policies formed for the Lithuanian citizenship should not discriminate aspirants on the grounds of race, colour, language, religion and ethnic origin" (European Commission against Racism and Intolerance Report 2006). As a matter of fact, the Constitutional Court of Lithuania declared the Citizenship Law of 2002 unconstitutional on the basis of the legal provision of the country. According to the law it is mandatory to hold a referendum to amend any provision of the Law on dual citizenship (Marcinkevicius 2007: 68).

However, this proposal of constitutional court of the state to organize a referendum on dual citizenship was alleged by political parties across the nation as a threat to Lithuania's sovereignty. The leading political parties of Lithuania argued that the nationwide protest and debate on the new citizenship law shows the nation is not ready to lose its sovereignty of this small state once again to any foreign power. It is considered a national interest by all the parties irrespective of their ideological differences. National identity was in the priority for the political parties, be it left wing or the right wing, while this new law on citizenship was proclaimed by the court of the state as discriminatory in nature.

The Law of 1989 on Ethnic Minorities allows them to "develop their culture freely", to get financial assistance from the state government for their cultural and educational activities including teaching the official language in minority schools.

To protect the interest of minorities and ethnic groups of the state the Law of 1989 on Ethnic Minorities was formulated which gave freedom to develop their culture freely. Minorities were given state sponsored financial assistance to hold the cultural activities and it also supported teaching the official language in the minority schools.

The attempt to make amendments to the legislation was initiated in 1997 and 2002. Thus, later in 1990s, it was argued about what is an "ethnic minority" and whose rights must be ensured and protected by the state. The resultant product of this debate was a new definition of ethnic minorities. However, these revisions were not accepted by the ethnic minorities because they felt that the national authorities of state are not actually interested to secure the interests of the ethnic minorities residing in Lithuania.

Another attempt to amend the law was made in 2002 by forming a working group. The "Department of National Minorities and Lithuanians Living Abroad" came up with a new draft of the Law on Ethnic Minorities, which gave individuals the freedom to decide as to whether or not they wanted to come under the category of ethnic minority. However, representatives of the minority community of Lithuania protested that their opinions were not asked before drafting the bill. Thus, no agreement could be reached on the final draft of the bill between the politicians and the administrators until the end of 2007.

The political parties of Lithuania have not exhibited the political will to expedite the process while the minority representatives have failed to correspond efficiently with the pro-government authorities who were in favour of protecting their rights. There is consensus at the global platform between some International organizations and local non-governmental organizations (NGOs) that the political institutions do not have strong platform to represent minorities in Lithuania and hence it has been difficult to formulate and implement the policies for the minority rights.

Conclusion

The European Union has been influential in the protection and promotion of minority rights in the Baltic states. Despite ongoing problems like immigration, Britain exiting from Europe and euro crisis, substantial efforts continue all over Europe to improvise the condition of minorities. In fact, European Union enlargement has been closely associated to the minority rights condition in Europe. For the applicant country to enter in the European Union as mentioned in the Copenhagen criteria it is mandatory to acquire certain benchmarks on their promotion of minorities. European Union enlargement has also encouraged applicant countries to follow the rule of law, democratic reforms and efficient policymaking regarding minority issues as conditionality to enter EU. These Baltic states as many other post-communist countries were obliged to have efficient policymaking on minority rights as a condition to enter EU. These procedures were mentioned in the Copenhagen criteria in 1993 for membership as part of accession. Despite less or lack of EU legislation on minority rights, the OSCE and the Council of Europe were the two main monitoring agencies as discussed above in detail.

In conclusion, it can be said that minority rights in Baltic states have always been one of the major concerns because of their history and European Union has been playing an active role to accommodate these minority questions diligently. However, the method of approach has been changed since the inception of the idea. Baltic states like other EU member states possess only general powers to take decisions about minorities. The EU gives power to all the member states to use all legal mechanisms to assure the fundamental rights including minority rights and human rights, which are effectively protected in accordance with their constitutional order and obligations under international law.

References

Adomenas, M. et al. (2007), *The Lithuanian Nation: Its Current Status and Its Future,* Vilnius: Versus Aureus.

Baltic Institute for Social Science (2006), *Research on Human Rights in Lativia: A Report in Graphics*, Riga: BJSS.

Council of Europe (2007), Country Specific Information, Strasbourg: Council of Europe, 6 July, retrieved from www.coe.int/t/e/human_rights/minorities/Country_specific_eng.asp#P428_22391.

Dorodnova, J. (2003), Challenging Ethnic Democracy: Implementation of the Recommendations of the OSCE High Commissioner on National Minorities to Latvia, 1993-2001, Centre for OSCE Research Working Paper 10, 7 July, retrieved from: www.core.hamburg.de/english/publications/workingpapers.

Elsuwege, P. (2004), "Russian-speaking Minorities in Estonia and Latvia: Problems of Integration on the Threshold of the EU", ECMI Working Paper, 20: 1-56, 7 July, retrieved from: http://www.ecmi.de/download.working paper 20.pdf.

European Commission (1997), "Agenda 2000- Commission Opinion on Lithuania's Application for Membership of the European Union", 6 July, retrieved from: http://ec.europa.eu/enlargement/archives.pdf/dwn/opinions/lithuania/li-op_en. pdf.

European Commission (1999), Regular Report from the Commission on Estonia's Progress Towards Accession, Brussels: European Commission.

European Commission (2007), "The Charter of Fundamental Rights of the EU- all personal, civil, political, economic and social rights in one simple text", 28 May, 60 retrieved from: http://ec.europa.eu/justice_home/fsj/rights/charter/fsj_rights_ charter_ en. htm.

European Commission against Racism and Intolerance (2006), "Third Report on Lithuania", 6 July, retrieved from http://www.coe.int/t/e/human_rights/ecri/1-ECRI/2-Country-by-Country_approach/Lithuania/Lithuania_CBC_3.asp.

European Council (1998), "Council Decision on the Principles, Priorities, Intermediate Objectives and Conditions Contained in the Accession Partnerships with the Republic of Estonia", *Official Journal of the European Communities*, 121: 26-30.

European Council (2002), Council Decision on the Principles, Priorities, Intermediate Objectives and Conditions Contained in the Accession Partnership with the Republic of Estonia", *Official Journal of the European Communities*, 44: 29-36.

Grabbe, Heather (1999), "A Partnership for Accession? The Implications of EU Conditionality for the Central and East European Applicants", Robert Schuman Centre Working Paper, 12(9), 1-34 retrieved from http://www.cer.org.uk/pdf/grabbe_conditionality_99.pdf.

Hughes, J. (2005), "Exit in Deeply Divided Societies: Regimes of Discrimination in Estonia and Latvia and the Potential for Russophone Migration", *Journal of Common Market Studies*, 43(4): 739-762.

Hughes, James and Gwendolyn Sasse (2003), "Monitoring the Monitors: EU Enlargement Conditionality and Minority Protection in the CEEs" *Journal on Ethnopolitics and Minority Issues in Western Europe*, 1: 1-37.

Kelley, J. (2003), "Does Domestic Politics Limit the Influence of External Actors on Ethnic Politics?" *Human Rights Review*, 4: 35-54.

Kemp, W.A. (2001), *Quiet Diplomacy in Action: The OSCE High Commissioner on National Minorities*, The Hague: Kluwer Law International.

Kubicek, P.J. (2003), *The European Union and Democratisation. Europe and the Nation State*, London: Routledge.

Kuus, M. (2004), "Those Goody Goody Estonians: Towards Rethinking Security in the European Union Candidate States", *Society and Space*, 22: 191-207.

Lukurniete, D. (2005), Racism in Latvia: ENAR Shadow Report 2005, Brussels: European Network Against Racism, 6 July, retrieved from: www.enar• eu.org/en/national/latvia/Latvia_2005.pdf.

Marcinkevicius, R. (2007), "Dual Citizenship may lead to a Second Independence Movement", 6 July, retrieved from: www.ivaizdis.lt/res_zinlpr_det.php?id=14456..

Mitrofanovs, M. et al. (2006), *The Last Prisoners of the Cold War: The Stateless People of Latvia in Their Own Words*, Riga: Averti-R Ltd.

Muižnieks, Nils and Ilze Brands Kehris (2003), "The European Union, democratization and minorities in Latvia", in Paul Kubicek (ed.), *The European Union and Democratization. Europe and the Nation State*, London: Routlege.

Ozolins, U. (2003), "The Impact of European Accession upon Language Policy in the Baltic states", *Language Policy*, 2: 217-238.

Rechel, Bernd (2009), *Minority Rights in Central and Eastern Europe*, London; New York: Routledge.

Simane, M. and N. Muiznieks (2005), UNDP Latvia 1992-2005: *Easing the Transition,* Riga: UNDP.

Van der Stoel, M. (1993), "Letter to Trivmi Velliste, Minister of Foreign Affairs, Republic of Estonia", 5 July, retrieved from http://www.osce.org/documents/hcnm/1993/04/2728_en.Pdf.

Zaagman, R. (1999), "Conflict Prevention in the Baltic states: The OSCE High Commissioner on National Minorities in Estonia, Latvia and Lithuania", Working Paper, Monograph Series no. 1, Flensburg: European Centre for Minority Issues. retrieved from http://www.eurac.edu/en/pages/default.aspx.

Index